Kaplan Publishing are constantly finding new ways to su~~~ dents looking for exam success and our online resour~~ n extra dimension to your studies.

This book comes with free MyKaplan c study anytime, anywhere. **This free on. separately and is included in the pric**

Having purchased this book, you have access to the following online study materials:

CONTENT	AAT	
	Text	Kit
Electronic version of the book	✓	✓
Knowledge Check tests with instant answers	✓	
Mock assessments online	✓	✓
Material updates	✓	✓

How to access your online resources

Received this book as part of your Kaplan course?
If you have a MyKaplan account, your full online resources will be added automatically, in line with the information in your course confirmation email. If you've not used MyKaplan before, you'll be sent an activation email once your resources are ready.

Bought your book from Kaplan?
We'll automatically add your online resources to your MyKaplan account. If you've not used MyKaplan before, you'll be sent an activation email.

Bought your book from elsewhere?
Go to **www.mykaplan.co.uk/add-online-resources**
Enter the ISBN number found on the title page and back cover of this book.
Add the unique pass key number contained in the scratch panel below.
You may be required to enter additional information during this process to set up or confirm your account details.

This code can only be used once for the registration of this book online. This registration and your online content will expire when the examinations covered by this book have taken place. Please allow one hour from the time you submit your book details for us to process your request.

Please scratch the film to access your unique code.

Please be aware that this code is case-sensitive and you will need to include the dashes within the passcode, but not when entering the ISBN.

PUBLISHING

BUSINESS TAX

STUDY TEXT

Qualifications and Credit Framework

Q2022

Finance Act 2023

For assessments from February 2024 until January 2025

This Study Text supports study for the following AAT qualifications:

AAT Level 4 Diploma in Professional Accounting

AAT Diploma in Professional Accounting at SCQF Level 8

KAPLAN PUBLISHING'S STATEMENT OF PRINCIPLES

LINGUISTIC DIVERSITY, EQUALITY AND INCLUSION

We are committed to diversity, equality and inclusion and strive to deliver content that all users can relate to.

We are here to make a difference to the success of every learner.

Clarity, accessibility and ease of use for our learners are key to our approach.

We will use contemporary examples that are rich, engaging and representative of a diverse workplace.

We will include a representative mix of race and gender at the various levels of seniority within the businesses in our examples to support all our learners in aspiring to achieve their potential within their chosen careers.

Roles played by characters in our examples will demonstrate richness and diversity by the use of different names, backgrounds, ethnicity and gender, with a mix of sexuality, relationships and beliefs where these are relevant to the syllabus.

It must always be obvious who is being referred to in each stage of any example so that we do not detract from clarity and ease of use for each of our learners.

We will actively seek feedback from our learners on our approach and keep our policy under continuous review. If you would like to provide any feedback on our linguistic approach, please use this form (you will need to enter the link below into your browser).

https://forms.gle/U8oR3abiPpGRDY158

We will seek to devise simple measures that can be used by independent assessors to randomly check our success in the implementation of our Linguistic Equality, Diversity and Inclusion Policy.

British Library Cataloguing-in-Publication Data

A catalogue record for this book is available from the British Library.

Published by:

Kaplan Publishing UK
Unit 2, The Business Centre
Molly Millar's Lane
Wokingham
Berkshire
RG41 2QZ

ISBN 978-1-83996-574-6

CONTENTS

STUDY TEXT

Chapter

KAPLAN PUBLISHING

Chapter

INTRODUCTION

HOW TO USE THESE MATERIALS

These Kaplan Publishing learning materials have been carefully designed to make your learning experience as easy as possible and to give you the best chance of success in your AAT assessments.

They contain a number of features to help you in the study process.

The sections on the Unit Guide, the Assessment and Study Skills should be read before you commence your studies.

They are designed to familiarise you with the nature and content of the assessment and to give you tips on how best to approach your studies.

STUDY TEXT

This study text has been specially prepared for the revised AAT qualification introduced in 2022.

It is written in a practical and interactive style:

- key terms and concepts are clearly defined

- all topics are illustrated with practical examples with clearly worked solutions based on sample tasks provided by the AAT in the new examining style

- frequent activities throughout the chapters ensure that what you have learnt is regularly reinforced

- 'assessment tips' help you avoid commonly made mistakes and help you focus on what is required to perform well in your assessment

- 'Test your understanding' activities are included within each chapter to apply your learning and develop your understanding.

ICONS

The chapters include the following icons throughout.

They are designed to assist you in your studies by identifying key definitions and the points at which you can test yourself on the knowledge gained.

 Definition

These sections explain important areas of knowledge which must be understood and reproduced in an assessment.

 Example

The illustrative examples can be used to help develop an understanding of topics before attempting the activity exercises.

 Test your understanding

These are exercises which give the opportunity to assess your understanding of all the assessment areas.

 Foundation activities

These are questions to help ground your knowledge and consolidate your understanding on areas you're finding tricky.

 Extension activities

These questions are for if you're feeling confident or wish to develop your higher level skills.

Quality and accuracy are of the utmost importance to us so if you spot an error in any of our products, please send an email to mykaplanreporting@kaplan.com with full details.

Our Quality Coordinator will work with our technical team to verify the error and take action to ensure it is corrected in future editions.

Progression

There are two elements of progression that we can measure: first how quickly learners move through individual topics within a subject; and second how quickly they move from one course to the next. We know that there is an optimum for both, but it can vary from subject to subject and from learner to learner. However, using data and our experience of learner performance over many years, we can make some generalisations.

A fixed period of study set out at the start of a course with key milestones is important. This can be within a subject, for example 'I will finish this topic by 30 June', or for overall achievement, such as 'I want to be qualified by the end of next year'.

Your qualification is cumulative, as earlier papers provide a foundation for your subsequent studies, so do not allow there to be too big a gap between one subject and another.

We know that exams encourage techniques that lead to some degree of short term retention, the result being that you will simply forget much of what you have already learned unless it is refreshed (look up Ebbinghaus Forgetting Curve for more details on this). This makes it more difficult as you move from one subject to another: not only will you have to learn the new subject, you will also have to relearn all the underpinning knowledge as well. This is very inefficient and slows down your overall progression which makes it more likely you may not succeed at all.

In addition, delaying your studies slows your path to qualification which can have negative impacts on your career, postponing the opportunity to apply for higher level positions and therefore higher pay.

You can use the following diagram showing the whole structure of your qualification to help you keep track of your progress.

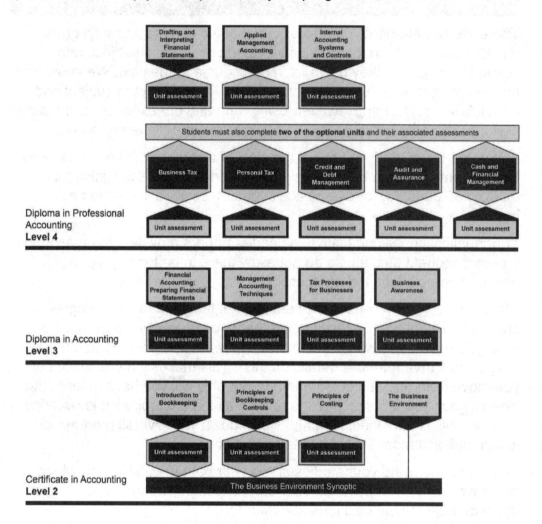

UNIT GUIDE

Introduction

This unit introduces learners to UK taxation relevant to businesses. Learners will understand how to compute business taxes for sole traders, partnerships and limited companies. They will also be able to identify tax planning opportunities while understanding the importance of maintaining ethical standards.

In learning how to prepare tax computations, learners will gain the skills required to identify expenditure as revenue or capital and adjust accounting profits for tax purposes. Learners will allocate profits between partners in a partnership and will calculate National Insurance (NI) contributions for the self-employed, advising clients on the tax implications of making losses.

Learners will understand the administrative requirements of UK tax law, including the implications of errors in tax returns, late filing of returns, late payment of tax and not retaining records for the required period. Learners will compute corporation tax and gains on the sale of capital assets by companies and will understand the capital gains implications of the sale of a business and the tax reliefs available to businesses.

Tax advice is an important part of many accountancy roles in recognising tax planning opportunities for businesses. Learners will discuss the ethical issues facing business owners and managers in reporting their business tax and the responsibilities that an agent has in giving advice on tax issues to business clients.

This unit is **optional** in the Level 4 Diploma in Professional Accounting.

Learning outcomes

On completion of this unit the learner will be able to:

- Prepare tax computations for sole traders and partnerships.

- Prepare tax computations for limited companies.

- Prepare tax computations for the sale of capital assets by limited companies.

- Understand administrative requirements of the UK's tax regime.

- Understand the tax implications of business disposals.

- Understand tax reliefs, tax planning opportunities and agent's responsibilities in reporting taxation to HM Revenue & Customs.

Scope of content

The unit consists of six learning outcomes, which are further broken down into assessment criteria. These are set out in the following table with reference to the relevant chapter within the text.

In any one assessment, learners may not be assessed on all content, or on the full depth or breadth of a piece of content. The content assessed may change over time to ensure validity of assessment.

Chapter

1   Prepare tax computations for sole traders and partnerships

1.1   Adjusting accounting profits and losses for tax purposes

Learners need to understand:

- how to identify deductible and non-deductible expenditure   8

- how expenditure is classified as either revenue or capital.   8

Learners need to be able to:

- adjust accounting profit and losses for tax purposes.   8

Chapter

1.2 Prepare capital allowances computations

Learners need to understand:

- which capital allowances apply to different assets: 8

    – plant and machinery

    – structures and buildings.

Learners need to be able to:

- prepare capital allowance computations for accounting periods: 8

    – longer than 12 months

    – shorter than 12 months

    – equal to 12 months

    – including adjustments for private usage.

1.3 Calculating taxable profits and losses of partners

Learners need to be able to:

- allocate profits between partners   9

1.4 Calculate the national insurance contributions (NICs) payable by self-employed taxpayers

Learners need to understand:

- what income class 2 and class 4 NICs are payable on.   12

Learners need to be able to:

- calculate NICs: 12

    – class 2

    – class 4.

2 **Prepare tax computations for limited companies**

2.1	**Adjusting accounting profits and losses for tax purposes**	
	Learners need to understand:	
	• how to identify deductible and non-deductible expenditure	3
	• how expenditure is classified as either revenue or capital.	3
	Learners need to be able to:	
	• adjust accounting profits and losses for tax purposes.	3
2.2	**Prepare capital allowances computations**	
	Learners need to understand:	
	• Which capital allowances apply to different assets:	4
	– plant and machinery	
	– structures and buildings.	
	Learners need to be able to:	
	• prepare capital allowance computations for accounting periods:	4
	– longer than 12 months	
	– shorter than 12 months	
	– equal to 12 months.	
2.3	**Calculate taxable profits and corporation tax payable**	
	Learners need to be able to:	
	• calculate the taxable total profits from trading income, property income, investment income, chargeable gains and qualifying charitable donations for accounting periods:	2, 5
	– longer than 12 months	
	– shorter than 12 months	
	– equal to 12 months	
	• calculate corporation tax payable.	5

KAPLAN PUBLISHING

3 **Prepare tax computations for the sale of capital assets by limited companies**

3.1 **Calculate chargeable gains and allowable losses**

Learners need to be able to:

- calculate: 13
    - chargeable gains and allowable losses
    - rollover relief
    - indexation allowance.

3.2 **Calculate chargeable gains and allowable losses for shares**

Learners need to be able to:

- apply matching rules for companies   14
- account for: 14
    - bonus issues
    - rights issues
    - indexation allowance.

4 **Understand administrative requirements of the UK's tax regime**

4.1 **The administrative requirements of UK tax law**

Learners need to understand:

- tax return filing deadlines for sole traders, partnerships and companies   7, 11
- tax payment dates for sole traders, partners and companies   7, 11
- time limits for notifying chargeability to tax   7, 11
- the enquiry window   7, 11
- the time period within which amendments to a tax return can be made   7, 11
- what records need to be maintained and for what time period.   7, 11

4.2 **Penalties and interest for non-compliance**

Learners need to understand:

- penalties for: 7, 11
  - late filing
  - late payment
  - failing to notify chargeability
  - errors in tax returns
  - not providing records in an enquiry
  - not retaining records.

Learners need to be able to:

- calculate penalties and interest for non-compliance.   7, 11

5 **Understand the tax implications of business disposals**

5.1 **Business disposals**

Learners need to understand:

- the income tax and capital gains tax implications of disposing of an unincorporated business   15

- the capital gains tax reliefs (gift relief, business asset disposal relief) available on the disposal of: 15
  - an unincorporated business
  - shares in a personal company.

Learners need to be able to:

- calculate capital gains on the disposal of: 15
  - trade and assets
  - shares in a personal company
  - capital gains tax reliefs available on disposal of:
    - trade and assets
    - shares in a personal company
  - post-tax proceeds following a business disposal.

6 **Understand tax reliefs, tax planning opportunities and agent's responsibilities in reporting taxation to HM Revenue & Customs**

6.1 **Trading losses**

Learners need to understand:

- options available to sole traders, partnerships and companies to utilise trading losses: 6, 10
    - opening years
    - carry back
    - current year
    - carry forward
    - terminal

- the best use of a trading loss for sole traders, partnerships and limited companies.   6, 10

Learners need to be able to:

- calculate available loss relief using: 6, 10
    - carry back
    - current year
    - carry forward.

6.2 **Badges of trade**

Learners need to understand:

- how to identify if clients are trading through the application of the badges of trade.   8

6.3	**Tax planning for businesses**	
	Learners need to know:	
	• the tax rates which apply:	16
	– to sole traders	
	– to companies	
	– on extraction of profits from companies.	
	Learners need to understand:	
	• implications of different business structures on tax planning	16
	• impact on tax when using different methods of extracting profits, including salary and dividends	16
	• tax planning opportunities to ensure taxable income is optimally allocated between spouses/civil partners.	16

6.4   **Ethical guidelines**

Learners need to understand:

•	the definitions of:	1
	– tax planning	
	– tax avoidance	
	– tax evasion	
•	ethical implications of tax avoidance and tax evasion	1
•	the requirement to report suspected tax evasion	1
•	the ethical principle of confidentiality.	1

KAPLAN PUBLISHING

LINKS WITH OTHER UNITS

This unit has close links with:

- Level 3 Tax Processes for Businesses
- Level 4 Personal Tax

THE ASSESSMENT

Test specification for this unit assessment

Assessment type	Marking type	Duration of assessment
Computer based unit assessment	Partially computer/ partially human marked	2 hours

The assessment for this unit consists of 10 compulsory, independent, tasks.

The competency level for AAT assessment is 70%.

Learning outcomes		**Weighting**
1	Prepare tax computations for sole traders and partnerships	19%
2	Prepare tax computations for limited companies	19%
3	Prepare tax computations for the sale of capital assets by limited companies	17%
4	Understand administrative requirements of the UK's tax regime	15%
5	Understand the tax implications of business disposals	10%
6	Understand tax reliefs, tax planning opportunities and agent's responsibilities in reporting taxation to HM Revenue & Customs	20%
Total		100%

Assessment tasks

An analysis of the areas covered in each task and the marks available is set out below.

Task	Marks	Topic
1	8	Adjusting accounting profits and losses for tax purposes
2	12	Capital allowances (part human marked)
3	8	Analysing profits and losses of a partnership and calculating NICs
4	8	Chargeable gains and allowable losses of companies
5	9	Calculating chargeable gains and allowable losses in company disposal of shares (human marked)
6	10	Calculating taxable profits and corporation tax payable
7	15	The administrative requirements for UK tax law
8	12	Tax planning and the responsibilities of the business and agent (human marked)
9	8	Trading losses (part human marked)
10	10	Business disposals

STUDY SKILLS

Preparing to study

Devise a study plan

Determine which times of the week you will study.

Split these times into sessions of at least one hour for study of new material. Any shorter periods could be used for revision or practice.

Put the times you plan to study onto a study plan for the weeks from now until the assessment and set yourself targets for each period of study – in your sessions make sure you cover the whole course, activities and the associated test your understanding activities.

If you are studying more than one unit at a time, try to vary your subjects as this can help to keep you interested and see subjects as part of wider knowledge.

When working through your course, compare your progress with your plan and, if necessary, re-plan your work (perhaps including extra sessions) or, if you are ahead, do some extra revision/practice questions.

Effective studying

Active reading

You are not expected to learn the text by rote, rather, you must understand what you are reading and be able to use it to pass the assessment and develop good practice.

A good technique is to use SQ3Rs – Survey, Question, Read, Recall, Review:

1   **Survey the chapter**

    Look at the headings and read the introduction, knowledge, skills and content, so as to get an overview of what the chapter deals with.

2   **Question**

    Whilst undertaking the survey ask yourself the questions you hope the chapter will answer for you.

3   Read

Read through the chapter thoroughly working through the activities and, at the end, making sure that you can meet the learning objectives highlighted on the first page.

4   Recall

At the end of each section and at the end of the chapter, try to recall the main ideas of the section/chapter without referring to the text. This is best done after a short break of a couple of minutes after the reading stage.

5   Review

Check that your recall notes are correct.

You may also find it helpful to re-read the chapter to try and see the topic(s) it deals with as a whole.

Note taking

Taking notes is a useful way of learning, but do not simply copy out the text.

The notes must:

- be in your own words
- be concise
- cover the key points
- be well organised
- be modified as you study further chapters in this text or in related ones.

Trying to summarise a chapter without referring to the text can be a useful way of determining which areas you know and which you don't.

Three ways of taking notes

1   Summarise the key points of a chapter

2   Make linear notes

A list of headings, subdivided with sub-headings listing the key points.

If you use linear notes, you can use different colours to highlight key points and keep topic areas together.

Use plenty of space to make your notes easy to use.

3   **Try a diagrammatic form**

The most common of which is a mind map.

To make a mind map, put the main heading in the centre of the paper and put a circle around it.

Draw lines radiating from this to the main sub-headings which again have circles around them.

Continue the process from the sub-headings to sub-sub-headings.

Annotating the text

You may find it useful to underline or highlight key points in your study text – but do be selective.

You may also wish to make notes in the margins.

Revision phase

Kaplan has produced material specifically designed for your final assessment preparation for this unit.

These include pocket revision notes and practice questions that include a bank of questions specifically in the style of the new syllabus.

Further guidance on how to approach the final stage of your studies is given in these materials.

Further reading

In addition to this text, you should also read the 'Accounting Technician' magazine every month to keep abreast of any guidance from the assessors.

REFERENCE MATERIAL

AAT reference material

Reference material is provided in this assessment. During your assessment you will be able to access reference material through a series of clickable links on the right of every task. These will produce pop-up windows which can be moved or closed.

The reference material has been included in this study text (below). This is based on the version of the reference material that was available at the time of going to print.

The full version of the reference material is available for download from the AAT website.

Level 4 Business Tax (BNTA)
reference material

Finance Act 2023 - for assessments from 29 January 2024

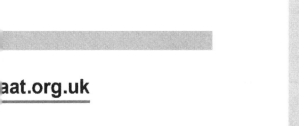

Reference material for AAT assessment of Business Tax

Introduction

This document comprises data that you may need to consult during your Business Tax computer-based assessment.

The material can be consulted during the practice and live assessments by using the reference materials section at each task position. It's made available here so you can familiarise yourself with the content before the assessment.

Do not take a print of this document into the exam room with you*.

This document may be changed to reflect periodical updates in the computer-based assessment, so please check you have the most recent version while studying. This version is based on **Finance Act 2023** and is for use in AAT Q2022 assessments from **29 January 2024**

*Unless you need a printed version as part of reasonable adjustments for particular needs, in which case you must discuss this with your tutor at least six weeks before the assessment date.

Contents

1. Income tax

Trading allowance			£1,000
Personal allowance			£12,570
	Basic rate (0-£37,700)	Higher rate (£37,701 - £125,140)	Additional rate (Above £125,140)
Salary	20%	40%	45%
Dividends	8.75%	33.75%	39.35%
Trading income	20%	40%	45%

- Income tax computations will not be required in the assessment, but the rates may be used in tax planning discussions.

2. National Insurance (NI)

Class 2 contributions	£3.45 per week
Lower profits threshold	£12,570
Class 4 contributions on trading profits between £12,570 and £50,270	9%
Class 4 contributions on trading profits above £50,270	2%

- Dividends are not subject to NI
- Salaries are subject to:
    - employee NI at 12% between £12,570 and £50,270 and 2% above £50,270
    - employer NI at 13.8% above £9,100 (an employment allowance of £5,000 is available)

  Calculations of NI on salaries will not be required in the assessment but the rates may be used in tax planning discussions

3. Capital gains tax

Annual exempt amount	£6,000
Basic rate	10%
Higher rate	20%
Business asset disposal relief rate	10%
Business asset disposal relief lifetime allowance	£1,000,000

4. Corporation tax

Rate of corporation tax prior to 1 April 2023	19%
Main rate of corporation tax from 1 April 2023	25%
Small profits rate of corporation tax from 1 April 2023	19%
Upper limit	£250,000*
Lower limit	£50,000*
Marginal small company relief	3/200 x (upper limit -TTP)

*reduced if:
- accounting period <12 months
- associated companies.

5. Capital allowances

Assets other than cars:	
Annual investment allowance	£1,000,000
Writing down allowance	18%
Full expensing – expenditure by companies after 1 April 2023	100%

Cars:	
Writing down allowance:	
- CO2 emissions 0g/km	100%
- CO2 emissions up to 50 g/km	18%
- CO2 emissions over 50 g/km	6%

Small pools allowance	£1,000
Structures and buildings allowance	3%

6.   Disallowed expenditure

Type of expense	Disallowable in calculation of trading profit	Notes
Fines and penalties	Fines on the business Fines on directors/owners	Employee fines are not disallowed if incurred in the course of their employment.
Donations	Political donations Donations to national charities	Donations to local charities allowable (these will only b examined for unincorporate businesses).
Capital expenditure	Depreciation Loss on disposal Capital items expensed	Capital allowances may be availabl
Legal and professional	Relating to: - capital items - purchase/renewal of a long lease - purchase of a short lease (50 years or less) - breaches of law/regulations.	Legal fees on the renewal of short lease (50 years or less) are allowable.
Entertaining and gifts	Customer gifts (unless <£50 per annum, not food, drink, tobacco, or cash vouchers and contains business advertising). Customer/supplier entertaining.	Staff gifts and staff entertainin are allowable.
Cars	Depreciation. Private use by owners. 15% of lease cost if leased car >50g/km CO2 emissions.	
Private expenditure of owner (unincorporated businesses only)	Goods taken for own use. Salary of owners. Private use % by owners. Private expenditure, e.g., Class and 4 NICs, legal and professional fees for personal expenditure.	Reasonable salaries of family members are allowable.

Trading losses

Loss option	Sole trader/Partner	Company
Carry forward	Against future profits of the same trade only. Applies automatically to first available profits. Applies after any other elections or if no elections are made.	Losses not relieved in the current accounting period or previous 12 months are carried forward and an election can be made to set against total profits in future periods.
Current year/carry back	Against total income in the current and/or previous tax year in any order. If opted for in either year, the amount of loss used cannot be restricted to preserve the personal allowance. Make claim by 31 January 2026 for 2023/24 tax year.	Can elect to set trading losses against current accounting period 'total profits'. Qualifying charitable donations will remain unrelieved. If the above election is made, can also carry back trading loss to set against 'total profits' within the previous 12 months. Claim within 2 years of the end of the loss-making period.
Opening year loss relief – loss in first four years of trade	Against total income of the previous three tax years on a FIFO basis. If opted for, losses will be used to reduce total income as much as possible in each year and cannot be restricted to preserve the personal allowance. Make claim by 31 January 2026 for 2023/24 tax year.	N/A
Terminal loss relief	Against trading profits of the previous 3 years on a LIFO basis. Claim within 4 years from the end of the last tax year of trade.	Against total profits of the previous 3 years. Claim within 2 years of the end of the loss-making period.

8.   Chargeable gains – Reliefs

Relief	Conditions
Replacement of business assets (Rollover) relief	Available to individuals and companies. Examinable for companies. Qualifying assets (original and replacement) – must be used in a trade and be land and buildings or fixed plant and machinery. Qualifying time period – replacement asset must be purchased between one year before and three years after the sale of the original asset. Partial reinvestment – if only some of the sales proceeds reinvested then the gain taxable is the lower of the full gain and the proceeds not reinvested.
Gift relief (holdover relief)	Available to individuals only. Qualifying assets – assets used in the trade of the donor or the donor's personal company, shares in any unquoted trading company or shares in th donors personal trading company. A personal trading company is one where the donor has at least 5%.
Business asset disposal relief	Available to individuals only. Gain taxable at 10%. £1m lifetime limit For 2023/24 a claim must be made by 31 January 2026. Qualifying assets: - the whole or part of a business carried on by the individual (alone or in partnership). The business must have been owned for 24 months prior to sale - assets of the individual's or partnership's trading business that has now ceased. The business must have been owned for 24 months prior to cessation and sale must be within 3 years of cessation - shares in the individual's 'personal trading company' (own at least 5%). The individual must have owned the shares and been an employee of the company for 24 months prior to sale.

9. Payment and administration

	Sole traders/partners	Company
Filing date	31 October following the end of the tax year if filing a paper return. 31 January following the end of the tax year if filing online. Amendments can be made within 12 months of the filing deadline.	Filed on the later of 12 months after end of AP or 3 months after the notice to deliver a tax return has been issued. Amendments can be made within 12 months of the filing deadline.
Payment date	31 January following the end of the tax year. If payments on accounts are due: • first POA – 31 January during tax year • second POA – 31 July after tax year • balancing payment – 31 January after tax year. POA's are each 50% of the previous years income tax and class 4 NICS due by self-assessment. POA's are not required for capital gains or class 2 NICs. POA's are not due if prior year tax payable by self-assessment is less than £1,000 OR if >80% of prior year tax was collected at source.	Small companies (annual profits less than £1.5 million): 9 months + 1 day after end of the accounting period (AP). Large companies (annual profits greater than £1.5 million) must estimate the year's tax liability and pay 25% of the estimate on the 14th day of each of the 7th, 10th, 13th and 16th month from the start of the accounting period.
Interest	Charged daily on late payment	Interest charged daily on late payment. Overpayment of tax receives interest from HMRC. Interest is taxable/tax allowable as interest income.
Penalties for late filing	£100. After 3 months, £10 per day for up to 90 days. After 6 months, 5% tax due (or £300 if greater). After 12 months, 5% tax due (or £300 if greater) if not deliberate. After 12 months, 70% of tax due (or £300 if greater) if deliberate and not concealed. After 12 months, 100% tax due (or £300 if greater) if deliberate and concealed.	£100. After 3 months, £100. After 6 months, 10% of unpaid tax. After 12 months, 10% of unpaid tax.
Late payment	30 days late – 5% of tax outstanding at that date. 6 months days late – 5% of tax outstanding at that date. 12 months late – 5% of tax outstanding at that date.	N/A

	Sole traders/partners	Company
Notify of chargeability	5 October following the end of the tax year.	Within 3 months of starting to trade.
Enquiry	Within 12 months of submission of return. Penalty for failure to produce enquiry documents = £300 + £60 per day.	Within 12 months of submission of return. Penalty for failure to produce enquiry documents: £300 + £60 per day.
Record retention	Five years from filing date. Penalty for failure to keep records is up to £3,000.	Six years after the end of the relevant accounting period. Penalty for failure to keep proper records is up to £3,000.

10. Penalties for incorrect returns

Type of behaviour	Maximum	Unprompted (minimum)	Prompted (minimum
Careless error and inaccuracy are due to failure to take reasonable care	30%	0%	15%
Deliberate error but not concealed	70%	20%	35%
Deliberate error and concealed	100%	30%	50%

AAT
30 Churchill Place
London E14 5RE

aat.org.uk

AAT is a registered charity. No. 1050724

Introduction to business tax

1

Introduction

This chapter presents an overview of business tax and an outline of some of the ethical guidelines that must be followed by tax advisers.

ASSESSMENT CRITERIA	CONTENTS
Definitions of: – tax planning – tax avoidance – tax evasion (6.4) Ethical implications of tax avoidance and tax evasion (6.4) The requirement to report suspected tax evasion (6.4) The ethical principle of confidentiality (6.4)	1 Contents of the study text 2 Types of business entity 3 Ethical guidelines 4 Confidentiality 5 Money laundering 6 Tax planning, avoidance and evasion

1 Contents of the study text

1.1 Four categories

The study text can be split into four specific categories:

	Chapters
• Companies	2 – 7
• Unincorporated traders (sole traders and partnerships)	8 – 12
• Chargeable gains	13 – 15
• Tax planning for businesses	16

The aim is to gradually consider each of the ways of taxing a business.

We also consider in this chapter the ethical implications for a tax adviser when giving advice.

Business taxation depends on how a business has been set up. An individual can decide to set up a business as a:

- company
- sole trader, or
- partnership.

2 Types of business entity

2.1 Company

A company is a legal entity, separate from its owners and managers.

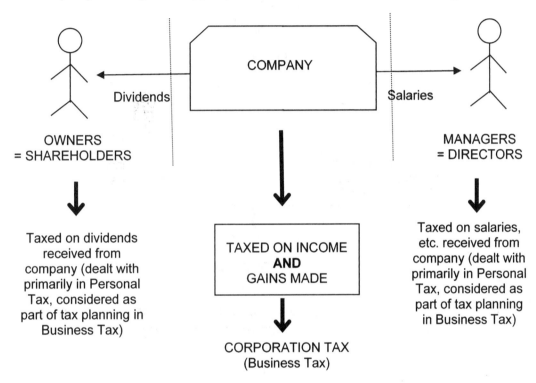

OWNERS = SHAREHOLDERS

Dividends

COMPANY

Salaries

MANAGERS = DIRECTORS

Taxed on dividends received from company (dealt with primarily in Personal Tax, considered as part of tax planning in Business Tax)

TAXED ON INCOME **AND** GAINS MADE

CORPORATION TAX (Business Tax)

Taxed on salaries, etc. received from company (dealt with primarily in Personal Tax, considered as part of tax planning in Business Tax)

Note: In a lot of cases the shareholders and directors are the same people. However, this will only be relevant when considering tax planning in the Business Tax assessment.

2.2 Sole trader

An individual setting up an unincorporated business (i.e. not a company) alone, is known as a sole trader.

A sole trader is not a separate legal entity.

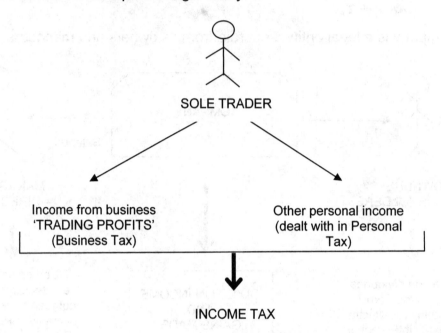

In the Business Tax assessment, you won't need to complete a full income tax computation. You will only deal with the business aspects.

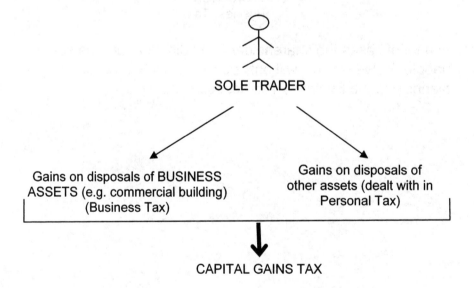

In the Business Tax assessment, you may be required to complete a capital gains tax computation. However, the sole trader will only have disposed of business assets or shares in a personal company.

2.3 Partnership

A partnership is another form of unincorporated business, but it is not a separate legal entity.

A partnership is formed when a number of individuals carry on a business together with a view to profit, i.e. a partnership is effectively a collection of sole traders working together.

Each partner pays their own income tax and capital gains tax on their share of the partnership's profits and gains.

3 Ethical guidelines

3.1 AAT expectations

The AAT expects its members to:

- master skills and techniques through learning and maintain them through continuing professional development

- adopt an ethical approach to work as well as to their employers and clients

- acknowledge their professional duty to society as a whole

- maintain an objective outlook

- provide professional, high standards of service, conduct and performance at all times.

These expectations are discussed in greater depth in the 'Code of Professional Ethics' that can be found on the website (www.aat.org.uk).

A person advising either a company or an individual on taxation issues has duties and responsibilities towards both:

- the company or the individual, and

- HM Revenue and Customs.

An adviser owes the greatest duty to the client.

4 Confidentiality

4.1 Dealings with third parties

A tax adviser has an overriding duty of confidentiality towards their client. Under normal circumstances a client's tax affairs should not be discussed with third parties. This duty remains even after the adviser no longer works for the client.

The exceptions to this rule mentioned in the guidelines are where:

- authority has been given by the client, or
- there is a legal, regulatory or professional duty to disclose (e.g. in the case of suspected money laundering).

4.2 Dealings with HM Revenue and Customs

The duty of confidentiality also relates to dealings with HMRC.

However, the tax adviser must ensure that, whilst acting in the client's best interests, they consult with HMRC staff in an open and constructive manner.

5 Money laundering

5.1 What is money laundering?

Money laundering is the process of concealing funds obtained from criminal activity within a legitimate business.

The AAT and its members are required to comply with the money laundering laws and regulations.

5.2 Requirements under the laws and regulations

A tax adviser should check the identity of prospective clients via a review of appropriate documentation, for example, a passport.

A firm of accountants must appoint a money laundering officer.

Suspicion that a person is involved in money laundering should be reported to the money laundering officer who will determine whether it needs to be reported to the appropriate authorities.

KAPLAN PUBLISHING

Test your understanding 1

Which of the following statements is **not** correct?

A   Accountants need to follow the rules of confidentiality even in a social environment.

B   If money laundering is suspected; accountants are allowed to break the rules of confidentiality.

C   Rules of confidentiality towards a client must be followed even after the business relationship has ended.

D   Accountants must follow the rules of confidentiality irrespective of the situation.

 6 Tax planning, tax avoidance and tax evasion

6.1   Tax planning and tax avoidance

Tax planning

This means arranging your tax affairs, using legal methods, so that you pay less tax.

For example, individuals and businesses can reduce their tax bills by claiming all the reliefs and allowances to which they are entitled. Sometimes a transaction can be timed to give maximum tax advantage.

Tax planning is legal.

Tax avoidance

Tax avoidance is legal but is not following the intent of the law.

For example, individuals and businesses may use unintended loopholes in the law, or artificially use foreign jurisdictions with low tax rates.

6.2   Tax evasion

Tax evasion is a criminal offence.

Tax evasion means using illegal methods to reduce tax due.

Typically this might be through concealing a source of income, deliberately understating income or over-claiming expenses and reliefs.

6.3 Dealing with problems

In spite of guidelines being available, there can be situations where the method of resolving an ethical issue is not straightforward.

In those situations additional advice should be sought from:

- a supervisor
- a professional body, or
- a legal adviser.

6.4 Dealing with errors in clients' tax returns

Where a tax adviser realises that an error has been made in a client's or employer's tax return he, she or they must recommend that the client/employer informs HMRC.

If the client/employer refuses to do so, the member must not act for them in connection with that return or related matters. The member may also have to consider whether to cease acting for the client.

Dishonestly retaining funds acquired as a result of an error or omission amounts to money laundering. Tax evasion is a criminal activity, and concealment of this leads to a duty to report.

 Test your understanding 2

When an accountant is advising a client, to whom does the accountant owe the greatest duty of care?

A   HMRC

B   The professional body to which the accountant belongs

C   The client

D   The public

7 Summary

There are three types of business entity to consider:

- company
- sole trader
- partnership.

Each has its own special rules for calculating profits, gains and tax.

A tax adviser has an overriding duty of confidentiality towards their client.

However, the tax adviser's responsibilities include openness in dealing with HMRC and reporting suspicion of money laundering.

Tax planning is the legal use of reliefs and allowances for the purpose they were intended for, tax avoidance is legal but not using the law as it was intended, whilst tax evasion is illegal such as concealment of income or over-claiming of reliefs.

Test your understanding answers

 Test your understanding 1

The answer is **D**.

The duty of confidentiality can be overridden if the client gives authority or if there is a legal, regulatory or professional duty to disclose.

 Test your understanding 2

The correct answer is **C**.

Principles of corporation tax

Introduction

Task 6 in the assessment will test the calculation of taxable profits and corporation tax payable. This chapter sets the scene.

<table>
<tr><td colspan="2">ASSESSMENT CRITERIA</td></tr>
<tr><td>Calculate the total profits from given trading income, property income, investment income, chargeable gains and qualifying charitable donations for periods:
–   longer than 12 months
–   shorter than 12 months
–   equal to 12 months (2.3)</td></tr>
</table>

CONTENTS

1 Introduction to corporation tax

2 The principle of accounting periods

3 Pro forma corporation tax computation

1 Introduction to corporation tax

1.1 Corporation tax

Corporation tax is paid by companies. A company can be recognised in the assessment because its name will end with:

- Ltd (which means limited company), or

- plc (which means public limited company).

Sole traders and partnerships do not pay corporation tax.

 Example

Which of the following businesses pay corporation tax?

(a) Amy's Motor Dealers Ltd

(b) Bert & Sons

(c) Fozia Diamond plc

(d) Salman & Co

Solution

Corporation tax is paid by companies:

(a) Amy's Motor Dealers Ltd (name ends in Ltd), and

(c) Fozia Diamond plc (name ends in plc).

1.2 Corporation tax computation

Companies pay corporation tax on the total of their income and gains. Firstly, the period covered by the computation must be identified and then the income and gains to be included in the computation are calculated.

2 The principle of accounting periods

2.1 Accounting period

A 'period of account' is the period for which a company prepares a set of financial accounts.

However, a company must prepare a corporation tax computation for an 'accounting period' (AP).

In a normal situation, a company prepares a 12-month set of financial accounts and has a matching AP for corporation tax purposes.

 Example

Fast Ltd has prepared accounts for the year ended 31 December 2023. Smart plc has prepared accounts for the year ended 31 March 2024.

For what period will the companies prepare their corporation tax computations?

Solution

Fast Ltd – computation for year ended 31 December 2023.

Smart plc – computation for year ended 31 March 2024.

2.2 Accounts of less than 12 months

An AP can be any length up to 12 months.

Where a company prepares a set of financial accounts of less than 12 months, there is a short AP for corporation tax purposes.

 Example

Tardy Ltd has previously prepared accounts to 31 December, until 31 December 2022. The company has now changed to preparing accounts to 30 September.

What is its first accounting period using the new date?

Solution

Tardy Ltd has an AP of 9 months ended 30 September 2023.

2.3 Accounts of more than 12 months

An AP can never exceed 12 months.

Therefore, when a company prepares financial accounts for a period of more than 12 months, there must be two APs for corporation tax purposes.

The two APs are:

- AP for the first 12 months, and

- a separate AP for the balance of the period.

No other combination is acceptable.

A corporation tax computation is prepared for each AP.

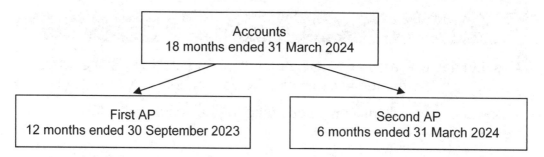

The method of allocating profits from the accounts between the two periods is covered in Chapter 5.

 Test your understanding 1

Ice Ltd has prepared accounts for the 15 months ended 31 July 2023.

What is/are the accounting period(s)?

A   15 months ended 31 July 2023

B   3 months ended 31 July 2022 and 12 months ended 31 July 2023

C   12 months ended 30 April 2023 and 3 months ended 31 July 2023

D   11 months ended 31 March 2023 and 4 months ended 31 July 2023

3 Pro forma corporation tax computation

In the assessment you may be expected to complete a corporation tax computation using a similar layout to the pro forma set out below.

The pro forma will become more familiar as you work through the chapters.

The pro forma includes references to the chapters in the textbook where each entry is considered in detail.

Company name

Corporation tax computation for XX months ended.......(the AP)

	£	Chapter(s)
Trading profit	X	3, 4
Non-trade interest (investment income)	X	5
Property income	X	5
Chargeable gains	X	5, 13
	—	
Total profits	X	
Less: Qualifying charitable donations	(X)	5
	—	
Taxable total profits (TTP)	X	
	—	
Corporation tax liability (at relevant rate)	X	5
	—	

4 Summary

A corporation tax computation must be prepared for each accounting period.

Identifying the correct accounting period(s) is an essential first step in correctly calculating corporation tax.

Test your understanding answers

 Test your understanding 1

The correct answer is C.

Explanation

The financial accounting period must be split into the first 12 months and then the remaining period.

Ice Ltd therefore has the following accounting periods:

12 months ended 30 April 2023, and

3 months ended 31 July 2023.

Two corporation tax computations must be prepared.

Adjusted trading profits

Introduction

Task 1 in the assessment will involve the computation of adjusted profits for sole traders, partnerships and limited companies.

This chapter deals with adjustments for companies.

See Chapter 8 for further information on the taxation of trading profits for a sole trader or partnership.

ASSESSMENT CRITERIA	CONTENTS
How to identify deductible and non-deductible expenditure (2.1)	1 Introduction to adjusted trading profits
How expenditure is classified as either revenue or capital (2.1)	2 Adjustment of profits calculation
Adjust accounting profit and losses for tax purposes (2.1)	3 Disallowable expenditure
	4 Income included in the accounts but not taxable as trading profits
	5 Detailed pro forma adjustment of profits

1 Introduction to adjusted trading profits

The first entry shown on the pro forma corporation tax computation is the adjusted trading profits of the company.

The starting point in determining the amount of adjusted trading profits is the net profit (this is the profit before tax) as shown in the accounts (i.e. the statement of profit or loss, formerly known as the income statement). However, the accounts may, for example, contain expenditure items which are not allowable for tax purposes.

The net profit shown in the accounts of the company must be adjusted for tax purposes to give the adjusted trading profit.

The rules in this chapter are also largely applicable to the calculation of the adjustment of profits for an unincorporated business. The differences in that calculation are set out in Chapter 8.

2 Adjustment of profits calculation

2.1 Pro forma adjustment of profits calculation

	£	Detail in:
Net profit as per accounts	X	
Add: Disallowable expenditure	X	Section 3
	X	
Less: Income included in the accounts but not taxable as trading profit	(X)	Section 4
Adjusted trading profit before capital allowances	X	
Less: Capital allowances	(X)	Chapter 4
Adjusted trading profit	X	

The three categories of adjustment are considered in turn, in the sections and chapter indicated above. In this chapter you will calculate the 'adjusted trading profit before capital allowances'.

An adjustment of profits will be required in the assessment. It is essential that you understand the entries made.

3 Disallowable expenditure

3.1 The principle of disallowable expenditure

Expenditure included in the accounts has the effect of reducing the profits of the company.

However, some items of expenditure are acceptable deductions for financial accounting purposes but are not acceptable for corporation tax purposes.

As a result, the reduction that was made in the accounts must be reversed for corporation tax purposes (i.e. the expenditure must be added back).

This is known as 'disallowable expenditure'.

The general principle to be applied in relation to any particular item of expenditure is that it will only be allowable in arriving at the taxable trading profits if it has been incurred 'wholly and exclusively' for the purposes of the trade.

If the expense is too remote from the trade it fails the remoteness test and will not be allowable. Expenditure is regarded as being too remote from the trade when it is incurred in some capacity other than that of trading.

Example

Jersey Ltd has the following statement of profit or loss for its year ended 31 March 2024:

	£
Sales	100,000
Less: Cost of sales	(40,000)
Gross profit	60,000
Less: Expenditure (Note)	(35,000)
Net profit per accounts	25,000

Note: The expenditure can be analysed as follows:

	£
Wholly and exclusively for the purposes of the trade	33,000
Not wholly and exclusively for the purposes of the trade (i.e. disallowable expenditure)	2,000
	35,000

Calculate the adjusted trading profits of Jersey Ltd for the year ended 31 March 2024.

Solution

Jersey Ltd – Adjusted trading profit – year ended 31 March 2024

	£
Net profit per accounts	25,000
Add: Disallowable expenditure	2,000
Adjusted trading profits	27,000

3.2 Examples of disallowable expenditure

The general principle of expenditure being incurred 'wholly and exclusively' for the purposes of the trade can be used in the assessment if you are in doubt.

However, there are many common examples of disallowable expenditure that tend to appear regularly in assessments. The common examples are set out in the remainder of section 3.

3.3 Fines

Fines on the business should be disallowed as the business is expected to operate within the law. Typical examples are penalties for late payment of VAT or for breaking health and safety regulations.

In practice, however, HM Revenue and Customs usually allow a deduction for parking fines incurred by employees while on company business. This does not, however, apply to directors' parking fines. Nor does it apply to any form of speeding or other motoring fines (irrespective of who they are incurred by).

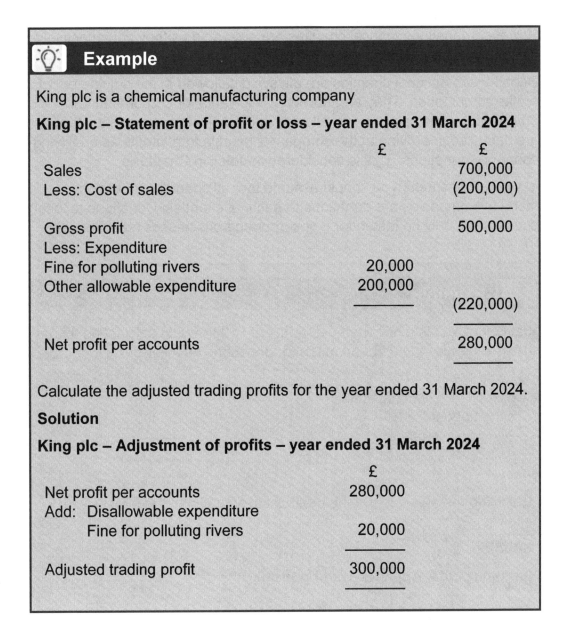

Example

King plc is a chemical manufacturing company

King plc – Statement of profit or loss – year ended 31 March 2024

	£	£
Sales		700,000
Less: Cost of sales		(200,000)
Gross profit		500,000
Less: Expenditure		
Fine for polluting rivers	20,000	
Other allowable expenditure	200,000	
		(220,000)
Net profit per accounts		280,000

Calculate the adjusted trading profits for the year ended 31 March 2024.

Solution

King plc – Adjustment of profits – year ended 31 March 2024

	£
Net profit per accounts	280,000
Add: Disallowable expenditure	
Fine for polluting rivers	20,000
Adjusted trading profit	300,000

3.4 Fraud

Fraud undertaken by directors is disallowed. This is because the loss does not relate to the company's trading activities.

However, petty theft by non-senior employees which is not covered by insurance is generally allowable.

3.5 Donations

Donations to charity usually fail the wholly and exclusively test.

In practice, this means that there is no deduction for donations to national charities or political parties, unless there is some clear benefit to the trade.

However, donations to local charities are allowable as they can effectively be classed as advertising.

Donations to national charities are always disallowed in the adjustment of profits computation. They are, however, allowable for corporation tax purposes, but instead of being allowed in the adjustment of profits, they are deducted in arriving at the company's taxable total profits as qualifying charitable donations. This is considered in detail in Chapter 5.

In your assessment, you should assume that all charitable donations made by companies are donations to national charities. Donations to local charities will only be tested for unincorporated businesses (see Chapter 8).

Example

Larkspur Ltd has a net profit before tax of £123,000. In calculating this profit, a deduction has been made for donations as follows:

	£
To NSPCC – national charity	7,000
To the Labour Party	300
	7,300

Calculate the adjusted trading profit assuming all other expenses are allowable.

Solution

Larkspur Ltd – Adjusted trading profit

	£
Net profit per accounts	123,000
Add: Donation to national charity	7,000
Donation to political party	300
Adjusted trading profit	130,300

3.6 Capital expenditure

As a rule, capital expenditure charged to the statement of profit or loss (e.g. depreciation, purchase of small capital items) is not an allowable expense for tax purposes.

For this reason, 'repairs' expenditure requires careful review, as it often contains items of a capital nature.

In general, repairs and redecoration are considered to be revenue expenditure and are therefore allowable. Improvements, however, are disallowable.

In practice, the distinction between a repair and an improvement is not clear-cut. Repairs usually involve restoring an asset to its original condition or replacing part of an asset with a modern equivalent. Improvements usually involve enhancing the asset in some way.

For example, the replacement of a single glazed window with a double glazed window would be a repair, whilst installing a new window in a brick wall would be an improvement.

Second-hand non-current assets

If a non-current asset (i.e. fixed asset) is purchased in a dilapidated state, and the purchase price reflects this, then initial 'repairs' expenditure to bring the asset to a fit state for use in the business will not be allowable.

Two cases illustrate the difficulty of applying this rule in practice.

In *Law Shipping Co Ltd v CIR (1923)* the company purchased a ship which was not in a seaworthy condition. Expenditure on making the ship seaworthy was held to be capital and therefore disallowed.

In *Odeon Associated Theatres Ltd v Jones (1971)* the company purchased some cinemas which were in a run-down condition. Expenditure incurred in renovating the cinemas was held to be revenue and therefore allowable.

These two cases can be distinguished. In the *Law Shipping* case, the ship was not usable until the repairs were undertaken and the purchase price reflected the condition it was in. By contrast, in the Odeon case, the cinemas were capable of being used for the purpose of the trade prior to their renovation. In addition, the repairs were to remedy normal wear and tear.

You do not need to remember the names of the legal cases mentioned but the principle of the decision made is important.

Legal expenses of a capital nature

The general rule to determine whether legal expenses are allowable is to look at the nature of the expense.

If they relate to a capital item, such as the purchase of a building, then the expenses will be disallowed.

Note that for tax purposes, leases are always treated as capital in this context, therefore legal expenses relating to leases will normally be disallowed (subject to some exceptions).

If they relate to a revenue item, such as the collection of trade receivables or employee issues such as drawing up contracts of employment, then they will be allowable.

There are some exceptions to the capital rule.

The following expenses are allowable:

- the legal costs of renewing a short lease (i.e. 50 years or less)
- the cost of registering a patent
- the legal costs of defending title to a non-current asset (e.g. disputes over land boundaries).

Depreciation

Depreciation, together with any loss on the sale of non-current assets, is disallowed and must be added back.

Relief for capital expenditure may be given through capital allowances instead of depreciation (see Chapter 4).

Test your understanding 1

For each of the following items of expenditure, state if they would be treated as capital or revenue items for tax purposes.

1	Purchase of new office furniture	Revenue / Capital
2	Rates	Revenue / Capital
3	Repair to make asset usable after purchase	Revenue / Capital
4	Legal costs re purchase of new offices	Revenue / Capital
5	Legal costs re renewal of 20-year lease	Revenue / Capital

3.7 Irrecoverable debts (also known as impaired debts or bad debts)

Debts written off

The write off of a trade debt (e.g. receivables) in the accounts is an allowable deduction from trading profits. Consequently, the recovery of a trade debt previously written off is taxable.

The write off of a non-trade debt (e.g. a loan to a former employee or a supplier), is not an allowable deduction from trading profits.

Provisions

A provision for bad debts, which is calculated in accordance with IFRS® Standards is allowable when computing adjusted trading profits.

As a company's accounts are required to be prepared using IFRS Standards and these standards require objective evidence of impairment in a debt, a bad debt provision in a company's accounts will be specific in nature and allowable for tax purposes. This may be different in an unincorporated business (see Chapter 8).

It is possible that a company's accounts could include a provision relating to matters other than receivables (e.g. inventory provision). Any movement in a provision described as general should be disallowed for tax purposes.

Example

The impaired debts account of Greenidge Ltd for the year ended 30 April 2024 appears as follows:

	£		£
		Provision for irrecoverable debts b/f	445
Written off:			
– Trade debts	274		
– Former employee	80	Recoveries – trade debts	23
Provision for irrecoverable debts c/f	419	Statement of profit or loss	305
	___		___
	773		773
	___		___

Show any adjustments required for tax purposes.

Solution

In this example, the information is presented in the form of a 'T' account.

The first stage is to establish a breakdown of the statement of profit or loss charge of £305.

Remember that this figure comprises amounts written off and recovered, and movements in provisions.

Statement of profit or loss charge:

	£	Allowable?
Decrease in provision for irrecoverable debts (£445 – £419)	(26)	✓
Amounts written off:		
Trade debt	274	✓
Former employee	80	✗
Recoveries – trade debts	(23)	✓
	___	
	305	
	___	

The write off of the debt owed by the former employee is disallowed.

The recovery of the trade debts is taxable.

The *decrease* in the provision for irrecoverable debts will be specific in nature and is therefore not adjusted for.

The adjustment to the trading profits for tax purposes is therefore:

Add: Former employee debt written off   £80

Write-offs of non-trading loans (such as here to the former employee) are not allowable deductions from trading profits, however they are allowed as a deduction from non-trade related interest income – take care, as it is easy to miss this point (see Chapter 5).

3.8 Interest payable

For the purpose of computing a company's adjusted trading profits you need to distinguish between trading and non-trading payments.

Interest payable on trading loans is an allowable expense in calculating trading profits. For example, interest payable on bank overdrafts or loan notes (also referred to as debentures) used for trading purposes.

Interest payable on non-trading loans is not an allowable expense in calculating trading profits. A loan to purchase an investment would be an example of a non-trading loan. Interest on such a loan should be added back in the adjustment to profits computation.

3.9 Other miscellaneous adjustments

Pre-trading expenditure

Expenditure incurred up to seven years before a trade starts is allowed as an expense of the first accounting period of trading, provided it would have been allowable had the trade existed at the time the expenditure was incurred.

Gifts

Gifts to employees are allowable (but may be taxed on employees).

Other gifts, for example gifts to customers, are only allowable if they fulfil the following three conditions.

- They incorporate a conspicuous advertisement for the business.

- The total cost per donee is not more than £50 per annum.

- The gift is not food, drink (alcoholic or otherwise) or tobacco or a voucher.

Note that if the cost exceeds the £50 limit, the whole amount is disallowed.

Therefore, desk diaries or pens embossed with the company name usually qualify, but a bottle of whisky carrying an advert for the company would not.

 Test your understanding 2

What adjustment, if any, should you make for the following items included in a company's statement of profit or loss when calculating adjusted trading profits?

State 'Add back' or 'No adjustment required'.

1   Managing director's salary (he owns 99% of the shares)

2   Overdraft interest

3   Interest on a loan to purchase an investment property

4   Gifts of diaries to customers, costing £5 each and embossed with the company's name

5   Gifts of bottles of wine to customers, costing £5 each and embossed with the company's name

Entertaining

The cost of entertaining customers and suppliers is disallowed. However, the cost of entertaining staff is allowable.

Trade samples

Trade samples which are not for resale are allowable.

 Test your understanding 3

The following items are charged against profit in the accounts of Saturn Ltd for the year ended 31 March 2024:

1   A payment of £616 to the Royal National Lifeboat Institution (a registered national charity).

2   The write off of £8,000 against a trade debt of the company, being 80% of the debt. The liquidator of the debtor company had advised Saturn Ltd of this figure but in the event £5,000 of the debt was paid in May 2024.

3   Trade samples costing £7,000 in total which are put through the letter boxes of 2,000 homes in the East Midlands.

State how you would deal with each of the items when preparing the company's computation of adjusted trading profits for the year ended 31 March 2024.

Hire or lease charges

The rules for disallowing part of the leasing charges for cars are based on the level of CO_2 emissions.

Leasing charges for cars with CO_2 emissions of 50g/km or less are allowed in full.

There is a standard disallowance of 15% of the leasing charges for a lease on a car with CO_2 emissions over 50g/km.

 Example

BSG Ltd started to lease two cars on 1 May 2023. The details of the leased cars are as follows:

(1)   The first car has a retail price of £21,000 and CO_2 emissions of 65g/km. The leasing charges up to 31 December 2023 are £6,400.

(2)   The other car has a retail price of £15,000 and CO_2 emissions of 45g/km. The leasing charges up to 31 December 2023 are £4,700.

Show the amount disallowed for the purposes of calculating the adjusted trading profits in the year ended 31 December 2023.

Solution

The only disallowance is for the first car as the CO_2 emissions exceed 50g/km.

The disallowed amount is (15% of £6,400) = £960.

Test your understanding 4

The following items are charged against profit in the accounts of Uranus Ltd for the year ended 31 March 2024:

1   Running expenses of the managing director's BMW totalling £10,000 (including depreciation of £6,000). His total mileage in the year was 12,000 of which 6,000 was private. The car was owned by Uranus Ltd.

2   Entertainment expenditure totalling £25,000 of which £10,000 was incurred on overseas customers, £11,000 on UK customers and £4,000 on the annual company dinner for 200 employees.

3   Lease rental of £6,000 on sales director's car costing £20,000. The lease commenced on 1 April 2023. The car has CO_2 emissions of 85g/km.

State how you would deal with each of the above items when preparing the company's computation of adjusted trading profits for the year ended 31 March 2024.

Legal and professional fees

Legal and professional fees are allowable to the extent that they are related to the trade (e.g. debt collection fees).

Any professional costs relating to disputing a fine, tax penalty or connected with an enquiry into a return will usually be disallowable. HMRC guidance states that if the enquiry relates specifically to trading income and no additional profits are brought within the charge to tax, then the associated costs of dealing with the enquiry will be allowable.

3.10   Dividends

Dividends are paid out of profits after they have been subjected to tax. They are not expenses incurred in earning those profits. They are therefore not allowable expenditure.

However, there is normally no adjustment required as the computation starts with the 'net profit' which for a company is before the deduction of dividends paid. In a correctly prepared statement of profit or loss dividends have not been deducted from net profit and so do not need to be added back.

An adjustment is only required if a question specifically tells you that the net profit given is **after** dividends have been deducted.

3.11 Summary

Common items of allowable and disallowable expenditure are summarised below.

Expenditure	Allowable	Disallowable
Fines	Employee parking fines	Other fines and penalties
Fraud	Petty theft by non-senior employees	By directors
Donations	Donations to local charities	Political donations Donations to national charities
In relation to non-current assets	Capital allowances	Depreciation Loss on sale
Repairs	Revenue expenditure Repairs and redecoration	Capital expenditure Improvements Work required on a newly-purchased asset to make it fit for use
Legal expenses	Relate to revenue matters – debt collection, employee contracts	Relate to capital matters – but note exceptions Relate to breaking the law
Irrecoverable debts	Trade debts	Non-trade debts
Interest payable	On trading loans	On non-trading loans
Entertaining	Staff	Customers and suppliers
Gifts	To employees Other gifts provided conditions satisfied	All other gifts
Car leasing	CO_2 emissions of 50g/km or less	Other cars – disallow 15% of leasing costs

Reference material

Some information about disallowable expenses can be found in the 'Disallowed expenditure' section of the reference material provided in the real assessment, so you do not need to learn it.

Why not look up the correct part of the reference material in the introduction to this text book now?

Test your understanding 5

1   Jamaica Ltd operates a business selling high quality second-hand clothes.

Which of the following costs is NOT deductible in arriving at the tax adjusted trading profits?

A   Repairs to shop premises, carried out two weeks after the shop opened.

B   Advertising in the local paper.

C   Parking fine incurred by the Managing Director for parking outside the shop.

D   Cost of writing off stock that wouldn't sell.

2   Bakers R Us Ltd incurred the following expenses for the year ended 31 March 2024, but is unsure of their treatment for tax purposes.

Which of the following is NOT deductible in arriving at Bakers R Us Ltd's tax adjusted trading profit?

A   The cost of new plant and machinery that is used in the bread making process.

B   The write off of a trade debt owed by a customer.

C   Legal fees in chasing the debt owed by a customer.

D   A provision against the debt owed by a customer.

 4   Income included in the accounts but not taxable as trading profits

4.1   Types of income

The following are examples of income which may be included in the statement of profit or loss, but which is not taxable as trading profits.

*   Income taxed in another way, for example rental income (property income), interest receivable.

*   Profits on sales of non-current (i.e. capital) assets.

4.2   Effect

As these types of income are not taxable as trading profits, they must be deducted to arrive at the correct adjusted trading profits.

5 Detailed pro forma adjustment of profits

5.1 Pro forma for a company

	+ £	– £
Net profit per accounts	X	
Add: Disallowable expenditure:		
Depreciation	X	
Loss on sale of non-current assets	X	
Capital expenditure	X	
Legal expenses of capital nature	X	
Fines and penalties	X	
Political donations	X	
Donations to national charities	X	
Entertaining (other than staff)	X	
Gifts to customers	X	
Proportion of high emission car leasing costs	X	
Less: Income in accounts but not trading profits:		
Rental income		X
Profit on sale of non-current assets		X
Interest receivable		X
	―――	―――
	X	X
	(X)	―――
	―――	
Adjusted trading profit before capital allowances	X	
	―――	

Example

The statement of profit or loss of SND Ltd for the year ended 31 March 2024 showed a net profit of £42,000 after accounting for the following items:

Expenditure:	£	Income:	£
Depreciation	9,500	Insurance recovery	
Loan note interest (Note 1)	8,000	re flood damage to	
Irrecoverable debts:		trading inventory	6,500
– Trade debts written off	4,000	Profit on sale of	
– Increase in provision	1,000	machine	3,200
Entertainment expenses			
(Note 2)	2,700		
Legal fees re new lease	3,200		
General expenses (Note 3)	1,800		

Notes:

(1) The loan note was issued to raise finance to purchase plant and machinery for the purpose of the trade.

(2) Entertainment consists of expenditure on:

	£
Entertaining customers	1,200
Staff dance (30 people)	900
Gifts to customers of food hampers	600

(3) General expenses comprise:

	£
Parking fines	
(relating to employees on company business)	300
Fees for employees attending training courses	1,500

Compute the adjusted trading profit for the above period.

Solution

Step 1: Start your solution with the company's net profit:

	+	−
	£	£
Net profit	42,000	

Step 2: Add back any disallowable items of expenditure

Go through each expense in turn and decide whether or not it needs to be added back. If it does require adding back, add the figure to the plus column of your pro forma.

If you do not know how to treat a particular item, guess. You have a good chance of getting the right answer.

Step 3: Deduct income in the accounts which is not taxable as trading profits

Deal with any income in the order in which it appears in the accounts. For each item, ask yourself whether it relates to the company's trade.

If it does, no action is required. If it does not, include the figure in the minus column.

Step 4: Finish by totalling the pro forma

Note that it is not essential for you to put headings such as 'disallowable expenditure' on your pro forma. You could simply state 'add' and 'less'.

You do, however, need to list each adjusted item in words as well as figures.

Approach in computer based assessment (CBA)

You might be given a pro forma and will not have to type in expense headings and numbers. Instead you may have to select correct headings and numbers from drop down menus.

Alternatively, an assessment task may require you to drag and drop each item which needs adjustment into the appropriate part of the computation.

SND Ltd – Adjustment of profit for the year ended 31 March 2024

	+ £	– £
Net profit	42,000	
Depreciation	9,500	
Entertainment expenses	1,800	
Legal fees	3,200	
General expenses	–	
Profit on sale of machine		3,200
	─────	─────
	56,500	(3,200)
	(3,200)	─────
	─────	
Adjusted trading profit	53,300	
	─────	

Explanation

1   Depreciation (capital expenditure) is not an allowable deduction.

2   Loan note interest is allowable (assuming the loan note proceeds were used for trading purposes).

3   Write-offs of trade debts and provisions in a company's accounts are allowable.

4   Expenditure on entertaining customers is not allowable. Expenditure on entertaining staff is allowable. The cost of the hampers is not allowable as they contain food.

5   The legal fees in respect of the new lease are a capital item, and are therefore not allowable.

6   Parking fines incurred by employees will generally be allowed. Training course fees are also allowable, assuming the course relates to the company's trade.

7   The insurance recovery is in respect of trading inventory. It is therefore taxable as trading profits, and no adjustment needs to be made.

8   Profits on the sale of non-current assets (such as plant and machinery) are effectively negative depreciation and are therefore not taxable.

In an assessment task you should try to work methodically through the statement of profit or loss and ensure you deal with all relevant items.

Example

The statement of profit or loss of DTS Ltd for the year ended 31 March 2024 showed a net profit of £53,000 after accounting for the following items:

Expenditure:	£	Income:	£
Depreciation	8,300	Rents received	8,400
Loss on sale of lorry	6,000	Profit on sale of	
Legal fees re employees'		machine	7,400
service contracts	600		
Penalty for late VAT return	2,200		
Repairs (Note)	6,400		

Note:

Included in the figure for repairs is an amount of £5,000 incurred in installing new windows in a recently acquired second-hand warehouse.

This building had suffered fire damage resulting in all of its windows being blown out shortly before being acquired by DTS Ltd. Other repairs were of a routine nature.

Compute the adjusted trading profit for the above period.

Solution

DTS Ltd – Adjustment of profit for the year ended 31 March 2024

	+ £	– £
Net profit	53,000	
Depreciation	8,300	
Loss on sale of lorry	6,000	
Legal fees re employees' service contracts	–	
Penalty for late VAT return	2,200	
Repairs	5,000	
Rents received		(8,400)
Profit on sale of machine		(7,400)
	74,500	(15,800)
	(15,800)	
Adjusted trading profit	58,700	

Explanation

1   Depreciation (capital expenditure) is not an allowable deduction.

2   Losses on the sale of non-current assets are treated in the same way as depreciation – they are added back. Conversely, profits on the sale of non-current assets are deducted.

3   Legal fees in connection with the service contracts are wholly and exclusively for the trade and are therefore allowable.

4   VAT penalties are not allowable.

5   The cost of new windows is not allowable. It is capital expenditure required to put a new asset into a usable state (*Law Shipping* case).

6   Rents received are taxable as property income and not trading profits, therefore deduct.

In an assessment you should try to work methodically through the information given and ensure you deal with all relevant items.

Test your understanding 6

The following is the statement of profit or loss of Brazil Ltd for the year ended 30 April 2024:

	£	£
Sales		240,458
Less: Cost of sales		(183,942)
Gross profit		56,516
Other income		5,000
Salaries and wages	24,174	
Rent and rates	8,560	
Legal and professional charges	3,436	
General expenses	1,211	
Depreciation	3,047	
		(40,428)
Net profit		21,088

The following further information is given:

(1) **Other income**

This comprises bank deposit interest for the year received on 30 April 2024.

(2) **Legal and professional charges**

This item includes the following:

	£
Legal fees in connection with new lease	325
Legal fees in connection with action by employee for unfair dismissal	830
Payment to employee for unfair dismissal	1,200
Accountancy charges	1,081

(3) **General expenses**

These include a donation of £25 to Save the Children, a national charity.

Calculate the adjusted trading profit for the year for tax purposes.

📝 Test your understanding 7

The following is the statement of profit or loss of Cashew Ltd for the year ended 31 March 2024:

	£	£
Gross profit		47,214
Other income		4,000
Salaries and wages	20,509	
Repairs to premises	3,263	
Travelling and entertaining expenses	1,964	
Irrecoverable debts	(630)	
Depreciation	2,120	
		(27,226)
Net profit		23,988

The following further information is given:

(1)   Other income

This comprises bank deposit interest for the year which was received on 31 March 2024.

(2)   Repairs to premises

Included in this item is £1,450 incurred in fitting a new shop-front to a former office and £250 for the initial repainting of a new shop.

(3)   Travelling and entertaining expenses

These include expenses of entertaining UK customers of £326 and gifts to customers of Christmas hampers costing £528 (cost £48 each).

(4)   Irrecoverable debts

The figure in the accounts is made up as follows:

	£
Trade debt recoveries	(232)
Decrease in provision for irrecoverable trade debts	(398)
	(630)

Calculate the adjusted trading profit for the year for tax purposes.

Test your understanding 8

Tricks Ltd's statement of profit or loss for the year ended 31 March 2024 was as follows:

	£	£
Sales		370,150
Loan note interest receivable		4,100
Rent receivable		12,000
Profit on the sale of an investment		2,750
		———
		389,000
Allowable trading expenses	125,750	
Disallowable trading expenses	5,900	
Loan note interest payable (Note)	8,100	
	———	(139,750)
		———
Net profit		249,250
		———

Note: The funds raised by the issue of the loan note were used to purchase machinery for use in the business.

Calculate Tricks Ltd's adjusted trading profits for the year ended 31 March 2024.

6 Summary

You should now be able to successfully attempt questions requiring you to calculate the adjusted trading profit for corporation tax purposes.

The starting point for computing adjusted trading profits is the net profit shown in the company's accounts. This must be adjusted in respect of the following items:

- Disallowable expenditure.

    The main types of disallowable expenditure are:

    - expenditure not wholly and exclusively for the purpose of the trade

    - expenditure disallowed under the detailed rules.

- Income included in the accounts but not taxable as trading profits. For example:

    - rents and interest

    - profits on the sale of capital assets.

When writing out answers on paper, it is advisable to use a '+' and '−' column and deal with each adjustment as you work methodically through the question. There is no need to arrange your answer into the two types of adjustment shown above. Either presentation may be seen in the assessment.

Test your understanding answers

Test your understanding 1

1	Capital	The purchase of a new non-current asset is capital expenditure
2	Revenue	Rates are payable every year and are revenue expenditure
3	Capital	As the asset was purchased in a damaged condition and needed to be repaired before use, it is capital expenditure
4	Capital	Legal fees in relation to a capital purchase are treated as capital expenditure
5	Revenue	Legal fees in relation to the renewal of a short lease are specifically allowed as revenue expenditure

Test your understanding 2

Adjustment of profits

1   No adjustment required – allowable expense.

2   No adjustment required – allowable expense.

3   Add back – not allowable deduction from trading profits.

4   No adjustment required – allowable expense.

5   Add back – gift of drink.

   Note that the gift of any type of drink is not allowable (not just alcohol).

Test your understanding 3

Saturn Ltd

1 Donations to national charities are disallowed and treated as qualifying charitable donations. Therefore, add back £616.

2 No adjustment is required.

   The write-off of a trade debt is allowable. There will be a credit in the following year's accounts, when the £5,000 is recovered, which will be taxable as part of the trading profit.

3 Trade samples, which are not for resale, are allowable. So no adjustment required.

 Test your understanding 4

Uranus Ltd

1 Running expenses, except for depreciation, are an allowable deduction. The depreciation must be disallowed but relief for the cost of the car will be available through capital allowances.

   The private use of the car by an employee of a company is irrelevant for profit adjustment purposes.

   Therefore, add back £6,000.

2 Disallow all entertaining except staff entertaining.

   Therefore, add back £21,000.

3 Part of this lease cost will be disallowed as the car has CO_2 emissions exceeding 50g/km.

   The disallowable portion added back is as follows:
   $(15\% \times £6,000) = £900$

Test your understanding 5

Jamaica Ltd

1   The correct answer is C.

Bakers R Us Ltd

2   The correct answer is A.

Explanation

1   Fines incurred by directors are not deductible.

Parking fines incurred by employees whilst on business activity are generally deductible, but not those incurred by directors.

The other costs are deductible.

2   A is a capital cost, whereas the others are revenue costs, all of which are allowable as trading expenses, given the context.

The cost of plant and machinery will qualify for capital allowances (see Chapter 4).

Test your understanding 6

Brazil Ltd

Adjusted trading profits for the year ended 30 April 2024

	£	£
Net profit as per accounts	21,088	
Add: Legal fees re new lease	325	
National charity donation	25	
Depreciation	3,047	
Less: Bank deposit interest		(5,000)
	24,485	(5,000)
	(5,000)	
Adjusted trading profit	19,485	

Explanation

- Legal fees and payment in connection with unfair dismissal are allowable, as part of the cost of employing staff.

- Any donation to a national charity is not allowable.

Test your understanding 7

Cashew Ltd

Adjusted trading profits for the year ended 31 March 2024

	£	£
Net profit as per accounts	23,988	
Add: New shop-front	1,450	
Entertaining customers	326	
Gifts	528	
Depreciation	2,120	
Less: Bank deposit interest		(4,000)
	28,412	(4,000)
	(4,000)	
Adjusted trading profit	24,412	

Explanation

- The £250 initial repainting costs in respect of the new shop are considered to be allowable, following the decision in the *Odeon Theatres case*.

- Although the hampers cost less than £50 each, the cost is disallowed as the gift is of food.

- Recoveries of trade debts relate to the trade and are therefore taxable and no adjustment is required. As a company, Cashew Ltd's accounts are prepared using IFRS Standards, therefore the movement in the provision for irrecoverable trade debts would be specific in nature and also taxable. No adjustment is required.

Test your understanding 8

Tricks Ltd

Adjusted trading profits for the year ended 31 March 2024

	£
Net profit	249,250
Add: Disallowable expenses	5,900
	255,150
Less: Loan note interest receivable	(4,100)
Rent receivable	(12,000)
Profit on sale of investment	(2,750)
Adjusted trading profits	236,300

The funds raised by the issue of the loan note were used for the purposes of the trade and the interest paid is therefore an allowable deduction in computing the adjusted trading profits.

Note that this alternative presentation to the two columns shown previously is also acceptable.

Capital allowances

4

Introduction

In the assessment, Task 2 will test capital allowances. This task will be partly manually marked.

Capital allowances are a very important topic.

ASSESSMENT CRITERIA	CONTENTS
Which capital allowances apply to different assets: – plant and machinery – structures and buildings (2.2) Prepare capital allowance computations for accounting periods: – longer than 12 months – shorter than 12 months – equal to 12 months (2.2)	1 Introduction to capital allowances 2 Qualifying expenditure 3 The allowances 4 Calculating the allowances 5 Capital allowances treatment of cars 6 Pro forma computation for capital allowances on plant and machinery 7 Impact of the length of the accounting period 8 Business cessation 9 Structures and buildings allowances

1 Introduction to capital allowances

1.1 Capital allowances

Capital allowances are a form of depreciation that is allowable for tax purposes. The allowances are only given on certain items of capital expenditure. This syllabus includes plant and machinery capital allowances and structures and buildings allowances (SBAs). We will consider SBAs separately at the end of this chapter.

The rules in this chapter are also largely applicable to the calculation of capital allowances for an unincorporated business. The differences in that calculation are set out in Chapter 8.

1.2 Capital allowances v depreciation

Each business can decide its own rate of depreciation for accounting purposes. In theory, identical businesses with the same assets could have different amounts of depreciation.

In order for everyone to be treated the same, HMRC use a standard calculation of capital allowances for tax purposes.

The capital allowances are deducted instead of depreciation, to arrive at the adjusted trading profit.

 Example

Opalite Ltd and Pyrite Ltd are two companies making the same products. In the year ended 31 December 2023, both companies made profits before depreciation/capital allowances of £200,000. Both have only one piece of machinery that they bought in the year for £150,000.

The companies have different methods of calculating depreciation, giving the following amounts:

Opalite Ltd	£25,000
Pyrite Ltd	£35,000

For tax purposes, both companies would have capital allowances of £150,000.

Compare the accounting profits and adjusted trading profits of both companies.

Solution

	Opalite Ltd £	Pyrite Ltd £
Profit before depreciation	200,000	200,000
Less: Depreciation	(25,000)	(35,000)
Accounting profits	175,000	165,000

Adjustment of profits computation

Accounting profits	175,000	165,000
Add: Depreciation	25,000	35,000
Adjusted profit before capital allowances	200,000	200,000
Less: Capital allowances	(150,000)	(150,000)
Adjusted trading profit	50,000	50,000

In reality there are likely to be many more adjustments that could give rise to different adjusted trading profits for tax purposes (as per Chapter 3).

However, this example illustrates that identical businesses could have different accounting profits, but have the same adjusted trading profits on which their tax is calculated.

2 Qualifying expenditure

2.1 What qualifies as plant and machinery?

There is no automatic right to tax relief for capital expenditure.

In order to qualify for capital allowances, expenditure must usually be in respect of plant or machinery.

There is no statutory definition of plant, however the courts have established a **function test**:

Does the asset perform:	This means that the asset is:	Plant and machinery?
An active function	Apparatus **with which** the business is carried on	Yes
A passive function	The setting **in which** the business is carried on	No

The dividing line between an asset that is functional and one that is merely setting is not always clear. Examples below show how the courts have reacted to claims for capital allowances in these circumstances.

- A canopy covering petrol filling pumps was held to be part of the setting and not plant and machinery. (It did not assist in serving petrol to customers.)

- False ceilings in a restaurant were not plant. (All they did was hide pipes.)

- Swimming pools at a caravan park were held to be plant and machinery – the caravan park as a whole was the setting.

The most common types of capital expenditure found in a set of financial accounts that are treated as 'plant and machinery' for tax purposes are:

- plant and machinery including moveable partitioning

- fixtures and fittings

- motor vehicles including cars, vans and lorries

- computer equipment and software.

In addition, the cost of alterations to buildings needed for the installation of plant qualifies as plant and machinery.

3 The allowances

3.1 Main types of capital allowances

The following are the main types of capital allowances that may be available to a company in respect of plant and machinery.

(a) Writing down allowance (WDA)

- given at 18% on a reducing balance basis on most assets

- given at 6% on a reducing balance basis for items in the special rate pool.

(b) Annual investment allowance (AIA)

- a 100% allowance for the first £1,000,000 of expenditure incurred by a company on plant and machinery in a 12-month period

- where a company spends more than the maximum AIA, the excess expenditure may qualify for a WDA.

(c) First year allowance (FYA)

- a 100% allowance is available on cars purchased with CO_2 emissions of 0g/km (see section 5).

(d) Full expensing

- 100% relief is available to companies on the purchase of **new** plant and machinery between 1 April 2023 and 31 March 2026.

 Example

Howlite Ltd purchased a used machine costing £1,210,000 on 1 March 2023 in its year ended 31 December 2023. This is its only capital item.

Calculate the capital allowances for the first three years of ownership.

Assume the rates of allowances for the year ended 31 March 2024 continue into the future.

Solution

Howlite Ltd – Capital allowances

	£	Allowances £
Year ended 31 December 2023		
Cost	1,210,000	
AIA (max)	(1,000,000)	1,000,000
	210,000	
WDA (18% × £210,000)	(37,800)	37,800
	172,200	1,037,800
Year ended 31 December 2024		
WDA (18% × £172,200)	(30,996)	30,996
	141,204	
Year ended 31 December 2025		
WDA (18% × £141,204)	(25,417)	25,417
	115,787	

4 Calculating the allowances

4.1 General pool (or main pool)

Most items of plant and machinery go into the general pool (also known as the main pool). Once an asset enters the pool, it loses its identity. This means that the writing down allowance (WDA) is calculated on the balance of the whole pool of assets, rather than on the individual assets.

When a new asset is acquired, the purchase price increases the value of the pool. When an asset is disposed of, the pool value is reduced by the lower of the sale proceeds or the original cost of the asset (see section 4.7).

Allowances are given for accounting periods. Allowances commence in the year in which the expenditure is incurred. A full WDA is given in the year of purchase irrespective of the date of purchase within that year.

4.2 Expenditure not pooled

As companies may have many assets, it would be extremely time-consuming to calculate allowances separately for each asset. Therefore, all qualifying expenditure is added to the general pool, apart from cars with CO_2 emissions exceeding 50g/km. These are added to the special rate pool, which operates in the same way as the general pool except that:

- the WDA is 6% for a 12-month period.

4.3 Annual investment allowance (AIA)

The AIA is a 100% allowance for expenditure incurred by a company on plant and machinery. The precise amount of AIA depends on the date to which a company is making up its accounts.

The AIA:

- is not available for expenditure on cars

- is available for expenditure on other vehicles

- applies for a 12-month accounting period. The allowance is time apportioned for short accounting periods.

Where expenditure on plant and machinery in an accounting period exceeds the maximum AIA, the excess is added to the pool balance on which a WDA can be claimed. If the expenditure incurred in the period is less than the available AIA, the remaining balance of any AIA is wasted.

 Example

Marble Ltd started trading on 1 March 2023. In its first year of trading the company made the following purchases:

- used plant and machinery (purchased 1 March 2023) £1,137,500

- a car for the office manager (CO_2 emissions 40g/km)   £11,000

(a)   Calculate how much of Marble Ltd's capital expenditure is eligible for writing down allowances after deduction of the AIA.

(b)   What would your answer to part (a) be if the plant and machinery had cost £780,000?

Solution

(a) **Marble Ltd – Capital allowances – year ended 29 February 2024**

	AIA	General pool
	£	£
Additions:		
Not qualifying for AIA		
Car		11,000
Qualifying for AIA		
Plant and machinery	1,137,500	
AIA	(1,000,000)	
	————	
Balance eligible for 18% WDA		137,500
		————
Eligible for WDA		148,500
		————

(b) **If the plant and machinery had cost £780,000**

	AIA	General pool
	£	£
Additions:		
Not qualifying for AIA		
Car		11,000
Qualifying for AIA		
Plant and machinery	780,000	
AIA (Note)	(780,000)	
	————	0
		————
Eligible for WDA		11,000
		————

Note

The unused AIA of £220,000 (£1,000,000 – £780,000) is lost.

Test your understanding 1

Which of the following acquisitions will qualify for the annual investment allowance?

A   A warehouse

B   Display equipment in a shop

C   A car used partly for business purposes by an employee

D   A pool car used exclusively for business use

4.4   First year allowance (FYA)

A first year allowance is given in the year that a qualifying asset is purchased.

A 100% FYA is given for expenditure on new zero-emission cars (see section 5).

First year allowances are given in full in the period of purchase, **regardless** of the length of the accounting period (i.e. the FYA is never time apportioned).

4.5   Full expensing

A 100% first year allowance is available to companies that purchase **new** (not second-hand) plant and machinery between 1 April 2023 and 31 March 2026. Full expensing is not available for expenditure on cars.

The relief is given in full in the period of purchase, regardless of the length of the accounting period (i.e. the relief is never time apportioned). Unlike AIA, there is **no limit** on the amount of full expensing relief that can be claimed in any 12-month period.

In practice, it is beneficial to claim the AIA in preference to full expensing. Although the relief is exactly the same on acquisition, claiming the AIA avoids the balancing charge which will arise on the disposal of an asset on which full expensing relief has been claimed (see section 4.7).

However, in your assessment, equal credit will be given for claiming either the AIA (within the limit) or full expensing.

4.6 Writing down allowances (WDA)

A WDA of 18% is given on a reducing balance basis for a 12-month period.

It is given on:

- the unrelieved expenditure in the pool brought forward at the beginning of the accounting period (known as the tax written down value (TWDV))

- plus any additions eligible for WDAs

- less disposals of plant and machinery.

The TWDV brought forward includes all prior period expenditure, less capital allowances already claimed.

 Example

Plaster Ltd started trading on 1 January 2023 preparing accounts to 31 December each year.

On 1 May 2023 the company purchased £1,115,000 of new machinery and a car costing £22,000 with CO_2 emissions of 45g/km.

Calculate the capital allowances available to Plaster Ltd for the year ended 31 December 2023.

Solution

Plaster Ltd – Capital allowances – year ended 31 December 2023

	FYA – Full expensing £	General pool £	Allowances £
Addition not qualifying for AIA/FYA			
Car		22,000	
Addition qualifying for full expensing	1,115,000		
Full expensing (Note)	(1,115,000)		1,115,000
WDA (18% × £22,000)		(3,960)	3,960
TWDV c/f		18,040	
Total allowances			1,118,960

Note

Alternatively, the AIA could be claimed for the first £1,000,000 of expenditure on the new machinery with full expensing for the remaining £115,000, to give the same total allowances. In the assessment, equal credit would be given for either approach.

4.7 Disposals

When a pool item is sold, the sale proceeds are deducted from the pool. However, this deduction cannot exceed the asset's original cost.

The exception to this rule is when disposing of an asset on which full expensing relief has been claimed. In this situation, the proceeds are not deducted from the pool. Instead, an immediate balancing charge (see section 4.8) will arise, equal to 100% of the disposal proceeds.

The following example illustrates the working of the general pool, including disposals.

Example

Apple Ltd prepares accounts to 31 March each year.

On 1 May 2023 Apple Ltd incurred expenditure of £10,000 on the purchase of new shop fittings and machinery. On 1 June 2023 the company sold some equipment for £6,000 (cost £4,000).

On 5 May 2024 the company sold equipment for £2,395 which had cost £11,200 in May 2018.

The tax written down value of the pool at 1 April 2023 was £8,260.

Compute the capital allowances for the years ended 31 March 2024 and 31 March 2025.

Assume the rates of allowances for the year ended 31 March 2024 continue into the future.

Solution

Step 1: **Identify the balance brought forward at the beginning of the accounting period**

This is the *tax written down value* (Tax WDV or TWDV).

	Pool £
Year ended 31 March 2024	
TWDV brought forward	8,260

Step 2: **Identify the accounting periods in which the additions and disposals occur**

In the year ended 31 March 2024, Apple Ltd acquired plant costing £10,000 and sold plant for £6,000 (cost £4,000).

The second disposal occurs in the second accounting period.

Step 3: **Identify any additions on which full expensing/AIA can be claimed**

The plant acquired on 1 May 2023 qualifies for AIA and also qualifies for full expensing. In this example, AIA has been claimed; however, in the assessment, equal credit would be given for claiming either the AIA or full expensing.

Step 4: **Prepare the capital allowances computation**

Deal with one accounting period at a time.

	AIA £	General pool £	Allowances £
Year ended 31 March 2024			
TWDV b/f		8,260	
Additions qualifying for AIA	10,000		
AIA	(10,000)		10,000
	───────		
Disposals			
1 June 2023			
(proceeds restricted to cost)		(4,000)	
		───────	
		4,260	
WDA @ 18%		(767)	767
		───────	
TWDV c/f		3,493	
		───────	
Total allowances			10,767
			───────

	General pool £	Allowances £
Year ended 31 March 2025		
TWDV b/f	3,493	
Disposals		
5 May 2024	(2,395)	
	───────	
	1,098	
WDA @ 18%	(198)	198
	───────	
TWDV c/f	900	
	───────	
Total allowances		198
		───────

4.8 Balancing charges

If, on the disposal of an asset in the general pool, the disposal proceeds exceed the pool balance (after additions to the pool in the period have been added) a negative balance will be left on the pool.

This gives rise to a 'balancing charge'.

A balancing charge is added to the pool to bring the pool balance back to £Nil.

A balancing charge is treated as a negative capital allowance (i.e. added to the adjusted trading profit).

4.9 Small pools writing down allowance

The WDA is claimed each accounting period and if there are no additions in an accounting period to be added to the pool, the WDA will be claimed on an ever-decreasing amount for many years. It will be quite common in many small businesses and companies for there to be no additions to the pool, since any purchases in the period are usually covered by the AIA.

To prevent the inconvenience of keeping records of small balances of expenditure, a 'small pool WDA' can be claimed.

The small pool WDA available:

- applies to the general pool and special rate pool

- is any amount up to £1,000, and

- applies for a 12-month accounting period. The WDA is time apportioned for short accounting periods.

Therefore, an allowance of up to £1,000 can be claimed on the general or special rate pool where the unrelieved expenditure on the pool (after dealing with additions and disposals in the period) is £1,000 or less. This allows the balance on a 'small pool' to be written off at once.

The claim is optional. However, it is likely that the taxpayer will want to claim as much as possible and reduce the remaining balance on the pool to £Nil.

Example

Eden Ltd prepares accounts to 31 December. During the year ending 31 December 2023 it incurred the following expenditure:

Purchased new office furniture for £23,000 on 1 June 2023.

In addition, on 1 July 2023 it sold office equipment for £10,000 (original cost £18,000).

As at 1 January 2023 the tax written down value on its general pool was £10,800.

Calculate Eden Ltd's capital allowances for the year ended 31 December 2023.

Solution

	AIA £	General pool £	Allowances £
Year ended 31 December 2023			
TWDV b/f		10,800	
Additions qualifying for AIA	23,000		
AIA (Note)	(23,000)		23,000
Disposals			
1 July 2023		(10,000)	
		800	
Small pool WDA		(800)	800
TWDV c/f		0	
Total allowances			23,800

Note

In the assessment, equal credit would be given for claiming either the AIA or full expensing on the acquisition of the office furniture.

4.10 Not claiming allowances

It is not compulsory to claim capital allowances. If profits are low, it may be preferable not to claim writing down allowances in the current year and instead to carry forward a higher tax written down value. Larger writing down allowances will then be available in the future when profits may be higher.

5 Capital allowances treatment of cars

5.1 Capital allowances treatment of cars

The capital allowances available in respect of cars depend on the level of the car's CO_2 emissions.

- Cars with CO_2 emissions between 1 and 50g/km are added to the general pool and attract a WDA of 18%.

- If the car has emissions exceeding 50g/km then it must be added to the special rate pool where the WDA is only 6%.

- New zero-emission cars are however eligible for a first year allowance (FYA) in the year of purchase.

  The rate of the FYA is 100% and it is only for new cars with zero CO_2 emissions (including electric cars).

  Second-hand zero-emission cars are treated as cars with CO_2 emissions between 1 – 50g/km, however, if the question does not specify, you should assume that the car is new.

You will be told the level of CO_2 emissions for each car in the assessment.

Remember also that cars **never** qualify for the AIA or full expensing.

The capital allowances task in the assessment often mentions private use of vehicles by an employee. No adjustment is required for private use within a company.

5.2 Disposals of cars

(a) *General pool cars*

Deduct lower of disposal proceeds and original cost from general pool balance before WDA is calculated (i.e. like normal pool disposals).

(b) *Zero-emission cars*

As for (a).

(c) *Special rate pool cars*

Deduct lower of disposal proceeds and original cost from special rate pool balance.

If a positive balance remains – give WDA at 18% (general pool cars) or 6% (special rate pool cars).

If a negative balance remains – a balancing charge applies (see section 4.8).

 Example

Thistle Ltd has a year ended 31 March 2024. Its general pool had a TWDV brought forward of £31,000 at 1 April 2023.

In the year ended 31 March 2024, it purchased two assets:

(a) a new car (CO_2 emissions 49g/km) costing £9,000; and

(b) a new van costing £4,000 (on 1 February 2024).

There were no disposals in the year.

(a) Calculate the capital allowances for the year.

(b) What would your answer be to (a) if the car was zero-emission?

Solution

(a) **Thistle Ltd – Capital allowances – year ended 31 March 2024**

	AIA £	General pool £	Allowances £
TWDV b/f		31,000	
Addition: no AIA or FYA		9,000	
Addition qualifying for AIA			
Van	4,000		
AIA	(4,000)		4,000
		40,000	
WDA @ 18%		(7,200)	7,200
TWDV c/f		32,800	
Total capital allowances			11,200

(b) **Thistle Ltd – Capital allowances – year ended 31 March 2024**

	AIA £	FYA – Cars £	General pool £	Allowances £
TWDV b/f			31,000	
Addition: FYA				
Zero-emission car		9,000		
FYA @ 100%		(9,000)		9,000
Addition qualifying for AIA				
Van	4,000			
AIA	(4,000)			4,000
			31,000	
WDA @ 18%			(5,580)	5,580
TWDV c/f			25,420	
Total capital allowances				18,580

Example

Joist Ltd prepares accounts to 31 March each year.

In the year ended 31 March 2024 it purchased the following cars:

(1)   Car costing £16,000 with CO_2 emissions of 48g/km

(2)   Car costing £20,000 with CO_2 emissions of 120g/km

The TWDV brought forward on the general pool was £21,480.

Calculate Joist Ltd's capital allowances for the year ended 31 March 2024.

Solution

Joist Ltd – Capital allowances – year ended 31 March 2024

	General pool £	Special rate pool £	Allowances £
TWDV b/f	21,480		
Additions: no AIA or FYA			
Car – CO_2 1–50 g/km	16,000		
Car – CO_2 >50 g/km		20,000	
	37,480		
WDA @ 18%	(6,746)		6,746
WDA @ 6%		(1,200)	1,200
TWDV c/f	30,734	18,800	
Total capital allowances			7,946

Example

Grin Ltd prepares accounts to 31 March each year.

At 1 April 2023 the tax written down values brought forward were:

General pool £15,400
Special rate pool £17,000

During the year ended 31 March 2024 the company purchased new plant for £20,000 and two cars with CO_2 emissions of 110g/km costing £20,000 each.

There were no additions in the year ended 31 March 2025.

There were no disposals in the year ended 31 March 2024 but in the year ended 31 March 2025, one of the cars purchased in the previous year was sold for £13,500.

Calculate Grin Ltd's capital allowances for the years ended 31 March 2024 and 2025.

Assume the rates of allowances for the year ended 31 March 2024 continue into the future.

Solution

The first task is to decide how many columns are needed to answer this question. There are two balances brought forward which require their own columns and a column is required on the left to deduct the FYA/AIA/full expensing.

A pro forma can then be set up as below

	AIA	General pool	Special rate pool	Allowances
	£	£	£	£
Year ended 31 March 2024				
TWDV b/f		15,400	17,000	

Now the additions can be put into the appropriate column and the allowances calculated.

Grin Ltd – Capital allowances

	AIA	General pool	Special rate pool	Allowances
	£	£	£	£
Year ended 31 March 2024				
TWDV b/f		15,400	17,000	
Additions:				
Not qualifying for AIA or FYA				
Cars over 50g/km			40,000	
			———	
			57,000	
Qualifying for AIA				
Plant	20,000			
AIA (Note)	(20,000)			20,000
	———			
WDA @ 18%		(2,772)		2,772
WDA @ 6%			(3,420)	3,420
		———	———	
TWDV c/f		12,628	53,580	———
Total allowances				26,192
				———
Year ended 31 March 2025				
Disposals			(13,500)	
			———	
			40,080	
WDA @ 18%		(2,273)		2,273
WDA @ 6%			(2,405)	2,405
		———	———	
TWDV c/f		10,355	37,675	
		———	———	
Total allowances				4,678
				———

Note

In the assessment, equal credit would be given for claiming either the AIA or full expensing on the acquisition of the plant.

The example below demonstrates the full capital allowances working.

 Example

Polar Ltd started trading on 1 January 2023, preparing accounts to 31 December each year.

The following assets have been purchased since the company began trading.

Date of purchase	Asset	Cost £
15 January 2023	Plant and machinery	1,002,800
9 November 2023	Used car	1,472
10 December 2023	Used car	928
23 March 2024	New plant	40,500
8 June 2024	New car	19,500
20 October 2025	New car	19,571

The cars acquired on 9 November 2023 and 10 December 2023 have CO_2 emissions of between 1 – 50g/km.

The new car acquired on 8 June 2024 has CO_2 emissions of 120g/km and the one acquired on 20 October 2025 has CO_2 emissions of 0g/km.

All the cars are used by employees 60% for business and 40% privately.

Calculate the capital allowances due for the three years ending 31 December 2025.

Assume the rates of allowances for the year ended 31 March 2024 continue into the future.

Solution

The approach is as follows:

- Allocate additions and disposals to the relevant accounting periods. Any acquisitions made prior to the start of trading are treated as if made on the first day of trading.

- Identify which additions qualify for full expensing, AIA and FYA.

- Ignore information about private use as this is not relevant to companies.

Polar Ltd – Capital allowances computation

	AIA/ FYA £	General pool £	Special rate pool £	Total allowances £
Y/e 31 December 2023				
TWDV b/f				
Additions: No AIA				
Cars (£1,472 + £928)		2,400		
Qualifying for AIA				
Plant and machinery	1,002,800			
AIA (max)	(1,000,000)			1,000,000
	———	2,800		
		———		
		5,200		
WDA (18% × £5,200)		(936)		936
		———		
TWDV c/f		4,264		
				———
Total allowances				1,000,936
				———
Y/e 31 December 2024				
Additions: No AIA				
Car – CO_2 > 50g/km			19,500	
Additions qualifying for AIA				
Plant	40,500			
AIA (Note)	(40,500)			40,500
	———			
WDA @ 18%/6%		(768)	(1,170)	1,938
		———	———	
TWDV c/f		3,496	18,330	
				———
Total allowances				42,438
				———

Y/e 31 December 2025

Additions qualifying for FYA			
Zero-emission car	19,571		
FYA (100%)	(19,571)		19,571
	————		
WDA @ 18%/6%		(629) (1,100)	1,729
		———— ————	
TWDV c/f		2,867 17,230	
		———— ————	
Total allowances			21,300
			————

Note

The new plant purchased on 23 March 2024 qualifies for both AIA and full expensing. In the assessment, equal credit would be given for claiming either the AIA or full expensing on the acquisition of this plant.

 Test your understanding 2

Entrance Ltd prepares accounts to 31 December annually.

On 1 January 2023 the tax written down value of plant and machinery brought forward on the general pool was £24,000.

The following transactions took place in the year to 31 December 2023.

15 April 2023	Purchased car for £12,600 (emissions 120g/km)
30 April 2023	Sold plant for £3,200 (original cost £4,800)
16 July 2023	Purchased car for £9,200 (emissions 40g/km)
17 August 2023	Purchased car for £9,400 (emissions 45g/km)
12 December 2023	Purchased new car for £26,150 (emissions 0g/km)

In the following year to 31 December 2024, Entrance Ltd sold 2 cars, one for £7,900, originally purchased on 17 August 2023. And the car purchased on 15 April 2023 was sold for £9,400 on 9 November 2024. There were no other transactions.

Compute the capital allowances for the years ended 31 December 2023 and 31 December 2024.

Assume the rates of allowances for the year ended 31 March 2024 continue into the future.

6 Pro forma computation for capital allowances on plant and machinery

6.1 Plant and machinery allowances

Capital allowances are an important element of the syllabus. To answer capital allowances questions successfully, it is vital to use a methodical approach to work through the information in the question.

The following approach to computational questions together with the following pro forma will help you to deal with the information in the correct order.

Reference material

Some information about capital allowances can be found in the 'Capital allowances' section of the reference material provided in the real assessment, so you do not need to learn it.

Why not look up the correct part of the reference material in the introduction to this text book now?

6.2 Approach to computational questions

For plant and machinery capital allowances, adopt the following step-by-step approach:

1   Read the information in the question and decide which columns/pools you will require.

2   Insert the TWDV b/f if not already shown (does not apply in a new trade).

3   Insert additions not eligible for the AIA or FYA into the appropriate column.

4   Deal with additions qualifying for 100% FYA and full expensing.

5   Insert additions eligible for the AIA in the AIA column, and then allocate the AIA to the additions. You must time apportion the AIA if the accounting period is not 12 months

6   Deal with any disposal by deducting the lower of cost and sale proceeds.

7   Work out any balancing charge if proceeds exceed the amount in the general or special rate pools. Remember that if any balance remains in those pools then a WDA is given (unless it is the final accounting period)

8   Calculate the WDA at the appropriate rate on each of the pools. The rate of WDA will need to be time apportioned if the accounting period is not 12 months

9   Calculate the TWDV to carry forward to the next accounting period and add the 'total allowances' column.

10 Deduct the total allowances from the tax adjusted trading profits.

Pro forma capital allowances computation

	AIA £	FYA – Cars £	FYA – Full expensing	General pool £	Special rate pool £	Allowances £
TWDV b/f				X	X	
Additions:						
Not qualifying for AIA or FYA						
Cars (up to 50g/km)				X		
Cars (over 50g/km)					X	
Qualifying for FYA						
Zero-emission cars		X				
FYA @ 100%		(X)				X
Qualifying for full expensing						
New plant and machinery purchased from 1 April 2023			X			
Full expensing			(X)			X
Qualifying for AIA						
Used plant and machinery	X					
Plant and machinery purchased pre 1 April 2023	X					
AIA (do not exceed maximum)	(X)					X
	───					
Excess to general pool				X		
Disposals (lower of original cost and sale proceeds)				(X)	(X)	
				───	───	
				X	X	
WDA @ 18%				(X)		X
WDA @ 6%					(X)	X
				───	───	
TWDV c/f				X	X	
				───	───	───
Total allowances						X
						───

6.3 Approach to assessment questions

In the CBA, as part of Task 2, you will be given a grid to enter capital allowance figures. It is likely that this grid will show the headings for the columns, possibly with the TWDV brought forward already inserted, and may include some columns that are not required.

You should add the figures into the computation, following the layout used in this chapter. However, you will not have to enter underlines or lines marking totals. You may have to omit headings and abbreviate words if they will not fit in the cell.

It is recommended that you prepare the computation on the paper provided before entering it on screen.

This part of Task 2 will be manually marked.

 Test your understanding 3

Deni Ltd is a manufacturing business preparing accounts to 31 January each year.

At 1 February 2023, the tax written down value of plant and machinery in the general pool was £25,000.

During the year ended 31 January 2024, the following transactions were undertaken:

Purchases		£
1 May 2023	New machinery	1,011,250
15 June 2023	Second-hand machinery	10,000
20 August 2023	MD's car with CO_2 emissions of 40g/km (used 80% for business)	19,600

Sales		
25 February 2023	Machinery (cost £6,000)	1,750

Compute Deni Ltd's capital allowances for the accounting period ended 31 January 2024.

Test your understanding 4

Tense Ltd prepares accounts to 31 December annually. On 1 January 2023, the balance of plant and machinery brought forward was £16,000.

The following transactions took place in the year to 31 December 2023.

15 April 2023	Purchased a car for £15,000 (CO_2 emissions 45g/km)
30 April 2023	Sold plant for £2,000 (original cost £1,600)
26 July 2023	Purchased two new cars for £9,300 each. Both of these cars are zero-emission cars.

In the following year to 31 December 2024, Tense Ltd sold for £7,600 one of the cars originally purchased on 26 July 2023.

The car originally purchased on 15 April 2023 was sold for £8,000 on 9 May 2024. There were no other transactions.

Compute the capital allowances for the years ended 31 December 2023 and 31 December 2024.

Assume the rates of allowances for the year ended 31 March 2024 continue into the future.

7 Impact of the length of the accounting period

7.1 Short accounting periods

Capital allowances are computed for accounting periods and deducted in calculating trading profits.

The allowances calculated so far have all been for 12-month accounting periods.

Where the accounting period is less than 12 months long, the AIA and WDA must be scaled down accordingly. You must perform this calculation to the nearest month.

If the period for which accounts are prepared exceeds 12 months, the capital allowances are computed in two stages – the first 12 months, then the balance (see Chapter 2, section 2.3 and Chapter 5, section 2.7).

Note that the first year allowances (including full expensing) are never time apportioned.

Therefore, purchases of new zero-emission cars are always given the FYA in full, even if the length of the accounting period is less than 12 months.

Example

Kyanite Ltd started to trade on 1 January 2023 and, on that day, purchased a second-hand machine costing £1,005,000.

Calculate the capital allowances due for the first period of account on the assumption that accounts are prepared to

(a) 31 December 2023

(b) 31 October 2023

(c) 31 May 2024

Solution

	(a) 31 Dec 2023 (12 months) £	(b) 31 Oct 2023 (10 months) £	(c) 31 May 2024 (17 months) £
First period of account:			
First AP (max 12 months)			
Addition:			
Qualifying for AIA			
Plant and machinery	1,005,000	1,005,000	1,005,000
AIA	(1,000,000)		(1,000,000)
(max £1,000,000 × 10/12)		(833,333)	
	5,000	171,667	5,000
WDA (18%)	(900)		(900)
WDA (18% × 10/12)		(25,750)	
TWDV c/f	4,100	145,917	4,100
Second AP (part c only)			
(balance of period of account)			
WDA (18% × 5/12)			(308)
TWDV c/f			3,792

Note that in example (c) corporation tax is charged separately on an accounting period of 12 months ending on 31 December 2023 and on an accounting period of 5 months ending on 31 May 2024 (see Chapter 2).

Test your understanding 5

Ammolite Ltd buys a car costing £16,000 in its accounting period of nine months to 31 December 2023. The car has CO_2 emissions of 45g/km.

What capital allowances are available?

A   £2,880

B   £960

C   £720

D   £2,160

 Test your understanding 6

Booker Ltd trades as a manufacturer and prepares accounts to 30 June each year. The directors decided to change the company's year-end and prepared accounts for the 9-month period to 31 March 2024.

The balance on the general pool was £218,150 at 1 July 2023. In August 2023, the company sold for £4,900 a car bought for £7,800 (the car had CO_2 emissions of 47g/km). The company also purchased a new car with CO_2 emissions of 0g/km for £25,750 in August 2023. There was 10% private use of both cars by employees.

In December 2023 Booker Ltd purchased second-hand plant for £753,750.

Calculate Booker Ltd's capital allowances for the nine months ended 31 March 2024 and show the tax written down values carried forward.

8 Business cessation

8.1 Final accounting period

In the accounting period of cessation, no allowances are given other than balancing adjustments.

Any additions and disposals in the final period are allocated to the appropriate columns in the capital allowances working.

At the end of the period there will be no TWDV carried forward, so there must be a balancing adjustment on all columns in the capital allowances working.

- If there is a positive balance remaining, a balancing allowance is given.

- If there is a negative balance remaining, a balancing charge arises.

Please note that cessation is the only time a balancing allowance can occur on the general pool and the special rate pool.

 Example

Druzy Ltd, a company that had been trading for many years preparing accounts to 31 March, ceased trading on 30 September 2024.

The tax written down value of the pool at 1 April 2023 was £12,600. On 1 October 2023, Druzy Ltd purchased some second-hand plant for £4,600.

All items of plant were sold on 30 September 2024 for £8,000 (no item was sold for more than cost).

Calculate the capital allowances due for the year ended 31 March 2024 and the six months ended 30 September 2024.

Assume the rates of allowances for the year ended 31 March 2024 continue into the future.

Solution

Druzy Ltd – Capital allowances computation

	AIA	General pool	Allowances
	£	£	£
Year ended 31 March 2024			
TWDV b/f		12,600	
Addition qualifying for AIA			
1 October 2023	4,600		
AIA	(4,600)		4,600
WDA (18%)		(2,268)	2,268
TWDV c/f		10,332	
Total allowances			6,868
6 months ended 30 September 2024			
Disposal		(8,000)	
		2,332	
Balancing allowance		(2,332)	2,332

Note: If plant is not sold until after the date of cessation, the proceeds eventually realised are used as the market value on cessation.

In effect it is treated as if sold on cessation for market value.

Test your understanding 7

Jackal Ltd ceased trading on 31 March 2024 and sold all of its plant and machinery on that date. The tax written down value of the pool at 1 April 2023 was £2,000.

What capital allowances are due based on the disposal proceeds below?

Please tick whether it is a balancing allowance or balancing charge and complete the amount.

Disposal proceeds	Balancing allowance	Balancing charge	Amount £
Scrapped for no proceeds			
Sold for £500			
Sold for £2,200			

 9 **Structures and buildings allowances**

9.1 Structures and buildings allowances

Structures and buildings allowances (SBAs) are a type of capital allowance for commercial structures and buildings, not residential property.

SBAs are calculated on a straight line basis, so are not included in the main capital allowance computation.

- SBAs are calculated at 3% of qualifying cost (equivalent to a straight line allowance over a 33⅓ year period).

- Qualifying buildings include factories, offices, retail and wholesale premises, warehouses, hotels and care homes.

- Qualifying structures include roads, walls, bridges and tunnels.

- Costs of converting and renovating commercial property also qualify.

- The costs of land and planning permission do not qualify, but site preparation is a qualifying cost.

- Each building or structure has its own pool.

- SBAs can only be claimed from the day the building or structure first comes into use, and must be time apportioned if that is part way through an accounting period.

Test your understanding 8

Which of the following are qualifying costs when calculating a structures and buildings allowance?

A   Land on which a warehouse will be built

B   Moveable partition within office space

C   Costs relating to gaining planning permission to build a factory

D   External walls of an office building

 Example

Granite Ltd prepares accounts to 31 December.

On 1 June 2023 the company purchased new retail premises for £250,000 and began trading from those premises on 1 July 2023.

The cost included £70,000 for the land. One third of the premises is a flat occupied by Hema, the managing director and 100% shareholder.

Calculate the structures and buildings allowance available for the year ended 31 December 2023.

Solution

Granite Ltd – Structures and buildings allowances computation

	£
Year ended 31 December 2023	
Total cost	250,000
Less: Land	(70,000)
	———
Cost excluding land	180,000
Less: Residential portion (1/3)	(60,000)
	———
Qualifying cost	120,000
	———
SBA at 3% × 6/12	1,800
	———

Note: SBAs can only be claimed from 1 July 2023, the day the retail premises first came into use.

9.2 Disposals

On disposal, the seller time apportions the SBAs up to the date of disposal.

There is no balancing allowance or balancing charge as the purchaser takes over the remaining allowances for the remainder of the 33⅓ year period.

The SBAs for the new owner continue to be based on the original cost.

The seller will need to increase the proceeds for chargeable gains (see Chapter 13) by the amount of SBAs claimed.

 Example

Verdite Ltd prepares accounts to 31 May each year.

On 1 May 2023 the company purchased an office for £200,000 (excluding land) and brought it into use immediately. The office was sold to Magnolia Ltd on 31 October 2024 for £370,000 and brought into use immediately.

Magnolia Ltd prepares accounts to 31 December each year.

Calculate the structures and buildings allowances available to Verdite Ltd in respect of the office for the years ended 31 May 2023, 31 May 2024 and 2025; and those available to Magnolia Ltd for the year ended 31 December 2024.

Solution

Verdite Ltd – Structures and buildings allowances

	£
Year ended 31 May 2023	
SBA (£200,000 × 3% × 1/12)	500
Year ended 31 May 2024	
SBA (£200,000 × 3%)	6,000
Year ended 31 May 2025	
SBA (£200,000 × 3% × 5/12)	2,500

Magnolia Ltd – Structures and buildings allowances

	£
Year ended 31 December 2024	
SBA (£200,000 × 3% × 2/12)	1,000

Note

For capital gains purposes Verdite Ltd will increase the £370,000 proceeds for the sale of the office by the SBAs claimed (£500 + £6,000 + £2,500 = £9,000).

 Test your understanding 9

Relaxed Ltd prepares accounts to 31 December annually.

On 1 January 2023, the company purchased factory premises for £350,000 (including land costing £50,000) and began trading from those premises on 1 May 2023.

Calculate the structures and buildings allowance available for the year ended 31 December 2023.

10 Summary

Capital allowances are available, instead of depreciation, to give tax relief for the cost of plant and machinery and some structures and buildings over the life of the assets.

A tabular layout is essential for computing capital allowances on plant and machinery.

The table should have separate columns for each of the following:

- general pool

- special rate pool.

When an accounting period is less than 12 months long, the maximum annual investment allowance and writing down allowances must be scaled down accordingly.

First year allowances and full expensing are never scaled down.

Test your understanding answers

 Test your understanding 1

Annual Investment Allowance

The correct answer is B.

Explanation

The other acquisitions will not qualify for AIA because:

A   Buildings are not plant and machinery.

C/D   Cars do not attract the AIA regardless of whether they are for business or private use.

Test your understanding 2

Entrance Ltd – Capital allowances computation

	FYA – Cars	General pool	Special rate pool	Allowances
	£	£	£	£
Y/e 31 Dec 2023				
TWDV b/f		24,000		
Additions – no AIA/FYA				
Cars:				
15 April 2023			12,600	
16 July 2023		9,200		
17 August 2023		9,400		
Additions – FYA				
Car (zero-emission)	26,150			
FYA @ 100%	(26,150)			26,150
Disposals		(3,200)		
		———		
		39,400		
WDA @ 18%/6%		(7,092)	(756)	7,848
		———	———	
TWDV c/f		32,308	11,844	
				———
Total allowances				33,998
				———
Y/e 31 Dec 2024				
Disposals		(7,900)	(9,400)	
		———	———	
		24,408	2,444	
WDA @ 18%/6%		(4,393)	(147)	4,540
		———	———	
TWDV c/f		20,015	2,297	
		———	———	———
Total allowances				4,540
				———

Test your understanding 3

Deni Ltd

Capital allowances

	AIA	FYA – Full expensing	General pool	Allowances
	£	£	£	£
Y/e 31 January 2024				
TWDV b/f			25,000	
Additions:				
Not qualifying for AIA/FYA				
Car			19,600	
Qualifying for full expensing				
Machinery		1,011,250		
Full expensing (Note)		(1,011,250)		1,011,250
Qualifying for AIA				
Machinery	10,000			
AIA	(10,000)			10,000
Disposal			(1,750)	
			42,850	
WDA (18%)			(7,713)	7,713
TWDV c/f			35,137	
Total allowances				1,028,963

Note

Alternatively, the balance of the AIA (£1,000,000 – £10,000) could be claimed on the new machinery with full expensing for the remaining cost, to give the same total allowances. In the assessment, equal credit would be given for either approach.

Test your understanding 4

Tense Ltd

Capital allowances

	FYA – Cars	General pool	Allowances
Year ending 31 December 2023	£	£	£
TWDV b/f		16,000	
Additions not qualifying for AIA			
Car		15,000	
Additions qualifying for FYA			
Cars (£9,300 × 2)	18,600		
FYA @ 100%	(18,600)		18,600
Disposals			
Plant (restrict to cost)		(1,600)	
		29,400	
WDA @ 18%		(5,292)	5,292
TWDV c/f		24,108	
Total allowances			23,892
Year ending 31 December 2024			
Disposals (£7,600 + £8,000)		(15,600)	
		8,508	
WDA @ 18%		(1,531)	1,531
TWDV c/f		6,977	
Total allowances			1,531

Test your understanding 5

The correct answer is D.

Explanation

A WDA of (£16,000 × 18% × 9/12) = £2,160 is due.

Test your understanding 6

Booker Ltd

Capital allowances computation

	AIA	FYA – Cars	General pool	Allowances
	£	£	£	£
9 months to 31 March 2024				
TWDV b/f			218,150	
Additions:				
Qualifying for FYA				
Car		25,750		
FYA @ 100% (Note)		(25,750)		25,750
Qualifying for AIA				
Plant and machinery	753,750			
AIA (W)	(750,000)			750,000
			3,750	
Disposal			(4,900)	
			217,000	
WDA @ 18% × 9/12			(29,295)	29,295
TWDV c/f			187,705	
Total allowances				**805,045**

Working: AIA

The accounting period is only nine months long.

The maximum AIA for the period is:

(£1,000,000 × 9/12) = £750,000

Note: The FYA is not time apportioned for short accounting periods.

Test your understanding 7

Capital allowances computation

Disposal proceeds	Balancing allowance	Balancing charge	Amount £
Scrapped for no proceeds	✓		2,000
Sold for £500	✓		1,500
Sold for £2,200		✓	200

Test your understanding 8

Structures and buildings allowance

The correct answer is D

Explanation

A   Land is not a qualifying cost

B   Moveable partitioning performs an active function and qualifies for plant and machinery capital allowances, not SBAs

C   Costs relating to gaining planning permission do not qualify.

Test your understanding 9

Relaxed Ltd

Structures and buildings allowance

Year ended 31 December 2023	£
Total cost	350,000
Less: Land	(50,000)
Qualifying cost	300,000
SBA @ 3% × 8/12	6,000

Note: The SBA is available from 1 May 2023, the day the factory first came into use.

5

Calculation of corporation tax liability

Introduction

In the previous chapters we have been working towards calculating the adjusted trading profit of a company, the major source of income found on most corporation tax computations.

In this chapter we add to that knowledge to enable a full computation of a company's corporation tax liability.

ASSESSMENT CRITERIA	CONTENTS
Calculate the total profits from given trading income, property income, investment income, chargeable gains and qualifying charitable donations for periods:	1 Pro forma corporation tax computation
– longer than 12 months	2 Taxable total profits
– shorter than 12 months	3 The corporation tax liability
– equal to 12 months (2.3)	
Calculate corporation tax payable (2.3)	

1 Pro forma corporation tax computation

1.1 Pro forma

The first stage of a corporation tax computation is to work out the company's taxable total profits. This comprises income and gains, less qualifying charitable donations.

The pro forma that was set out in Chapter 2 is set out again below. It will be referred to throughout this chapter.

Company name

Corporation tax computation for XX months ended...(the AP)

	£
Trading profit	X
Non-trade interest (investment income)	X
Property income	X
Chargeable gains	X
Total profits	X
Less: Qualifying charitable donations	(X)
Taxable total profits	X
Corporation tax liability at relevant rate	X

2 Taxable total profits

2.1 Adjusted trading profit

The adjusted trading profit and capital allowances have been covered in the previous chapters, so you can now compute the trading profit that is entered in the computation of taxable total profits.

	Chapter	£
Adjusted trading profit	3	X
Less: Capital allowances	4	(X)
Trading profit		X

2.2 Interest income (the loan relationship rules)

We consider the loan relationship rules at this point because of their relevance to the computation of trading profit and non-trade interest.

The loan relationship rules apply when a company pays or receives interest, or incurs any cost relating to a loan.

The legislation distinguishes between trading purposes and non-trading purposes, in relation to the interest.

For assessment purposes:

If a company **receives** interest you can normally assume that it is for non-trading purposes.

For example:

- interest received on a building society account

- interest received on a bank deposit account.

If a company **pays** interest you can normally assume that it is for trading purposes.

For example:

- interest paid on a bank overdraft

- interest paid on a loan to purchase new machinery.

Trading loans

Interest paid

All interest on trading loans deducted in the statement of profit or loss is an allowable deduction from trading profits.

This means you will not need to make any adjustments in converting the accounting profit into the adjusted trading profit.

Interest received

You are unlikely to see any interest received for trading purposes.

However, if you do, such interest is included in the trading profit and therefore needs no adjustment.

Non-trading loans

Interest paid

Interest deducted in the statement of profit or loss in relation to non-trading loans is disallowed in computing adjusted trading profits (i.e. add it back in the adjustment of profit computation). You may have to make this adjustment as part of Task 1 of your assessment, which tests the adjustment of profits.

Instead, the interest paid is an allowable deduction from non-trade interest income. However, the deduction of non-trade interest paid from interest income will not be tested in your assessment.

The main examples of non-trade interest paid would be interest paid on a loan to buy an investment property or shares.

Interest received

Interest income shown in the statement of profit or loss (e.g. interest on a deposit account) will be from a non-trade loan and therefore must be deducted from net profit in the adjustment of trading profit computation and instead treated as non-trade interest income. This may be referred to as 'investment income' in the assessment.

Accruals basis

All interest in corporation tax computations must be dealt with on an accruals basis (not received and paid basis).

The accruals basis means the amount due within the accounting period.

 Example

Slam Limited has received the following interest on its bank deposit account that was opened on 1 April 2023:

Date received	£
30 June 2023	1,000
31 December 2023	3,000
30 June 2024	4,000

Assuming interest accrues evenly between each date, calculate the non-trade interest income to be shown in the corporation tax computation for the year ended 31 March 2024.

Solution

1 April 2023 account opened	30 June 2023 received £1,000	31 December 2023 received £3,000	30 June 2024 received £4,000

31 March 2024

Interest accrued

£1,000   £3,000 $\frac{3}{6}$ × £4,000

Non-trade interest for year ended 31 March 2024
= (£1,000 + £3,000 + £2,000) = £6,000

The figure shown in the accounts will normally be the accrued amount. You are therefore unlikely to have to calculate this.

Test your understanding 1

The statement of profit or loss of Letter Ltd includes interest received on an investment in government securities.

How should this be dealt with in the computation of the taxable total profits?

A   Deducted from net profit only

B   Included as non-trading income only

C   Deducted from net profit and included as non-trading income

D   No adjustment

Test your understanding 2

Ballard Ltd prepares accounts for the year ended 31 March 2024. The following information is available:

	£
Adjusted trading profits before capital allowances	56,000
Bank interest receivable	3,000

The tax written down value of the general pool was £24,000 on 1 April 2023 and on 1 December 2023 the company purchased a second-hand lorry for £14,000.

What are Ballard Ltd's taxable total profits for the year ended 31 March 2024?

A   £40,680

B   £45,000

C   £21,000

D   £52,160

2.3   Property income

Property income in corporation tax computations must be dealt with on an accruals basis and is calculated as follows:

	£
Rental income accrued	X
Less: Allowable property expenses	X

Property income	X

Technical tax knowledge of allowable property expenses is not in the Business Tax syllabus. However, the above figures may be given for inclusion within the corporation tax computation.

2.4   Chargeable gains

A company's taxable total profits include chargeable gains as well as income.

The calculation of the chargeable gain or loss on the disposal of capital assets is covered in Chapter 13.

For the purpose of this chapter, all gains and losses on asset disposals are already computed. You will, however, need to be able to produce a summary of the position for the purpose of calculating taxable total profits.

This is shown as follows:

	£
Gain (transaction 1)	X
Gain (transaction 2)	X
Loss (transaction 3)	(X)
	X
Less: Capital losses brought forward	(X)
Net chargeable gains	X

Current period gains and losses are netted off automatically.

Excess capital losses are covered in Chapter 13.

Test your understanding 3

1   Gate Ltd made a chargeable gain on the disposal of shares during 2023 of £60,000. It had capital losses brought forward of £25,000.

   How much should be included in taxable total profits?

2   How would your answer differ if capital losses brought forward had amounted to £75,000?

2.5   Qualifying charitable donations

The final component in calculating taxable total profits is to deduct from the total profits (income and gains) any qualifying charitable donations.

The amount deductible for an 'accounting period' (AP) is the amount *paid* in that AP. This may be a different figure from the amount accrued in the accounts.

A qualifying charitable donation is basically any donation made by a company to a charity unless it already qualifies as a trading expense. Only donations that are 'small' and 'local in effect' will normally be allowed as a trading expense. It is therefore usually donations made to national charities which are treated as qualifying charitable donations.

In your assessment, donations made to local charities will only be tested for unincorporated businesses, so you should assume that any charitable donation made by a company is a donation to a national charity.

Test your understanding 4

Laserjet Ltd provided you with the following information for its year to 31 January 2024.

	£
Adjusted trading profit before capital allowances	500,600
Capital allowances	16,000
Rental income (net of expenses)	32,000
Building society interest receivable (accrued)	20,000
10% loan note interest receivable (accrued)	2,000
Donation paid to national charity	14,000

Calculate the taxable total profits for the year ended 31 January 2024.

Approach to the question

You need a methodical approach to calculate taxable total profits.

Step 1: Set up a skeleton CT computation pro forma (this may be given in the assessment)

	£
Trading profit (W1)	
Non-trade interest (W2)	
Property income	
	———
Total profits	
Less: Qualifying charitable donations	
	———
Taxable total profits	
	———

Note that the labels in the computation are not required to be in any particular order, but it is accepted best practice to put the trading profit first.

Step 2: Prepare any necessary workings separately from the pro forma

Work through the information methodically. The figure for trading profit may (though not in this example) require more than one working for the component parts of:

*   adjusted trading profit

*   capital allowances.

As you complete each working, slot the result into the pro forma.

Test your understanding 5

Pitch Ltd has the following results for the year ended 31 December 2023:

	£
Adjusted trading profits (before capital allowances)	693,601
Capital allowances	24,688
Chargeable gains	136,400
Capital loss brought forward	63,200
Rents receivable	3,500
Bank deposit interest receivable	2,400
Qualifying charitable donation paid	(1,000)

Show Pitch Ltd's taxable total profits for the year ended 31 December 2023.

 Test your understanding 6

The following details relate to the corporation tax computation of Griphook Ltd for the 12-month accounting period ended 31 March 2024:

	£
Tax adjusted trading profit (after disallowing a national charity donation of £1,800)	677,500
Bank interest receivable	2,200
Loan interest received	22,000

Calculate Griphook Ltd's taxable total profits for the year ended 31 March 2024.

2.6 Long periods of account

As you know, although a company can prepare financial accounts for a period of more than 12 months, a company's AP for corporation tax purposes can never exceed 12 months.

Therefore, if the financial accounts cover more than 12 months, two APs are required; one for the first 12 months and one for the balance.

This section tackles the allocation of income, chargeable gains and qualifying charitable donations between the two periods in finding taxable total profits.

Item	Method of allocation
Trading profit before deducting capital allowances	Time apportioned
Capital allowances (see Chapter 4)	Separate computation for each AP
Property income	Period in which accrued (Note)
Non-trade interest	Period in which accrued (Note)
Chargeable gains	Period of disposal
Qualifying charitable donation	Period in which paid

Note: If information to apply the strict accruals basis is not available, then time apportion.

Be very careful when calculating the number of months in the second period – double check it – as it is crucial for time apportioning calculations and easy to get wrong.

Example

Printer Ltd has prepared accounts for the 16 months to 31 August 2023, with the following information.

	£
Adjusted trading profit before capital allowances	381,000
Building society interest	
Received 30 June 2022 (of which £1,950 related to year ended 30 April 2022)	2,450
Received 30 June 2023	2,675
Accrued on 31 August 2023	200
Rents from property	26,010
Chargeable gains	
Disposal on 31 March 2023	25,700
Disposal on 1 May 2023	49,760
Qualifying charitable donations:	
Paid 31 July 2022	6,000
Paid 31 January 2023	6,000

Capital allowances for the two APs derived from the 16-month period of account are £20,000 and £6,250 respectively.

Show how the company's period of account will be divided into APs and compute the taxable total profits for each AP assuming, where relevant, that all income is deemed to accrue evenly.

Solution

The procedure to be followed is exactly the same as for a 12-month period, but incorporating the allocation rules.

	12 months to 30 April 2023 £	4 months to 31 August 2023 £
Trading profit (W1)	265,750	89,000
Non-trade interest (W2)	2,531	844
Property income (W3)	19,507	6,503
Chargeable gains	25,700	49,760
Total profits	313,488	146,107
Less: Qualifying charitable donations (W4)	(12,000)	0
Taxable total profits	301,488	146,107

Note: The chargeable gains are allocated according to the date of the transaction.

Workings

(W1) Trading profit

	Total £	12m £	4m £
Adjusted profit (see note)	381,000	285,750	95,250
Less: Capital allowances		(20,000)	(6,250)
Trading profit		265,750	89,000

Note: The adjusted trading profit before capital allowances is **time apportioned** (it is acceptable to apportion on a monthly basis in the assessment).

(W2) Non-trade interest – Building society interest

As the accrual at 30 April 2023 is not given, the total amount which would be included in the statement of profit or loss for the 16-month period on the accruals basis is calculated, then time apportioned:

		Total £	12m £	4m £
Received	30 June 2022	2,450		
	30 June 2023	2,675		
Add	Closing accrual	200		
Less	Opening accrual	(1,950)		
		3,375	2,531	844

(W3) Property income

Rental income is taxable as property income, which is assessed on an accruals basis for the 16 months and then time apportioned into the two APs:

	Total £	12m £	4m £
Property income	26,010	19,507	6,503

(W4) Qualifying charitable donations

	£
31 July 2022	6,000
31 January 2023	6,000
	12,000 In y/e 30 April 2023

£Nil in 4 months to 31 August 2023 as none paid.

Test your understanding 7

When a company has a period of account that exceeds 12 months, how are the following apportioned:

	Time apportioned	Separate computation	Period in which arises
Adjusted trading profits			
Capital allowances			
Rental income			
Interest income			
Chargeable gains			
Qualifying charitable donation paid			

Tick the appropriate treatment.

 Test your understanding 8

Chinny Ltd has for many years prepared accounts to 30 September, but changed its accounting date to 31 December by preparing accounts for the 15 months ended 31 December 2023.

The accounts show a profit, as adjusted for tax purposes (but before deducting capital allowances), of £250,000.

Capital allowances for the two APs based on the 15-month period of account were £13,450 and £5,818 respectively.

The company also had income in the period as follows:

		£
Building society interest receivable	1 Oct 2022 – 30 Sept 2023	4,420
	1 Oct 2023 – 31 Dec 2023	780
Chargeable gains	Disposal 15 Dec 2023	55,000
Rents received	31 July 2023	8,000

The rents accrued at 30 September 2022 and 31 December 2023 were £3,000 and £5,000 respectively.

Calculate the amounts of taxable total profits for this 15-month period of account.

3 The corporation tax liability

3.1 Calculating the corporation tax liability

Once you have computed a company's taxable total profits, the next stage of the computation is to calculate the corporation tax liability.

Corporation tax is calculated using the rate (or rates) in force during the accounting period.

The rates of tax are fixed for a financial year (FY), which is the year that runs from 1 April to the following 31 March. For example, FY2023 is the period from 1 April 2023 to 31 March 2024 (note that it is labelled based on the year in which the period starts).

For FY2023 the rate of corporation tax is determined based on the level of taxable total profits (TTP) of the company:

- A corporation tax rate of 25% (the main rate) applies if the company has TTP of greater than £250,000 (the upper limit).

- A corporation tax rate of 19% (the small profits rate) applies if the company has TTP of no more than £50,000 (the lower limit).

- Marginal relief applies (see section 3.2) for companies with TTP between £50,000 and £250,000.

The upper and lower limits must be:

- time apportioned for accounting periods of less than 12 months.

- shared equally between associated companies.

Broadly, companies are associated with each other if either one company controls the other, or they are both under common control.

In your assessment, you will be told the number of associated companies.

For example, if a company has two associated companies, the limits must be shared equally between the three associated companies (the company itself and its two associates).

Reference material

Some information about corporation tax can be found in the 'Corporation tax' section of the reference material provided in the real assessment, so you do not need to learn it.

Why not look up the correct part of the reference material in the introduction to this text book now?

 Example

Tile Ltd has taxable total profits of £200,000 in its year ended 31 March 2024. Tile Ltd has one associated company.

Calculate Tile Ltd's corporation tax liability.

Solution

The upper and lower limits must be shared between associated companies. As Tile Ltd has one associated company, the limits must be shared between two:

Lower limit (£50,000 ÷ 2) = £25,000

Upper limit (£250,000 ÷ 2) = £125,000

As Tile Ltd's taxable total profits are above the revised upper limit of £125,000, corporation tax is payable at 25%.

Corporation tax liability is (£200,000 × 25%) = £50,000.

 Test your understanding 9

Osmond Ltd has the following results for the year ended 31 March 2024. Osmond Ltd has two associated companies.

	£
Trading profit	510,000
Loan note (debenture) interest receivable	8,000
Chargeable gain on the sale of an investment	7,500

Calculate Osmond Ltd's corporation tax liability for the year ended 31 March 2024.

Example

Hammer Ltd has taxable total profits of £24,500 for the nine months ended 31 March 2024. Hammer Ltd has no associated companies.

Calculate Hammer Ltd's corporation tax liability.

Solution

The upper and lower limits need to be time apportioned because of the short accounting period.

Lower limit (£50,000 × 9/12) = £37,500

Upper limit (£250,000 × 9/12) = £187,500

As Hammer Ltd's taxable total profits are below the revised lower limit of £37,500, corporation tax is payable at the small profits rate.

Corporation tax liability is (£24,500 × 19%) = £4,655

 Test your understanding 10

Donnie Ltd has taxable total profits of £192,500 for the eight months ended 31 December 2023, and has no associated companies.

Calculate Donnie Ltd's corporation tax liability for the period ended 31 December 2023.

3.2 Marginal relief

Where taxable total profits fall between the upper and lower limits, the following approach is taken:

1   Calculate corporation tax on taxable total profits (TTP) at the main rate of 25%.

2   Deduct marginal relief using the formula:

   3/200 × (upper limit – TTP)

Note that the upper limit must be shared between associated companies and time apportioned for periods of less than 12 months (see section 3.1).

Example

Pliers Ltd has taxable total profits of £104,500 for the year ended 31 March 2024. It has no associated companies.

Calculate Pliers Ltd's corporation tax liability.

Solution

As the taxable total profits figure of £104,500 falls between the upper and lower limits, a marginal relief calculation is needed.

	£
Corporation tax at the main rate (£104,500 × 25%)	26,125
Less: Marginal relief	
3/200 × (£250,000 – £104,500)	(2,183)
Corporation tax liability	23,942

 Example

Uptown Ltd has taxable total profits of £110,000 for the year ended 31 March 2024. It has one associated company.

Calculate Uptown Ltd's corporation tax liability.

Solution

The upper and lower limits need to be shared between the two associated companies.

Lower limit (£50,000 ÷ 2) = £25,000

Upper limit (£250,000 ÷ 2) = £125,000

As the taxable total profits figure of £110,000 falls between the upper and lower limits, a marginal relief calculation is needed.

	£
Corporation tax at the main rate (£110,000 × 25%)	27,500
Less: Marginal relief	
3/200 × (£125,000 – £110,000)	(225)
Corporation tax liability	27,275

Test your understanding 11

Wahlberg Ltd has taxable total profits of £178,500 for the nine months ended 31 March 2024. Wahlberg Ltd has no associated companies.

Calculate Wahlberg Ltd's corporation tax liability for the period ended 31 March 2024.

 Test your understanding 12

RightStuff Ltd has taxable total profits of £82,000 for the year ended 31 March 2024. It has one associated company.

Calculate RightStuff Ltd's corporation tax liability for the year ended 31 March 2024.

3.3 Earlier financial years

The main rate of corporation tax (25%) and marginal relief were introduced for FY2023. For FY2022 and earlier financial years, the rate of corporation tax for all companies was 19%.

When dealing with an accounting period which falls into both FY2022 and FY2023, the profits would need to be time apportioned to enable some of the tax to be calculated using the FY2022 rate, and some using the FY2023 rates. For example, the year ended 31 December 2023 falls partly in FY2022 and partly in FY2023.

However, in the assessment, you will not be expected to deal with an accounting period that falls into two different financial years where this would involve a change in tax rates.

4 Summary

Make sure you are very familiar with the pro forma corporation tax computation.

Setting out your computations as shown in the pro forma will help to ensure that your computations and submissions to HM Revenue and Customs (HMRC) are always made in accordance with the current law and take account of current HMRC practice.

If you are given a period of account of more than 12 months, the first step is to split it into two APs and compile the two separate taxable total profit figures using the apportioning rules.

Each AP is then dealt with separately.

In FY2023 the rate of corporation tax is determined by the taxable total profits of the company.

Test your understanding answers

Test your understanding 1

Letter Ltd

The correct answer is C.

Explanation

The interest received will be included in the net profit per the accounts. It therefore needs to be deducted in the adjusted trading profit computation. It is then included as non-trade interest income in the calculation of taxable total profits.

Test your understanding 2

Ballard Ltd

The correct answer is A.

Explanation

	£
Adjusted trading profits	56,000
Less: Capital allowances (W)	(18,320)
Tax adjusted trading profits	37,680
Bank interest receivable	3,000
Taxable total profits	40,680

Working: Capital allowances

	AIA	General Pool	Allowances
	£	£	£
TWDV b/f		24,000	
Addition with AIA	14,000		
AIA	(14,000)		14,000
		0	
WDA (18% × £24,000)		(4,320)	4,320
TWDV c/f		19,680	
Total allowances			18,320

Test your understanding 3

Gate Ltd

1   £35,000

2   £Nil

Explanation

1   Gate Ltd would include chargeable gains of (£60,000 – £25,000) = £35,000 in taxable total profits.

2   No chargeable gains would be included in taxable total profits as the losses exceed gains by (£75,000 – £60,000) = £15,000. The excess loss will be carried forward and deducted from the next available future chargeable gains.

Test your understanding 4

Laserjet Ltd

Corporation tax computation – year ended 31 January 2024

	£
Trading profit (W1)	484,600
Non-trade interest (W2)	22,000
Property income	32,000
Total profits	538,600
Less: Qualifying charitable donations	(14,000)
Taxable total profits	524,600

Workings

(W1) Trading profit

	£
Adjusted trading profit	500,600
Less: Capital allowances	(16,000)
Trading profit	484,600

Take care not to adjust a profit which has already been adjusted.

(W2) Non-trade interest

	£
Building society interest receivable	20,000
Loan note interest receivable	2,000
Non-trade interest	22,000

Test your understanding 5

Pitch Ltd

Taxable total profits – year ended 31 December 2023

	£
Trading profit (W)	668,913
Property income	3,500
Non-trade interest	2,400
Chargeable gains (£136,400 – £63,200)	73,200
Total profits	748,013
Less: Qualifying charitable donations	(1,000)
Taxable total profits	747,013

Working: Trading profit

	£
Adjusted trading profit	693,601
Less: Capital allowances	(24,688)
Trading profit	668,913

Test your understanding 6

Griphook Ltd – Corporation tax computation – year ended 31 March 2024

	£
Trading profit	677,500
Interest income (£2,200 + £22,000)	24,200
Total profits	701,700
Less: Qualifying charitable donation	(1,800)
Taxable total profits	699,900

Test your understanding 7

Long period of account

	Time apportioned	Separate computation	Period in which arises
Trading income	✓		
Capital allowances		✓	
Rental income			✓
Interest income			✓
Chargeable gains			✓
Qualifying charitable donation paid			✓

Test your understanding 8

Chinny Ltd

Corporation tax computations

	Year ended 30 September 2023 £	3 months to 31 December 2023 £
Trading profit (W1)	186,550	44,182
Non-trade interest	4,420	780
Property income (W2)	8,000	2,000
Chargeable gains	–	55,000
Taxable total profits	198,970	101,962

Workings

(W1) Trading profit

	Year ended 30 September 2023 £	3 months to 31 December 2023 £
Adjusted trading profits (12/15:3/15)	200,000	50,000
Less: Capital allowances	(13,450)	(5,818)
Trading profit	186,550	44,182

(W2) Property income

Rent receivable for 15 months:

(£8,000 – £3,000 + £5,000) = £10,000

	Year ended 30 September 2023 £	3 months to 31 December 2023 £
Time apportioned	8,000	2,000

Test your understanding 9

Osmond Ltd

Corporation tax computation – year ended 31 March 2024

	£
Trading profit	510,000
Chargeable gain	7,500
Interest	8,000
Taxable total profits	525,500
Corporation tax liability (£525,500 × 25%)	£131,375

Workings

The upper and lower limits must be shared between associated companies:

Lower limit (£50,000 ÷ 3) = £16,667

Upper limit (£250,000 ÷ 3) = £83,333

The main rate of corporation tax applies as taxable total profits are above the upper limit.

 Test your understanding 10

Donnie Ltd

Corporation tax liability – period ended 31 December 2023

Corporation tax liability (£192,500 × 25%) = £48,125

Workings

The upper and lower limits need to be time apportioned because of the short accounting period.

Lower limit (£50,000 × 8/12) = £33,333

Upper limit (£250,000 × 8/12) = £166,667

The main rate of corporation tax applies as taxable total profits are above the upper limit.

Test your understanding 11

Wahlberg Ltd

Corporation tax liability – period ended 31 March 2024

	£
Corporation tax at the main rate (£178,500 × 25%)	44,625
Less: Marginal relief	
3/200 × (£187,500 – £178,500)	(135)
Corporation tax liability	44,490

Workings

The upper and lower limits need to be time apportioned because of the short accounting period.

Lower limit (£50,000 × 9/12) = £37,500

Upper limit (£250,000 × 9/12) = £187,500

As the taxable total profits figure of £178,500 falls between the upper and lower limits, a marginal relief calculation is needed.

Test your understanding 12

RightStuff Ltd

Corporation tax liability – year ended 31 March 2024

	£
Corporation tax at the main rate (£82,000 × 25%)	20,500
Less: Marginal relief	
3/200 × (£125,000 – £82,000)	(645)
Corporation tax liability	19,855

Workings

The upper and lower limits must be shared between associated companies:

Lower limit (£50,000 ÷ 2) = £25,000

Upper limit (£250,000 ÷ 2) = £125,000

As the taxable total profits figure of £82,000 falls between the upper and lower limits, a marginal relief calculation is needed.

KAPLAN PUBLISHING

Losses for companies

Introduction

This chapter covers the relief available to companies for trading losses and capital losses. The reliefs available to individuals are covered in Chapter 10.

Losses will be tested in Task 9 of the assessment, which will be partly manually marked.

ASSESSMENT CRITERIA
The options available to sole traders, partnerships and companies to utilise trading losses:
– opening years
– carry back
– current year
– carry forward
– terminal (6.1)
The best use of a trading loss for sole traders, partnerships and limited companies. (6.1)
Calculate available loss relief using:
– carry back
– current year
– carry forward (6.1)

CONTENTS

1 Trading losses

2 Capital losses

1 Trading losses

1.1 Adjusted trading losses

In Chapter 3 we considered how to calculate an adjusted trading profit.

An adjusted trading loss is computed in the same way. However, when a company makes an adjusted trading loss, its trading profit assessment for the accounting period is £Nil.

Example

Carlos Ltd had the following results for its year ended 31 March 2024:

	£	£
Gross profit		30,000
Less: Depreciation	5,000	
Allowable expenses	12,000	
		(17,000)
Net profit per accounts		13,000

The capital allowances for the year amount to £21,000.

Calculate the adjusted trading profit/(loss) for the year.

Solution

Step 1: Set up an adjustment of profits pro forma as in Chapter 3.

Step 2: Calculate the adjusted trading profit/(loss)

Work through the statement of profit or loss line by line as previously to calculate the adjusted trading profit/(loss).

Carlos Ltd

Adjustment of profit/(loss) – year ended 31 March 2024

	£
Net profit per accounts	13,000
Add: Disallowable expenses	
Depreciation	5,000
	18,000
Less: Capital allowances	(21,000)
Adjusted trading loss	(3,000)
Trading profit assessment	Nil

The trading profit figure to be entered onto the pro forma corporation tax computation is £Nil.

The accounts may show a net **loss** to be adjusted. If this is the case, adding disallowable expenses will **reduce** the loss.

Example

Assume Carlos Ltd in the previous example had a net loss per accounts of (£10,000). Calculate the adjusted trading loss.

Solution

	£
Net loss per accounts	(10,000)
Add: Depreciation	5,000
	(5,000)
Less: Capital allowances	(21,000)
Adjusted trading loss	(26,000)

1.2 Summary of trading loss reliefs

There are three forms of relief available to a company which makes a trading loss:

- current year relief

- carry back relief

- carry forward relief.

There are no extra forms of relief available to a company in its opening years.

 Reference material

Some information about reliefs can be found in the 'Trading losses' section of the reference material provided in the real assessment, so you do not need to learn it.

Why not look up the correct part of the reference material in the introduction to this text book now?

1.3 Current year relief

A trading loss can be relieved against total profits of the loss-making accounting period. The set off is against profits before the deduction of qualifying charitable donations.

A claim for current year (or carry back) relief must be made within two years of the end of the loss-making accounting period.

 Example

Sage Ltd had the following results for the year ended 31 March 2024.

	£
Adjusted trading loss	(40,000)
Property income	10,000
Chargeable gain	50,000
Qualifying charitable donation	10,000

Show how relief would be obtained for the loss in the current period.

Approach to the example

It is *essential* once a loss has been identified to set up a loss memorandum as a working and allocate the loss to it, so that the relief for the loss does not exceed the actual amount of loss available.

Even where there is a trading loss, this does not alter the basic approach to a question.

- Present the CT computation in the standard pro forma.
- Support it with workings where necessary (one of which will be the loss memorandum).

Solution

Sage Ltd – Corporation tax computation – y/e 31 March 2024

	£
Trading profit	Nil
Property income	10,000
Chargeable gain	50,000
	———
Total profits	60,000
Less: Loss relief – Current year	(40,000)
	———
	20,000
Less: Qualifying charitable donation	(10,000)
	———
Taxable total profits	10,000
	———

Working: Loss memorandum

	£
Year ended 31 March 2024	
Current period loss	40,000
Relieved in current period	(40,000)
	———
Loss c/f	Nil
	———

Setting off the loss before the deduction of qualifying charitable donations (QCDs) may result in the QCDs becoming unrelieved. Excess amounts of QCDs are lost.

Example

What if Sage Ltd in the previous example made a loss of £60,000?

Solution

	£
Total profits i.e. before QCDs (as before)	60,000
Less: Loss relief – Current year	(60,000)
	Nil
Less: QCDs	Wasted
Taxable total profits	Nil

The QCD is unrelieved. It has not been used as there are insufficient profits to set it against.

It is an important principle in the use of most loss reliefs that, where there is an available loss, no restriction in set off is permitted.

This means that it would *not* have been possible here to restrict the loss relief to (£50,000) so as to then relieve a QCD of (£10,000), and find an alternative use for the remaining (£10,000) loss.

Unused QCDs cannot be carried forward or back and are therefore wasted.

1.4 Carry back relief

A trading loss may be carried back for relief against total profits in the preceding 12 months, but only **after** the loss has first been relieved against any available current period total profits.

The loss is set off against total profits **before** deducting QCDs.

In other words, the order in which the loss is applied is as follows.

- First, against total profits of the current year (**before** QCDs).

- Second, against total profits of the previous 12 months (again, **before** the deduction of QCDs).

In questions this is often referred to as 'setting off the loss as soon as possible'.

Approach to losses questions

A longer style task in the assessment may involve utilising company losses over several years; a methodical approach is very important for these tasks.

- Lay out the years side by side in a table, leaving space to insert any loss reliefs.

- Keep a separate working for the trading loss – the memorandum.

- Firstly set the loss against the total profits (before QCDs) of the year of loss.

- Then carry the balance of the loss back against total profits (before QCDs) of the previous 12 months (36 months on cessation).

- State whether there is any unrelieved loss remaining.

- Keep a running tally in the loss memorandum working.

Here is a pro forma. The loss has been incurred in 2024.

Pro forma corporation tax loss computation

	2023 £	2024 £
Trading profit	X	Nil
Investment income	X	X
Property income	X	X
Chargeable gains	X	X
Total profits	X	X
Less: Loss relief		
– Current period		(X)
– Carry back	(X)	
	Nil	Nil
Less: QCDs	Wasted	Wasted
Taxable total profits	Nil	Nil

Loss memorandum:	£
Current year loss (2024)	X
Less: Current year relief	(X)
Carry back relief	(X)
Loss still available	X

Example

Marjoram Ltd has the following results for the three accounting periods to 31 December 2024.

Year ended 31 December	2022	2023	2024
	£	£	£
Trading profits/(loss)	11,000	9,000	(45,000)
Building society interest	500	500	500
Chargeable gains	–	–	4,000
Qualifying charitable donations	250	250	250

Show the taxable total profits for all periods affected, assuming that loss relief is taken as soon as possible.

Solution

Marjoram Ltd

Corporation tax computations

Year ended 31 December	2023	2024
	£	£
Trading profit	9,000	Nil
Investment income	500	500
Chargeable gains	Nil	4,000
Total profits	9,500	4,500
Less: Loss relief		
– Current period		(4,500)
– Carry back	(9,500)	
	Nil	Nil
Less: QCDs	Wasted	Wasted
Taxable total profits	Nil	Nil

Note: The year ended 31 December 2022 is not affected; the loss cannot be carried back that far.

Loss working

	£
Loss for the year ended 31 December 2024	45,000
Less: Current year relief	(4,500)
	40,500
Less: Carry back 12 months	(9,500)
Loss still available at 1 January 2025	31,000

Test your understanding 1

Banks Ltd has the following results:

Year ended 31 March	2023	2024
	£	£
Adjusted trading profit/(loss)	50,000	(120,000)
Bank interest	2,000	3,000
Qualifying charitable donation	1,000	500

On the assumption that Banks Ltd uses its loss as early as possible, what is the trading loss carried forward to the year ended 31 March 2025?

A   £117,000

B   £68,000

C   £66,500

D   £65,000

Short previous accounting period

Losses can be carried back 12 months. This usually means the loss can be deducted from the profits of the previous accounting period. However, if the previous accounting period is less than 12 months long, it will be possible to carry the loss back to cover a proportion of the profits for the period preceding that. The total profits of the earlier period must be time apportioned.

Example

Amla Ltd has the following results for the three accounting periods to 31 December 2023.

	12m to 30 April 2022	8m to 31 Dec 2022	12m to 31 Dec 2023
	£	£	£
Trading profits/(loss)	40,000	18,000	(100,000)
Bank interest	2,000	1,500	1,700
Qualifying charitable donations	1,000	1,000	1,000

Show the taxable total profits for all periods affected, assuming that loss relief is taken as soon as possible.

Solution

Amla Ltd

Corporation tax computations

	12m to 30 April 2022	8m to 31 Dec 2022	12m to 31 Dec 2023
	£	£	£
Trading profits	40,000	18,000	Nil
Investment income	2,000	1,500	1,700
Total profits	42,000	19,500	1,700
Less: Loss relief			
– Current period			(1,700)
– Carry back		(19,500)	
(max 4/12 × £42,000)	(14,000)		
	28,000	Nil	Nil
Less: QCDs	(1,000)	Wasted	Wasted
Taxable total profits	27,000	Nil	Nil

Note: The loss can be carried back 12 months. This covers the whole of the 8 months to 31 December 2022 and 4 months of the year ended 30 April 2022. The maximum loss that can be deducted for the year ended 30 April 2022 is equal to 4/12 of the total profits i.e. £14,000.

Loss working

	£
Loss for the year ended 31 December 2023	100,000
Less: Current year relief	(1,700)
	98,300
Less: Carry back 8m to 31 Dec 2022	(19,500)
	78,800
Carry back to year ended 30 April 2022	(14,000)
Loss still available at 1 January 2024	64,800

 Test your understanding 2

Undergrowth Ltd is a UK resident company that began trading on 1 July 2021. The company's results are summarised as follows:

	Year ended 30 Jun 2022	6 months to 31 Dec 2022	Year ended 31 Dec 2023
	£	£	£
Trading profit/(loss)	35,000	25,000	(350,000)
Non-trade loan interest receivable	–	15,000	22,000
Property income	25,000	–	–
Donation to national charity	1,000	1,000	1,000

Calculate the taxable total profits for all of the accounting periods in the question after giving maximum relief at the earliest time for the trading losses sustained and any other reliefs.

Also show any balance of losses carried forward.

1.5 Carry forward relief

Where any loss remains unrelieved after the current year and carry back claims have been made, the remaining loss can be carried forward indefinitely. This also applies where no current year and carry back claims are made, as there is no compulsory requirement to use such reliefs.

When trading losses are carried forward, provided the trade is still being carried on and has not become small or negligible, a claim can be made for them to be offset against **total profits** of the company.

Where this is the case losses do not have to be offset against the first available total profits – the company can choose how much, if any, to offset and how much to carry forward to future periods.

Example

Mint Ltd began trading on 1 April 2021 and has the following results:

Year ended 31 March	2022	2023	2024
	£	£	£
Adjusted trading profit/(loss)	15,000	(100,000)	40,000
Non-trade interest	5,000	10,000	10,000
Chargeable gain	–	40,000	–

Show how the loss relief would be claimed where relief is required as soon as possible.

Solution

Mint Ltd – Corporation tax computations

Year ended 31 March	2022	2023	2024
	£	£	£
Trading profit	15,000	Nil	40,000
Investment income	5,000	10,000	10,000
Chargeable gain	–	40,000	–
Total profits	20,000	50,000	50,000
Less: Loss relief			
– Current year		(50,000)	
– Carry back	(20,000)		
– Carry forward			(30,000)
Taxable total profits	Nil	Nil	20,000

Working: Loss memorandum

	£
Loss for the year ended 31 March 2023	100,000
Less: Current year relief	(50,000)
Carry back relief	
– Year ended 31 March 2022	(20,000)
	30,000
Less: Used in year ended 31 March 2024	(30,000)
Loss left to c/f	Nil

Test your understanding 3

The following is the income of Potter Ltd which commenced to trade on 1 October 2022.

Year ended 30 September	2023	2024
	£	£
Adjusted trading profit (loss)	(35,000)	94,000
Bank interest receivable	11,400	8,400
Rents receivable (after deducting expenses)	21,300	21,400
Donation to national charity paid 30 Sept	500	500

Calculate the taxable total profits for the years ending 30 September 2023 and 2024, indicating how you would obtain relief as soon as possible for the loss.

Test your understanding 4

Eldorado Ltd prepares accounts annually to 31 August in each year. The company started to trade on 1 September 2021.

The results for the first few years were as follows:

Year to 31 August	2022	2023	2024
	£	£	£
Trading profits/(loss)	18,000	(81,000)	(6,000)
Chargeable gain	3,000		
Property income	22,000	22,000	22,000

Show how relief is obtained for the trading losses, assuming that relief is claimed as soon as possible.

1.6 Terminal loss relief

When a company ceases to trade, a loss arising in the final 12 months of trade can be carried back for 36 months rather than 12.

After a current period claim, losses are set against total profits before QCDs of the previous 36 months, starting with the most recent period.

You will not have to calculate terminal loss relief in the assessment, but you may have to explain the options available to a company on cessation of trade.

 Reference material

Some information about terminal loss relief can be found in the 'Trading losses' section of the reference material provided in the real assessment, so you do not need to learn it.

Why not look up the correct part of the reference material in the introduction to this text book now?

1.7 Factors to be considered when choosing loss relief

Companies have the following choices when considering loss relief:

- current year claim then carry back claim then carry forward the remaining loss or

- current year claim then carry forward the remaining loss or

- carry forward all the loss.

When deciding which choice to make there are two main considerations:

(1) **Timing (cash flow)**

Where the company wants earliest relief, a current year and carry back claim would be preferred.

This enables the company to claim tax repayments for the previous year which is a useful cash flow for a company suffering losses.

(2) **Amount of relief**

Where the company wants to obtain the highest possible tax saving it would be preferable to avoid wasting QCDs.

Note that current year and carry back claims cannot be restricted to avoid wasting QCDs whereas the offset of brought forward losses is more flexible.

The company may also obtain a higher tax saving if carrying forward the loss as the rates of corporation tax have increased. The rate of corporation tax for all companies prior to FY2023 was 19%. From FY2023 the main rate of corporation tax is increased to 25%, applying to profits over £250,000 (see Chapter 5).

A company expecting to make high levels of profits in the future may prefer to carry forward losses to benefit from a greater tax saving.

You may have to make a choice of relief in the assessment and/or may be asked to select what factors a company should take into account when choosing the best relief.

2 Capital losses

Both trading and capital losses may be examined in the assessment.

Capital losses may occur in questions in isolation, but where a mixture of losses appear it is essential to distinguish the reliefs available.

The treatment of capital losses will be covered in detail in Chapter 13. However, in summary:

- A capital loss incurred in the current period is automatically relieved against current period gains. Any excess is then carried forward for relief against gains in future accounting periods.

- There is no carry back facility and a capital loss cannot be used against any other profit.

Test your understanding 5

Coriander Ltd began trading on 1 April 2021 and has the following results:

	Trading profit or (loss) £	Non-trade interest £	Qualifying charitable donation £	Capital gains or (losses) £
Year ended 31 Mar:				
2022	37,450	1,300	3,000	(5,000)
2023	(81,550)	1,400	3,000	
2024	20,000	1,600	3,000	12,000

Calculate taxable total profits for all years, assuming all reliefs are claimed at the earliest opportunity. State the amounts of losses carried forward.

Approach to the question

- Set up CT pro formas for all years leaving space to enter any loss reliefs.

- Set up a loss memorandum for the trading loss for the year ended 31 March 2023.

- There is also a capital loss to deal with which has more restrictive use than a trading loss.

 Test your understanding 6

Read the following statements and state whether they are **true** or **false**.

1 Trading losses can be relieved by carry back before being offset in the year of loss.

2 Trading losses are deducted from other income in the current period after deducting qualifying charitable donations.

3 Trading losses carried forward can only be carried forward for 12 months.

4 Capital losses can be offset against other income in the year of the loss, but only against chargeable gains in future years.

3 Summary

Losses appear in every assessment.

The rules depend on the type of loss:

- trading losses – current year and carry back relief against total profits before qualifying charitable donations, carry forward against total profits

- capital losses – current year against chargeable gains only, carry forward against chargeable gains only.

Test your understanding 1

Banks Ltd

The correct answer is D.

Explanation

When you are asked to use the loss 'as early as possible' it means the loss is set off against total profits before qualifying charitable donations in the current year and then total profits before qualifying charitable donations in the preceding 12 months.

A current year claim must be made before a carry back claim, as follows:

	£
Trading loss	120,000
Less: Utilised – Current year offset	(3,000)
– Carry back claim	(52,000)
	———
Available to carry forward	65,000
	———

Test your understanding 2

Undergrowth Ltd

	Year ended 30 Jun 2022 £	6 months to 31 Dec 2022 £	Year ended 31 Dec 2023 £
Trading profit	35,000	25,000	Nil
Investment income	–	15,000	22,000
Property income	25,000	–	–
Total profits	60,000	40,000	22,000
Less: Loss relief			
– Current year			(22,000)
– Carry back (W)	(30,000)	(40,000)	
	30,000	Nil	Nil
Less: QCDs	(1,000)	Wasted	Wasted
Taxable total profits	29,000	Nil	Nil

Balances carried forward

- There is a trading loss at 31 December 2023 to carry forward of £258,000 (W).

Working: Trading losses

		£
Loss for 12 months to 31 December 2023		350,000
Current year relief		(22,000)
Carry back relief –	6 months to 31 December 2022	(40,000)
–	12 months to 30 June 2022 (£60,000 × 6/12)	(30,000)
Carry forward at 31 December 2023		258,000

Test your understanding 3

Potter Ltd

Year ended 30 September	2023	2024
	£	£
Trading profit	Nil	94,000
Investment income	11,400	8,400
Property income	21,300	21,400
Total profits	32,700	123,800
Less: Loss relief – Current year	(32,700)	
Less: Losses b/f (£35,000 – £32,700)	–	(2,300)
	Nil	121,500
Less: QCDs	(Wasted)	(500)
Taxable total profits	Nil	121,000

Test your understanding 4

Eldorado Ltd

Corporation tax computations

Year to 31 August	2022	2023	2024
	£	£	£
Trading profit	18,000	Nil	Nil
Property income	22,000	22,000	22,000
Chargeable gain	3,000	–	–
Total profits	43,000	22,000	22,000
Less: Loss relief			
– Current year		(22,000)	(6,000)
– Carry back	(43,000)		
– Carry forward			(16,000)
Taxable total profits	Nil	Nil	Nil

Loss memorandum

	£		£
Loss – y/e 31 Aug 2023	81,000	Loss – y/e 31 Aug 2024	6,000
Offset: Current year	(22,000)	Offset: Current year	(6,000)
Carry back	(43,000)		
Carry forward	(16,000)		
Losses carried forward	Nil		Nil

Test your understanding 5

Coriander Ltd – Corporation tax computations

Year ended 31 March	2022 £	2023 £	2024 £
Trading profit	37,450	Nil	20,000
Investment income	1,300	1,400	1,600
Chargeable gains (£12,000 – £5,000 b/f)	Nil		7,000
Total profits	38,750	1,400	28,600
Less: Loss relief			
– Current year		(1,400)[1]	
– Carry back	(38,750)[2]		
– Carry forward			(25,600)[3]
	Nil	Nil	3,000
Less: QCDs	Wasted	Wasted	(3,000)
Taxable total profits	Nil	Nil	Nil

Loss memorandum

	£
Trading loss in the year ended 31 March 2023	81,550
(1) Current period relief	(1,400)
(2) Carry back relief – year ended 31 March 2022	(38,750)
	41,400
(3) Carry forward against total profits – year ended 31 March 2024	(25,600)
Loss to carry forward at 31 March 2024	15,800

Note that the use of losses in the year ended 31 March 2024 has been restricted to avoid wastage of QCDs.

Test your understanding 6

1	False	Trading losses can only be relieved by carry back after a claim for current year relief has been made.
2	False	Trading losses are deducted from other income before deducting qualifying charitable donations. Any excess QCDs remaining unrelieved are wasted.
3	False	Trading losses carried forward can be carried forward indefinitely.
4	False	Capital losses cannot be offset against other income. They can only be set against chargeable gains.

Payment and administration – companies

7

Introduction

This chapter looks at the payment and administration aspects of corporation tax (see Chapter 11 for sole traders and partnerships). Payment and administration will be tested in Task 7 of the assessment.

At the end of each section you will find a summary showing which information from that section is provided in the AAT reference material, and which information is not provided and therefore needs to be learnt.

ASSESSMENT CRITERIA

Tax return filing deadlines for sole traders, partnerships and companies (4.1)

Tax payment dates for sole traders, partners and companies (4.1)

Time limits for notifying chargeability to tax (4.1)

The enquiry window (4.1)

The time period within which amendments to a tax return can be made (4.1)

What records need to be maintained and for what time period (4.1)

Penalties for:

– late filing

– late payment

– failing to notify chargeability

– errors in tax returns

– not providing records in an enquiry

– not retaining records (4.2)

Calculate penalties and interest for non-compliance (4.2)

CONTENTS

1 Corporation tax self-assessment (CTSA)

2 HM Revenue and Customs' (HMRC) compliance checks

3 Record keeping requirements

4 Payment of corporation tax

1 Corporation tax self-assessment (CTSA)

1.1 Scope

Corporation tax self-assessment (CTSA) requires companies to submit a tax return for each accounting period (AP) and a self-assessment of any tax payable.

1.2 Filing the return

A company is required to file a return (form CT600) when it receives a notice requiring it to do so.

All companies must file their returns online and submit their accounts and any tax computations using iXBRL (inline eXtensible Business Reporting Language).

A company which is chargeable to tax, but which does not receive a notice requesting a return, must notify HMRC within 12 months of the end of the accounting period.

Failure to notify may result in a penalty. The penalty is calculated in broadly the same way as penalties for incorrect returns (see section 1.8) and is a maximum of 100% of the tax outstanding.

The return must include a calculation (self-assessment) of the corporation tax payable for the accounting period covered by the return.

The return must be submitted within:

- 12 months of the end of the period of account or, if later
- three months from the date of the notice requiring the return.

Long periods of account

The return filing date is based on the period of account (which may be more than 12 months long).

For a set of accounts of more than 12 months long, there will be two APs, two corporation tax computations and therefore two returns to file.

However, both returns will have the same filing date; 12 months after the end of the period of account.

Example

Edgar Ltd has prepared a set of accounts for the 15 months ended 31 March 2024.

Identify the period(s) for which return(s) must be completed and the filing date(s).

Solution

The period of account is the period for which accounts are prepared (i.e. 15 months to 31 March 2024).

Periods for returns	Filing date
(i) First 12 months	
– 12 months ended 31 December 2023	31 March 2025
(ii) Balance	
– 3 months ended 31 March 2024	31 March 2025

Penalties for late filing

Failure to submit a return by the due date will result in a penalty.

The system operates as follows:

• Less than 3 months overdue	£100
• Delay of more than three months	£200
• Delay of more than six months	£200 plus 10% of tax due
• Delay of more than 12 months	£200 plus 20% of tax due

If the return is late three times in a row then the £100 penalty is increased to £500 and the £200 penalty to £1,000.

A penalty will not be charged if the taxpayer has a reasonable excuse for the late filing, for example a serious illness. A lack of knowledge of the tax system is not a reasonable excuse.

 Reference material

Some information about dates, time limits and penalties can be found in the 'Payment and administration' section of the reference material provided in the real assessment, so you do not need to learn it.

Why not look up the correct part of the reference material in the introduction to this text book now?

Example

Flat Ltd received a notice to file Form CT600 for the year ended 30 June 2022 on 31 August 2022. The company submitted the corporation tax return on 29 February 2024 and paid its corporation tax liability of £35,000 on the same date.

What are the maximum penalties that can be charged in respect of the late filing of the return?

Solution

The corporation tax return was due to be filed on 30 June 2023, 12 months after the end of the period of account. The return was filed more than six months but less than 12 months late.

A fixed penalty of £200 will be charged plus 10% of any tax still outstanding. In this case that will be an additional penalty of £3,500 (£35,000 × 10%) making a total due of £3,700.

1.3 Notification of chargeability

A company which is liable to tax for the first time must notify HMRC within three months of the start of its first accounting period for tax.

A company which is chargeable to tax, but does not receive a notice to file a return, must notify HMRC within 12 months of the end of its accounting period.

Failure to notify may result in a penalty. The penalty is calculated in broadly the same way as penalties for incorrect returns (see section 1.8) and is a maximum of 100% of the tax outstanding.

1.4 Amending the return

A company can amend a return within 12 months of the filing due date.

HMRC can amend a return to correct obvious errors and anything else which they believe to be incorrect by reference to the information they hold within:

- nine months of the date it was filed, or
- nine months of the filing of an amendment.

If the company disagrees with HMRC's amendment it may reject it.

This rejection should be made within:

- the normal time limit for amendments or
- if this time limit has expired, within three months of the date of correction.

 Test your understanding 1

Read the following statements and state whether they are true or false.

1. The filing date for a company which prepares accounts for the 11 months to 30 April 2024 is 30 April 2025.

2. DEF Ltd filed its corporation tax return for the year ended 31 March 2024 on 19 May 2025. The latest date that it can amend the return is 19 May 2026.

3. The maximum penalty for not filing a corporation tax return on time is £100.

1.5 Recovery of overpaid tax

A company may claim a repayment of tax within four years of the end of an accounting period. An appeal against HMRC's decision on such a claim must be made within 30 days.

A company is not allowed to make such a claim if its return was made in accordance with a generally accepted accounting practice (GAAP) which prevailed at the time.

1.6 Interest on late payments of corporation tax

Interest is charged automatically on late paid corporation tax:

- from the due date
- to the date of payment.

Where there is an amendment to the self-assessment interest runs:

- from the date the tax would have been payable had it been correctly self-assessed in the first place.

Interest paid on late payments of corporation tax is allowable as a deduction from non-trade interest income.

1.7 Interest on overpaid corporation tax

If corporation tax is overpaid HMRC will pay interest:

- from the later of the normal due date and the date of overpayment

- to the date it is refunded.

Interest received on overpaid corporation tax is taxable as non-trade interest income.

Computations of interest will not be required in the assessment, but the principles must be understood.

1.8 Penalties for incorrect returns

A penalty will be charged where:

- an inaccurate return is submitted to HMRC or

- the company fails to notify HMRC where an under assessment of tax is made by them.

The penalty depends on the reason for the error.

Taxpayer behaviour	Maximum penalty % of tax lost
Genuine mistake: despite taking reasonable care	No penalty
Careless error and inaccuracy due to failure to take reasonable care	30%
Deliberate error but not concealed	70%
Deliberate error and concealed	100%

The penalties may be reduced at HMRC discretion where the taxpayer discloses information to HMRC. The reduction depends on the circumstances of the penalty and whether the taxpayer discloses the information before HMRC discover the error (unprompted disclosure) or afterwards (prompted disclosure).

	Minimum penalties	
Taxpayer behaviour	Unprompted disclosure % of tax lost	Prompted disclosure % of tax lost
Careless error and inaccuracy due to failure to take reasonable care	Nil	15%
Deliberate error but not concealed	20%	35%
Deliberate error and concealed	30%	50%

Reference material

Some information about incorrect returns can be found in the 'Penalties for incorrect returns' section of the reference material provided in the real assessment, so you do not need to learn it.

Why not look up the correct part of the reference material in the introduction to this text book now?

 Example

State the maximum and minimum penalties that may be levied on each of the following companies which have submitted incorrect tax returns.

L Ltd   Accidentally provided an incorrect figure even though the return was checked carefully. The company notified HMRC of the error three days after submitting the return.

S Ltd   Was unable to check the return due to staff being on holiday. The return included a number of errors. The return was checked thoroughly the following week and the company provided HMRC with the information necessary to identify the errors.

J Ltd   Deliberately understated its tax liability and attempted to conceal the incorrect information that had been provided. HMRC have identified the understatement and J Ltd is helping them with their enquiries.

Solution

Penalties for incorrect tax returns are a percentage of the under declared tax.

L Ltd   No penalty is charged where a taxpayer has been careful and has made a genuine mistake.

S Ltd   The maximum percentage for failing to take reasonable care is 30%. The minimum penalty for unprompted disclosure is £Nil.

J Ltd   The maximum percentage for a deliberate understatement with concealment is 100%. The minimum percentage for prompted disclosure of information (where the taxpayer provides information in response to HMRC identifying the error) in respect of deliberate understatement with concealment is 50%.

1.9 Summary of reference material

Item	Included in reference material	Not included in reference material
How to submit returns		✓
Deadline to notify HMRC if chargeable to tax but no return has been issued		✓
Filing deadline	✓	
Late filing penalties	✓	
Increases to late filing penalties where return is filed late three times in a row		✓
Deadline to notify chargeability	✓	
Penalties for failure to notify chargeability		✓
Deadline for company to amend return	✓	
Deadline for HMRC to amend return		✓
Rejections of amendments		✓
Recovery of overpaid tax		✓
Interest on late and overpaid tax	✓	
Dates between which interest is charged		✓
Penalties for incorrect returns	✓	

2 HM Revenue and Customs' (HMRC) compliance checks

2.1 Basic rules

HMRC have the right to enquire into a company's tax return under their compliance check powers. This may be a random check or because they have reason to believe that income or expenses have been misstated in the tax return.

Notice must normally be given within a year of the actual filing date. If the return is filed late, notice must be given by the quarter day following the 12-month anniversary of the actual filing date. The quarter days are 31 January, 30 April, 31 July and 31 October.

HMRC may also demand that the company produce documents for inspection. If the company fails to do so, a penalty of £300, plus up to £60 per day, may be imposed.

A compliance check (enquiry) ends when HMRC give notice that it has been completed and notify what amendments they believe to be necessary. The notice is referred to as a closure notice.

In more complex cases, if the compliance check covers several different aspects, then a partial closure notice (PCN) may be issued to bring one particular part of the compliance check to an end ahead of the final closure notice.

 Example

CTS Ltd has produced accounts for the year ended 30 June 2023. The company filed its return on 1 April 2024.

What is the latest date by which HMRC must give notice of a compliance check (enquiry)?

How would your answer differ if CTS Ltd had filed its return on 1 September 2024?

Solution

HMRC must give notice within a year of the actual filing date. Therefore, notice must be given by 1 April 2025.

If the company had filed its return on 1 September 2024, (i.e. after the due filing date of 30 June 2024) HMRC would need to give notice by 31 October 2025 (i.e. 12 months after 31 October following the actual date of delivery of the return).

2.2   Discovery assessments

A discovery assessment may be issued if HMRC believe that insufficient tax has been collected.

The taxpayer can appeal to the Tribunal against a discovery assessment.

2.3   Appeals procedure

The taxpayer can request an informal review of a disputed decision.

Alternatively, a formal appeal may be made to the Tax Tribunal within 30 days of the closure notice or PCN being issued.

Appeals from the Tax Tribunal on a point of law (but not on a point of fact) may be made to the Court of Appeal and from there to the Supreme Court.

The Tax Tribunal is independent of HMRC.

2.4   Summary of reference material

Item	Included in reference material	Not included in reference material
Reasons why HMRC may open an enquiry		✓
Deadline for HMRC to open an enquiry	✓	
Penalty for failure to produce enquiry documents	✓	
Details of closure notice/partial closure notice		✓
Discovery assessments		✓
Appeals		✓

3 Record keeping requirements

A company and its tax adviser must keep records to assist in dealings with and support evidence given to HMRC.

Companies must keep records until the latest of:

- six years from the end of the accounting period
- the date any enquiries are completed
- the date after which enquiries may not be commenced.

Failure to keep records can lead to a penalty of up to £3,000 for each accounting period affected.

Summary of reference material

Item	Included in reference material	Not included in reference material
Six year deadline for keeping records	✓	
Deadlines for keeping records where enquiries have taken place		✓
Penalty for failure to keep proper records	✓	

4 Payment of corporation tax

4.1 Payment date

All payments of corporation tax must be made electronically.

Companies must normally pay corporation tax within nine months and one day of the end of the accounting period (AP).

A company with a year ended 31 January 2024 must pay corporation tax by 1 November 2024.

Note that Edgar Ltd (in an earlier example) which had a long period of account of the 15 months ended 31 March 2024 would have two payment dates.

Edgar Ltd would pay corporation tax for:

* AP 1 = 12 months ended 31 December 2023, by 1 October 2024

* AP 2 = 3 months ended 31 March 2024, by 1 January 2025.

From this we can see that a company with a long period of account can have:

* two separate payment dates

* but one common filing date.

Note that the payment dates are earlier than the filing date.

This normal payment date rule does not however apply to large companies (see section 4.2).

4.2 Payment by instalments

Large companies are required to make quarterly payments on account of their corporation tax liability.

A 'large' company is one with profits of more than £1,500,000. This figure is time apportioned for short accounting periods.

Payment amounts and pay days

The quarterly payments should be based on the corporation tax liability for the current year.

The first payment is made on the 14th day of the seventh month of the accounting period.

The other quarterly payments are due on the 14th day of months 10, 13 and 16.

Note that the payments begin during the accounting period itself, not afterwards. So you must begin counting months from the start of the accounting period.

 Example

State the instalment payment dates for a company with a 12-month accounting period ending on 29 February 2024.

Solution

The payments on account are due on:

- 14 September 2023

- 14 December 2023

- 14 March 2024

- 14 June 2024

Each payment due is a quarter of the corporation tax liability for the year.

Therefore, estimates of the corporation tax liability for the year need to be made at each payment date.

At least the first three (and probably all four instalments) usually have to be estimated in practice.

The first instalment payment would be a quarter of the best estimate at that date.

The second payment would require a revised estimate to which an amount is added or deducted for any under or over payment in respect of the first instalment and so on.

HMRC may expect to see some proof that the estimates were made with care.

A penalty may be imposed where a company deliberately makes insufficient quarterly payments.

Test your understanding 2

Wendell plc has profits above £1,500,000 every year and has taxable total profits in the year ended 31 March 2024 of £2,400,000.

Calculate the corporation tax liability of Wendell plc for the accounting period to 31 March 2024 and state when this liability is due for payment.

4.3 Interest

Companies should revise the estimate of their corporation tax liability every quarter. It is a good idea to keep records showing how the estimate has been calculated. This will help to justify the size of a payment if HMRC should dispute the amount paid.

Interest runs from the due date on any underpayments or overpayments.

Interest paid by the company is a deductible expense. Interest received by the company is taxable income. Both are dealt with under the loan relationship rules as non-trade interest.

Penalties may be charged if a company deliberately fails to pay instalments of a sufficient size.

 Test your understanding 3

Space plc, which has taxable total profits of £2 million annually, is preparing its budget for the year ending 31 March 2024.

(a) Prepare a plan of projected corporation tax payments based on its results for the year, stating the amounts due and the due dates.

(b) Advise of any other administrative requirements for corporation tax purposes.

Approach to the question

Step 1: Calculate the corporation tax liability.

Step 2: Consider the impact of the instalment system on this large company.

Step 3: Consider the **returns** required, and the impact of late payments.

4.4 Summary of reference material

Item	Included in reference material	Not included in reference material
Due date for companies which are not large	✓	
Large company due dates	✓	
Definition of a large company	✓	
Need to revise estimates		✓
Penalties may be imposed where a company deliberately pays insufficient instalments		✓

5 Summary

There are numerous deadlines and penalties under CTSA.

The key points are:

- A company must file a return within

    - 12 months of the end of its period of account or

    - if later, three months from the date of the notice from HMRC.

- Failure to submit a return on time results in an immediate penalty of £100.

- A company which is liable to tax for the first time must notify HMRC of its chargeability within three months of the start of its accounting period.

- The company can amend a return within 12 months of the due filing date.

- HMRC can conduct a compliance check (enquiry) into a return provided they give written notice within a year of the actual filing date.

- Companies must keep records for six years from the end of the accounting period. Failure to do so can result in a penalty of up to £3,000.

- The due date for corporation tax is nine months and one day after the end of the accounting period.

- Companies with profits of more than £1,500,000 (adjusted for short accounting periods) must pay their liability in quarterly instalments, commencing on the 14th day of the seventh month of the accounting period.

KAPLAN PUBLISHING

Test your understanding 1

Administration

1   True   The filing date is 12 months from the end of the period of account regardless of the length of the accounting period.

2   False   The latest date that DEF Ltd can amend its return is 31 March 2026 (i.e. 12 months after the due filing date not the actual filing date).

3   False   The immediate penalty for late filing is £100. There can then be additional penalties once the delay exceeds three months.

Test your understanding 2

Wendell plc

Corporation tax liability and payment dates

	£
Corporation tax due:	
Taxable total profits	2,400,000
Corporation tax liability (£2,400,000 × 25%)	600,000
Due date of instalments:	
14 October 2023 (£600,000 × 1/4)	150,000
14 January 2024	150,000
14 April 2024	150,000
14 July 2024	150,000
	600,000

Test your understanding 3

(a) **Space plc**

Projected corporation tax payments – y/e 31 March 2024

Taxable total profits	£2,000,000
Corporation tax liability (at 25%)	£500,000

The accounting period will be subject to quarterly instalments as the company is large.

The liability for the year ended 31 March 2024 should be settled by four equal instalments of £125,000 (£500,000 ÷ 4).

		£
Instalment 1	14 October 2023	125,000
Instalment 2	14 January 2024	125,000
Instalment 3	14 April 2024	125,000
Instalment 4	14 July 2024	125,000

(b) **Administrative requirements**

(1) A return, including statutory accounts and computations, must be submitted online by 31 March 2025 (i.e. within 12 months of the accounting period end otherwise penalties will be charged).

(2) Late payments of tax will give rise to interest charges, which will be deductible from non-trade interest income.

Taxable trade profits for unincorporated businesses

Introduction

In Chapters 2 to 7 we have considered how we tax the profits and gains of one type of business entity – a company.

In the next few chapters we look at how we tax the profits of sole traders and partnerships (unincorporated businesses).

The assessment will include several tasks that consider the taxable trading profits of a sole trader or partner.

There are some differences in the computation of adjusted trading profits and capital allowances for unincorporated businesses compared to companies.

ASSESSMENT CRITERIA
How to identify deductible and non-deductible expenditure (1.1)
How expenditure is classified as either revenue or capital (1.1)
Adjust accounting profit and losses for tax purposes (1.1)
Which capital allowances apply to different assets:
–   plant and machinery
–   structures and buildings (1.2)
Prepare capital allowance computations for accounting periods:
–   longer than 12 months
–   shorter than 12 months
–   equal to 12 months
–   including adjustments for private usage (1.2)
How to identify if clients are trading through the application of the badges of trade (6.2)

CONTENTS

1 Introduction to sole traders and partnerships

2 Trading profits for individuals

3 Adjustment of trading profits

4 Capital allowances for individuals

5 Trading allowance

1 Introduction to sole traders and partnerships

1.1 Sole trader

A sole trader is an individual who has set up a business on their own. The business is not a separate legal entity.

1.2 Types of tax payable

The individual who sets up as a sole trader pays:

- income tax, on income including adjusted trading profits, and

- capital gains tax, on chargeable gains.

 Example

Which of the following business entities is a sole trader?

(a) Fred Flint, haulage contractor.

(b) Fred Flint Ltd, haulage contractor.

Solution

(a) Fred Flint is a sole trader. Fred pays income tax on his adjusted trading profit and capital gains tax on his gains.

(b) Fred Flint Ltd is a company (a separate legal entity). The company pays corporation tax on income and gains.

1.3 Partnership

A partnership is a group of individuals carrying on in business together. The business is not a separate legal entity.

1.4 Types of tax payable

Each partner individually pays:

- income tax, on their share of the partnership's adjusted trading profit in addition to any other personal income.

A partnership is effectively a collection of sole traders working together, each responsible for their own tax liability.

The allocation of partnership profits is considered further in Chapter 9.

2 Trading profits for individuals

2.1 Badges of trade

To determine whether an individual is trading, a number of tests, known as the 'badges of trade', are considered.

The badges of trade are as follows (and can be remembered by using two mnemonics 'SOFIRM', and 'FAST' as donated by the letters in the brackets below):

- **Subject matter (S)**

  Assets are generally acquired either for personal use, or as an investment, or as inventory used in a trade (i.e. stock) or as a non-current asset (i.e. fixed asset) used in a trade.

  An investment may be income generating (e.g. shares) or for pleasure (e.g. a painting). If an asset is clearly neither acquired as an investment or for the use of the owner (or the owner's family or friends), the inference of trading arises.

- **Length of ownership (O)**

  The shorter the period of ownership the more likely this is indicative of a trade.

- **Frequency of transactions (F)**

  The more frequent a transaction the more likely a trade is being conducted.

- **Improvements/Supplementary work (I)**

  An asset bought and enhanced in some way before sale is more likely to be a trading asset than a similar asset simply bought and sold without improvement.

- **Circumstances of realisation (R)**

  It can be argued that the forced sale of an asset to relieve a cash flow crisis is less likely to be a disposal in the course of a trade.

- **Motive (M)**

  The presence of a profit motive is indicative of a trade.

In addition to the above six badges of trade, HMRC guidance states that the following are also considered to indicate trading:

- **The source of finance (F)**

  If the purchase of the asset was funded by a loan which is to be paid off on disposal this is an indication of trading.

- **Method of acquisition (A)**

  If the asset was acquired through an inheritance or on a gift the existence of a trade is less likely to be assumed.

- **Existence of similar trading transactions (ST)**

  If the transaction is similar to an existing trade of the individual it is more likely that it will be held that a trade is being carried out than if the transaction is unrelated.

It is vital to appreciate that no one badge is conclusive. In any set of circumstances some badges may indicate trading whilst others may not.

All factors must be considered and an overall view taken.

As part of Task 8 in the assessment you may be asked to apply the badges of trade to a scenario and explain whether a trade is being carried on. This task will be manually marked.

 Example

Jameela renovates classic cars as a hobby in their spare time and exhibits them at classic car events. They have accepted the occasional offer to sell and usually make a profit if the time they have spent is ignored.

Explain whether you think Jameela will be treated as trading in cars by HMRC.

Solution

- The situation has to be measured against the 'badges of trade'.

- A car could be a trading asset or an investment or for personal use so the 'nature of asset' badge is inconclusive.

- If Jameela owns the cars for only a brief period and is constantly buying, renovating and selling, perhaps even advertising, there comes a point where the hobby becomes a trade.

2.2 Professions and vocations

The profits made by a self-employed person from a profession or vocation, such as accountancy, are taxed in the same way as the profits of a trade.

3 Adjustment of trading profits

3.1 Comparison between individuals and companies

The starting point in determining the amount of taxable trading profits is the net profit as shown in the accounts, but this must be adjusted for tax purposes in a similar way to companies.

We have already considered in Chapter 3 in the context of a company how to adjust the accounting profits to find the adjusted trading profits for tax purposes. The first part of this chapter will concentrate on approaching the topic from an individual trader's perspective.

Taxable trading profits for an individual comprise adjusted trading profits (Chapter 3) less capital allowances (Chapter 4) for an accounting period in much the same way as for a company.

This chapter covers the minor adjustments needed to the rules covered earlier in the context of companies.

Outline pro forma for adjustment of profits computation

		Section	£	£
Net profit per accounts				X
Add:	Disallowable expenditure	3.2	X	
	Income not included in the accounts but taxable as trading income	3.3	X	
			—	X
				X
Less:	Income included in the accounts but not taxable as trading income	3.4	X	
	Expenditure not in the accounts but allowable as a trading deduction	3.5	X	
			—	(X)
Adjusted trading profit (before deducting capital allowances)				X

The same profit adjustment rules for companies apply for individual (or 'sole') traders but with minor adjustments explained as follows.

Reference material

Some information about common adjustments can be found in the 'Disallowed expenditure' section of the reference material provided in the real assessment, so you do not need to learn it.

Why not look up the correct part of the reference material in the introduction to this text book now?

3.2 Disallowable expenditure differences

Adjustments for private expenditure

Any private expenditure of the owner of the business deducted in the accounts should be disallowed. This would include any payment of the trader's income tax or national insurance liabilities.

There will sometimes be an estimated proportion of business use, for example with motor expenses or telephone expenses. If this is the case, only the private element should be disallowed and therefore added back.

Under self-assessment the trader has to be prepared to justify the estimate of the private element if HMRC enquires into the trader's self-assessment return.

Salary to proprietor

The salary or drawings paid to the owner is the equivalent of a dividend paid by a company. It is an appropriation of profit, not a business expense, and must therefore be added back to profit.

Sole traders often employ spouses or other family members in their business. Salaries paid to family members are allowable provided the amount paid is reasonable for the work carried out. Any excessive salary payments are disallowed.

Example

Gordon has his own business as a motor dealer. His accounts for the year ended 31 December 2023 show the following results:

	£	£
Gross profit		80,000
Less: Expenses		
Salaries	30,000	
Motor expenses	3,000	
Allowable expenses	22,000	
	———	(55,000)
Net profit per accounts		25,000

Included in motor expenses is £1,000 relating to the cost of running Gordon's car which is used 60% for business purposes and included in salaries is Gordon's 'salary' of £20,000.

Calculate Gordon's adjusted trading profit.

Solution

	£
Net profit per accounts	25,000
Add: Disallowable expenses	
Gordon's 'salary'/drawings	20,000
Private motor expenses (£1,000 × 40%)	400
	———
Adjusted trading profit	45,400
	———

Note: Do not add back salaries or private motor expenses of employees. These are allowable expenses for the business (just as they are in a company's computation).

Bad debts/Irrecoverable debts

We saw in Chapter 3 that as companies are required to produce their accounts in accordance with internationally accepted accounting practice, any provisions for irrecoverable debts (bad debts) included within the accounts are specific in nature and therefore allowable for tax purposes.

The accounts of an unincorporated business however are not bound by the Companies Act requirements and therefore may contain **general** provisions which are not allowable for tax purposes.

Movements in general provisions, for example the **general** bad debt provision, are not allowable. An increase in a general provision must be added back, and a decrease in a general provision must be deducted, to arrive at adjusted trading profits.

Movements in **specific** provisions are allowable and do not need adjusting for in calculating the adjusted trading profits.

Note that movements in any other general provisions charged to the statement of profit or loss should also be disallowed (e.g. inventory/stock provisions).

Example

The bad debts account of Gregor, an interior designer, for the year ended 30 June 2023 appears as follows:

	£		£
Written off:		Balance brought down:	
Trade	274	Specific provision	185
Former employee	80	General provision	260
Balance carried down:		Recoveries – trade	23
Specific provision	194	Profit and loss account	305
General provision	225		
	───		───
	773		773
	───		───

Show the adjustment required in computing the adjusted trading profit.

Solution

The first stage is to establish a breakdown of the statement of profit or loss charge of £305.

Remember that this figure comprises amounts written off and recovered, and movements in provisions.

Statement of profit or loss charge:

	£	Allowable?
Increase in specific provision (£194 – £185)	9	✓
Decrease in general provision (£225 – £260)	(35)	✗
Trade debt written off	274	✓
Former employee loan written off	80	✗
Recoveries – trade	(23)	✓
	305	

The movement in the general provision and the amount owed by the former employee are both disallowed. In this case, the movement in the general provision is a **decrease**, so the adjustment made is to **deduct** it from the profit per the accounts.

The adjustments required to compute the adjusted trading profit are therefore as follows:

		£
Add:	Former employee, debt written off	80
Less:	Decrease in general provision	(35)

Charitable donations

An unincorporated business may make charitable donations. These fall into three categories:

- Small and to a local charity – allowed as trade expenses.

- Donations via the gift aid scheme – these are not allowed as a trade expense but the trader will get relief for the payment via their personal income tax computation. This relief is not tested in the business tax assessment.

- Other charitable donations – not allowed as a trade expense and no other relief is available.

For a company all charitable donations that are not relieved as trade expenses are given relief as qualifying charitable donations and are deducted from total profits on the face of the corporation tax computation.

Test your understanding 1

Manuel is a self-employed wholesale clothing distributor. His summarised accounts for the year ended 30 June 2023 are as follows:

	£	£
Sales		400,000
Opening inventory	40,000	
Purchases	224,000	
	264,000	
Closing inventory	(32,000)	
Cost of sales		(232,000)
Gross profit		168,000
Wages and National Insurance (Note 1)	84,655	
Car running expenses (Manuel's car) (Note 2)	2,000	
Lighting and heating	4,250	
Rent and business rates	31,060	
Repairs and renewals (all allowable)	3,490	
Legal expenses (Note 3)	1,060	
Depreciation	3,510	
Sundry expenses (all allowable)	5,770	
		(135,795)
Net profit		32,205

Notes to the accounts

(1) Wages

Included in wages are Manuel's drawings of £300 per week, his national insurance contributions of £179 for the year and wages and national insurance contributions in respect of his wife totalling £11,750. His wife worked full-time in the business as a secretary.

(2) Car running expenses

Manuel estimates that one-third of his mileage is private. Included in the charge is £65 for a speeding fine incurred by Manuel whilst delivering goods to a customer.

(3) Legal expenses

	£
Defending action in respect of alleged faulty goods	330
Defending Manuel in connection with speeding offence	640
Debt collection	90
	1,060

(4) Capital allowances for the year to 30 June 2023 are £2,480.

Calculate the taxable trade profits for the accounting period to 30 June 2023.

3.3 Income not included in the accounts but taxable as trading income

This category does not exist for the adjustment of profits for a company.

The most common example is goods taken from the business for the owner's personal use. The proprietor must be taxed on the profit that would have been made if the goods had been sold at market value (i.e. at retail or wholesale price as appropriate).

If the cost of sales in the statement of profit or loss has not been reduced for the goods taken for own use, then the amount to be added back to arrive at the adjusted profit will be the **selling price**.

If the cost of sales has been reduced by the cost of the goods taken for own use, then the amount added back will be the **profit**.

 Example

Samina operates a toy store and has taken goods for her own use costing £500 during the year ended 31 December 2023. An adjustment has already been made to reflect the cost of the goods taken.

What is the increase to net profit required if:

(a) Samina operates a mark-up basis of pricing of 40%, or alternatively

(b) Samina operates on a gross profit margin of 40%?

Read the requirement carefully in the assessment. These will give different results.

Solution

(a) Mark-up means that the cost of the goods represents 100% and that sales value is therefore 140%.

	%
Sales	140
Less: Cost	(100)
Profit	40

The profit is therefore (40% of £500) = £200.

(b) Where a gross profit margin is supplied, sales represent 100% of the value.

If the profit is 40% of sales then the cost of goods is 60%.

	%
Sales	100
Less: Cost	(60)
Profit	40

Therefore the profit element is (£500 × 40/60) = £333.

 Example

Ragna has taken £500 of goods from inventory. An adjustment has been made in the accounts for the cost of the goods taken.

An extract from the statement of profit or loss shows the following:

	£	£
Sales		450,000
Opening inventory	160,000	
Purchases	210,000	
Closing inventory	(120,000)	
Cost of sales		(250,000)
Gross profit		200,000

Explain the adjustments needed if the net profit shown in the accounts is £90,000.

Solution

The increase to net profit for the profit element of goods for own use must be calculated by reference to the correct relationship between cost and gross profit.

If cost of goods used is £500 and £250,000 of costs generates £200,000 of profit then:

Profit element = £500 × 200/250 = £400

Therefore, the net profit is adjusted as follows:

	£
Net profit	90,000
Add: Increase in profit for goods for own use	400
Adjusted profit	90,400

Test your understanding 2

Freda supplies furniture and furnishings. Her summarised accounts for the year ended 31 December 2023 are as follows:

	£	£
Sales of furniture and furnishings		300,000
Cost of sales (Note 1)		(200,000)
		100,000
Design fees		85,000
Gross profit		185,000
Wages and national insurance (Note 2)	75,000	
Rent and business rates	18,250	
Miscellaneous expenses (all allowable)	12,710	
Taxation (Freda's income tax)	15,590	
Depreciation	2,540	
Lease rental on car (Freda's car) (Notes 3 and 4)	8,400	
Car running expenses (Freda's car) (Note 4)	2,500	
Lighting and heating	1,750	
		(136,740)
Net profit		48,260

Notes to the accounts

(1) Cost of sales has been reduced by £1,000 reimbursed by Freda for furnishings taken from inventory. This reimbursement represented cost price.

(2) Wages include Freda's drawings of £1,000 per month and her national insurance contributions of £179 for the year.

(3) A lease for a BMW for Freda (list price £50,000, CO_2 emissions 90g/km) was entered into on 1 July 2023.

(4) Freda estimates that one-half of her mileage is private.

(5) Capital allowances for the year to 31 December 2023 are £1,200.

Calculate the taxable trade profits for the year ended 31 December 2023.

3.4 Income included in the accounts but not taxable as trading income

The following are examples of amounts which may be included in the statement of profit or loss, but which are not taxable as trading income. Hence they should be deducted when calculating taxable trading profits.

- Income taxed in another way (e.g. rent, interest receivable).

- Income exempt from income tax (e.g. interest received on delayed tax repayments).

- Profits on sales of non-current assets.

These adjustments are essentially the same as those for companies.

 Test your understanding 3

Adam's business accounts for the year to 31 March 2024 include the following items.

For each item state what adjustments, if any, are required?

1   Motor expenses for a car used by an employee, private use estimated at 30%.

2   Motor expenses for a car used by Adam, private use estimated at 30%.

3   Overdraft interest on the business bank account.

4   Bank interest received on the business deposit account.

5   Goods taken by Adam which he paid for at cost.

The choices available are:

A   None

B   Add back full amount

C   Deduct full amount

D   Add back 30%

E   Add back selling price

F   Add back profit

3.5 Expenditure not in the accounts but allowable

This category of adjustment does not arise for companies.

Any business expense not charged in the accounts but paid for or borne privately by the proprietor can be deducted as a business expense.

For example, where a home telephone is used for business calls the cost of the business calls can be deducted (although it is more common for the whole amount to be charged to the statement of profit or loss, in which case the private portion should be disallowed).

✳ Test your understanding 4

Alphonse is in business as a wine merchant and has prepared accounts to 30 June 2023. His statement of profit or loss was:

	£	£
Sales		183,658
Cost of sales		(119,379)
Gross profit		64,279
Dividend income		300
		64,579
Salaries	9,740	
Rent and business rates	9,860	
Repairs to premises	2,620	
Motor expenses	740	
Depreciation	4,150	
Bad and doubtful debts	6,030	
Sundry expenses	770	
Salary		
– Alphonse	14,000	
– Wife, as secretary	1,450	
		(49,360)
Net profit		15,219

The following information is given:

Repairs to premises	£
Alterations to flooring in order to install new bottling machine	1,460
Redecoration	1,160
	2,620

Bad and doubtful debts account

	£		£
Trade debts written off	1,300	Provision brought forward	
Loan to ex-employee		– General	1,850
written off	400	– Specific	580
Provisions carried forward		Statement of profit or loss	6,030
– General	5,200		
– Specific	1,560		
	8,460		8,460

Sundry expenses	£
Fine re breach of Customs bonding regulations	250
Subscription to Wine Retail Trade Association	50
Miscellaneous allowable expenses	470
	770

During the year Alphonse had withdrawn goods from inventory for his own consumption. The cost of this inventory was £455. The business makes a uniform gross profit of 35% on selling price. No entry had been made in the books in respect of the goods taken.

Compute Alphonse's adjusted trading profit before capital allowances for the period ended 30 June 2023, giving reasons for the adjustments made.

Note: Reasons for the adjustments will not be required in the assessment. It is likely that an adjustment of profits question will involve completing a pro forma, dragging items of expenditure to the appropriate part of the adjustment of profits calculation or choosing the correct adjustment from a few options.

However, understanding why adjustments are made will help you to remember them better.

4 Capital allowances for individuals

4.1 The general rules

The capital allowance rules for plant and machinery and the structures and buildings allowance have already been explained in detail for companies (Chapter 4). The modifications needed to apply these rules for sole traders are explained in this section.

4.2 Private use assets

Any item of plant or machinery used partly **by the proprietor/owner** for private purposes, such as a van, must be given a separate column in the capital allowances working.

The AIA, WDA or FYA on the asset is based on its full cost. However, the allowance actually **claimed** will be reduced for private use. Only the proportion relating to business use can be claimed.

Note that if applicable, the business can choose the expenditure against which the AIA is matched. It will be most beneficial for the AIA to be allocated against the general pool expenditure rather than any private use asset as only the business proportion of any AIA available can be claimed.

However, note that in the assessment the assets most commonly used for private purposes are cars, which are not eligible for the AIA.

On disposal, a balancing adjustment will be calculated. However, the balancing adjustment will be similarly reduced for private use. Only the business proportion can be claimed or is taxable.

The following example demonstrates this.

Example

Gerard is a trader preparing accounts for calendar years.

In May 2023 he bought a car for £7,200 which has CO_2 emissions of 45g/km. He sold this car in February 2025 for £5,000 replacing it with a car costing £18,800 which has a CO_2 emission rate of 110g/km.

Gerard uses his cars for both business and private purposes and estimates an 80% business use proportion.

Show the capital allowances and balancing adjustments on the cars for the years ended 31 December 2023, 2024 and 2025.

Assume the rates of allowances for the tax year 2023/24 continue into the future.

Solution

This example involves two private use cars.

Each car will have a separate column, as a private use asset.

The first stage is to calculate the allowances in the normal way. Then multiply these allowances by 80%, the business use proportion, to find the allowances that can be claimed.

On disposal, the balancing allowance or charge will be calculated as usual, and again multiplied by 80% to find the actual amount to be deducted or added back to adjusted trading profits.

The answer is therefore as follows:

Gerard – Capital allowances

	Private use Car 1 £	Private use Car 2 £	Allowances £
Year ended 31 December 2023			
Additions	7,200		
WDA @ 18%	(1,296)	× 80%	1,037
TWDV carried forward	5,904		
Year ended 31 December 2024			
WDA @ 18%	(1,063)	× 80%	850
TWDV carried forward	4,841		
Year ended 31 December 2025			
Additions		18,800	
Disposal proceeds	(5,000)		
	(159)		
Balancing charge	159	× 80%	(127)
WDA @ 6% (note)		(1,128) × 80%	902
TWDV carried forward		17,672	
Total allowances			775

Note: Gerard's new car has emissions of more than 50g/km. The rate of WDA is 6%.

Test your understanding 5

Georgina runs a business which she started on 1 September 2023. The first set of accounts were prepared to 31 May 2024.

On 1 October 2023, she purchased a car with CO_2 emissions of 47g/km for £10,500 which is used 30% for business purposes.

What are the capital allowances available for the period ended 31 May 2024?

A   £567

B   £1,418

C   £1,890

D   £425

 Test your understanding 6

Ernest prepares accounts to 31 March annually. On 1 April 2023 there is a qualifying general pool balance of plant and machinery brought forward of £24,000.

The following transactions took place in the year to 31 March 2024.

15 April 2023	Purchased car for £16,000 (wholly business usage)
30 April 2023	Sold plant for £3,200 (original cost £4,800)
16 July 2023	Purchased car for £9,200 (wholly business usage)
17 August 2023	Purchased car for £9,400 (30% private usage by Ernest)

In the following year to 31 March 2025, Ernest sold for £8,100 the car originally purchased on 17 August 2023. The car originally purchased on 15 April 2023 was sold for £9,400 on 9 March 2025. There were no other transactions.

All cars purchased had CO_2 emissions between 1 and 50g/km.

Compute the capital allowances and balancing adjustments for the years ended 31 March 2024 and 31 March 2025.

Assume the rates of allowances for the tax year 2023/24 continue into the future.

Test your understanding 7

Etta prepares accounts to 31 March annually. In the year to 31 March 2024, she bought three cars for use in her business as follows:

11 May 2023	Purchased car for £17,000 (wholly business usage)
21 June 2023	Purchased car for £8,800 (wholly business usage)
16 September 2023	Purchased car for £11,600 (30% private usage by Etta)

All the cars have CO_2 emissions between 1 and 50g/km.

She had never previously acquired any plant and machinery for her business.

In the following year to 31 March 2025, Etta sold for £9,700 the car originally purchased on 16 September 2023. The car originally purchased on 11 May 2023 was sold for £10,000 on 12 June 2024. There were no other transactions.

Compute the capital allowances and balancing adjustments for the years ended 31 March 2024 and 31 March 2025.

Assume the rates of allowances for the tax year 2023/24 continue into the future.

4.3 The impact of the length of the accounting period (sole traders)

As we have seen, capital allowances are computed for accounting periods and deducted in calculating taxable trading profits (Chapter 4).

Where the accounting period is more or less than 12 months long, the AIA, WDA and small pools WDA must be scaled up or down accordingly. You must perform this calculation to the nearest month.

Note the important difference between companies and sole traders. A company cannot have an accounting period greater than 12 months, but a sole trader can. Therefore, the allowances are scaled up where there is a long period of account for a sole trader.

Remember however, that first year allowances are given in full regardless of the length of the accounting period. They are never scaled up or down according to the length of the accounting period.

Full expensing on the purchase of new plant and machinery is **not available to sole traders**, this can only be claimed by companies.

Capital allowances for periods which are not twelve months long are very popular in the assessment and you should always watch out for them.

 Example

Kedarnath started to trade on 1 January 2023, and on that day three cars were purchased to be used by employees at a total cost of £21,900. Plant which cost £22,000 was also purchased. All the cars had CO_2 emissions of 40g/km.

Calculate the allowances due for the first two accounting periods on the assumption that the accounts are prepared to:

(a) 31 December 2023

(b) 31 October 2023

(c) 31 March 2024

and annually on those dates thereafter.

Assume the rates of allowances for the tax year 2023/24 continue into the future.

Solution

(a) **First accounts – 12 months to 31 December 2023**

	AIA	General pool	Allowances
	£	£	£
12 months to 31 December 2023			
Additions:			
No AIA: Cars		21,900	
Qualifying for AIA:			
Plant	22,000		
AIA	(22,000)		22,000
	——	Nil	
		21,900	
WDA @ 18%		(3,942)	3,942
		——	
TWDV c/f		17,958	
			——
Total allowances			25,942
			——

	General pool £	Allowances £
12 months to 31 December 2024		
TWDV b/f	17,958	
WDA @ 18%	(3,232)	3,232
TWDV c/f	14,726	

(b) **First accounts – 10 months to 31 October 2023**

	AIA £	General pool £	Allowances £
10 months to 31 October 2023			
Additions:			
No AIA: Cars		21,900	
Qualifying for AIA:			
Plant	22,000		
AIA (Note)	(22,000)		22,000
		Nil	
		21,900	
WDA @ 18% × 10/12		(3,285)	3,285
TWDV c/f		18,615	
Total allowances			25,285
12 months to 31 October 2024			
WDA @ 18%		(3,351)	3,351
TWDV c/f		15,264	

Note: Maximum AIA = (£1,000,000 × 10/12) = £833,333.

(c) **First accounts – 15 months to 31 March 2024**

	£	General pool £	Allowances £
15 months to 31 March 2024			
Additions:			
No AIA: Cars		21,900	
Qualifying for AIA:			
Plant	22,000		
AIA (Note)	(22,000)		22,000
	————	Nil	
		————	
		21,900	
WDA @ 18% × 15/12		(4,928)	4,928
		————	
TWDV c/f		16,972	
			————
Total allowances			26,928
			————
12 months to 31 March 2025			
WDA @ 18%		(3,055)	3,055
		————	
TWDV c/f		13,917	
		————	

Note: Maximum AIA = (£1,000,000 × 15/12) = £1,250,000.

Test your understanding 8

Anjula started trading on 1 May 2023 and prepares her first set of accounts to 31 August 2024.

On 2 June 2023 she purchased equipment costing £2,500 and a car costing £6,200 with carbon dioxide emissions of 45g/km and 100% business use.

What are the capital allowances available for the period ended 31 August 2024?

A £8,700

B £3,988

C £2,088

D £3,616

Test your understanding 9

On 1 May 2023, Raj began a small manufacturing business in a rented factory.

They subsequently purchased the following machinery:

		£
2 November 2023	Machinery	20,000
1 February 2024	Car (20% private use by Raj with CO_2 emissions 120g/km)	16,000
1 February 2024	New tool grinder	6,000
2 October 2024	Car for salesman (with CO_2 emissions 42g/km)	11,600

Accounts are prepared to 31 March in each year.

Compute the capital allowances for each accounting period up to 31 March 2025.

Assume the rates of allowances for the tax year 2023/24 continue into the future.

Test your understanding 10

Hudson has been carrying on a manufacturing business in a South London suburb since 1 April 2018 preparing accounts to 31 March each year.

He decided to retire on 31 October 2024, and prepared his final set of accounts for the 7-month period to 31 October 2024.

The balance on the general capital allowances pool as at 1 April 2023 was £6,500.

The following plant was acquired for cash on the dates shown:

1 May 2023	New plant costing	£10,858
1 June 2023	Second-hand plant costing	£1,000

On 10 July 2023, Hudson bought a car costing £16,000 through his business. Three-quarters of his usage of the car was for business purposes and one-quarter for private purposes. The car has CO_2 emissions of 45g/km.

No sale of plant took place during these periods, but at 31 October 2024, when the business closed down, all the plant was sold for £2,450 (no one item realising more than its original cost), and the car was disposed of to a dealer, who gave Hudson £14,000 for it.

Calculate the capital allowances for Hudson for the final two accounting periods to 31 October 2024.

Assume the rates of allowances for the tax year 2023/24 continue into the future.

 Test your understanding 11

Asha started trading on 1 November 2021, preparing accounts for the period to 30 April 2023. During this period the following acquisitions were made:

		£
1 November 2021	Machinery	40,000
1 February 2022	Car (60% business use by Asha with CO_2 emissions 95g/km)	16,000
1 December 2022	Plant	280,000

Compute the capital allowances for the accounting period to 30 April 2023.

4.4 Structures and buildings allowances

We have already seen that structures and buildings allowances (SBAs) are available only on commercial property, not residential property, and that the rate of SBAs is 3% (Chapter 4). As with capital allowances, SBAs are scaled up where there is a long period of account for a sole trader.

 Example

Adalia began trading on 1 January 2023 and prepares her first set of accounts to 31 March 2024.

On 1 January 2023 she purchased new retail premises for £240,000 and began trading from those premises on the same day.

The cost included £80,000 for the land. One quarter of the premises is a flat occupied by Adalia.

Calculate the structures and buildings allowance available for the period ended 31 March 2024.

Solution

Adalia – Structures and buildings allowances computation

	£
15 months ended 31 March 2024	
Total cost	240,000
Less: Land	(80,000)
Cost excluding land	160,000
Less: Residential portion (1/4)	(40,000)
Qualifying cost	120,000
SBA (3% × £120,000 × 15/12)	4,500

Test your understanding 12

Niamh prepares accounts to 31 March.

On 1 May 2023 Niamh purchased an office for £340,000 (including £140,000 for the land) and began trading from the office on 1 June 2023.

Calculate the structures and buildings allowance available for the year ended 31 March 2024.

5 Trading allowance

5.1 The trading allowance

A trading allowance of £1,000 is available to sole traders (not partnerships).

If a sole trader's trading income (not profit) is no more than £1,000 it is exempt and does not need to be declared.

If a sole trader's trading income is no more than £1,000 but trading expenses exceed receipts, the trader can choose not to claim the trading allowance in order to get relief for the trading loss that would arise without the allowance (see Chapter 10 for details).

If a sole trader's trading income is in excess of £1,000 then the trader can choose to deduct the trading allowance from trading income rather than the actual expenses incurred.

 Reference material

Some information about trading allowance can be found in the 'Income tax' section of the reference material provided in the real assessment, so you do not need to learn it.

Why not look up the correct part of the reference material in the introduction to this text book now?

Example

Anahera designs T-shirts in her spare time and sells them online.

Calculate Anahera's assessable trading profit assuming her income and expenses are as follows:

	Income	Expenses
	£	£
(a)	800	350
(b)	1,100	480
(c)	500	700

(a) **Income £800 and expenses £350**

As Anahera's income (not profit) is less than £1,000 it is exempt and she will not need to declare it to HMRC.

(b) **Income £1,100 and expenses £480**

Anahera's income is in excess of £1,000 so she can choose whether to deduct her actual expenses incurred or the trading allowance of £1,000.

	Actual expenses	Trading allowance
	£	£
Income	1,100	1,100
Less: Expenses/trading allowance	(480)	(1,000)
Trading profit	620	100

Deducting the trading allowance gives a lower taxable profit and so this is the method that should be chosen.

(c) **Income £500 and expenses £700**

Anahera's expenses exceed her income and create a trading loss. If she were to claim the trading allowance she would not receive the benefit of this trading loss.

Anahera should not claim the trading allowance and should deduct her expenses incurred instead to recognise a trading loss of £200.

	£
Income	500
Less: Expenses	(700)
Trading loss	(200)

Test your understanding 13

Meg receives trading income of £1,555 in the tax year 2023/24. Her allowable expenses are £500 for the tax year.

Calculate Meg's taxable trading income for the tax year 2023/24 assuming all beneficial elections are made.

6 Summary

Sole traders and partnerships:

- DO NOT pay corporation tax
- DO pay income tax and capital gains tax
- ARE NOT separate legal entities.

Sole traders (and partners) must adjust their accounting profits in the same way as companies:

- add back disallowable expenditure
- deduct allowable expenditure which is not shown in the accounts
- deduct income shown in the accounts not taxable as trading income
- add income taxable as trading income which is not shown in the accounts.

The main adjustments applying to individuals but not companies are the disallowance of the proprietor's salary and private expenses, and the adjustment of goods taken for the proprietor's own use.

Capital allowances are then deducted from the adjusted trading profits to give the taxable trading profits. The capital allowances must be restricted for the proprietor's own use of business assets.

A trading allowance is available which means sole traders with trading income of no more than £1,000 do not have to declare income or pay tax on it.

Test your understanding answers

Test your understanding 1

Manuel

Adjustment of profits for 12 months ended 30 June 2023

	£
Net profit per accounts	32,205
Manuel's drawings (£300 × 52)	15,600
Manuel's NIC	179
Speeding fine	65
Motor expenses (1/3 of balance) (£2,000 – £65) × 1/3	645
Legal expenses in connection with speeding offence	640
Depreciation	3,510
	52,844
Less: Capital allowances	(2,480)
Taxable trade profits	50,364

Test your understanding 2

Freda

Adjustment of profits for year ended 31 December 2023

	£
Net profit per accounts	48,260
Goods for own use (W1)	500
Freda's drawings (£1,000 × 12)	12,000
Freda's NIC	179
Taxation (Freda's income tax)	15,590
Lease rental on high emission car (W2)	4,830
Depreciation	2,540
Car running expenses (1/2 × £2,500)	1,250
	85,149
Less: Capital allowances	(1,200)
Taxable trade profits	83,949

Workings

(W1) Goods for own use

Where goods are taken for own use, the proprietor will be taxed on the profit that would have been made, had the goods been sold at market value.

Here, the cost of the goods has already been credited to the statement of profit or loss, but an additional credit is needed to reflect the profit that would have been made.

As no information is given about profit margins, an estimate will have to be used, based on the trading account.

	£
Sales	300,000
Less: Cost of sales	(200,000)
Gross profit	100,000

Gross profit as a percentage of cost = $\frac{100,000}{200,000}$ = 50%

Gross profit on goods taken for own use = 50% × £1,000 = £500

(W2) Lease rental on high emission car

Amount to be disallowed is 15% of hire charges:

Disallowed amount = 15% × £8,400 = £1,260

The car is also used privately so in addition to the disallowable amount calculated above, the private use element of the balance must also be disallowed.

Balance of expenditure £8,400 – £1,260 = £7,140

Private use element   £7,140 × 1/2   = £3,570

Total amount disallowed:

	£
High emission element	1,260
Private use element	3,570
	———
	4,830
	———

Alternative calculation:

Amount allowed = (£8,400 × 85% × 50%) = £3,570

Amount to be added back = (£8,400 – £3,570) = £4,830

Test your understanding 3

Adam

The correct answers are as follows:

1   A   These are fully allowable from the business point of view and, as they have already been deducted in the accounts, no adjustment is required. The employee may be assessed on the private use as a taxable benefit.

2   D   30% of the motor expenses should be added back as the private use is by the owner of the business.

3   A   This is an allowable trade expense and, as it has already been deducted in the accounts, no adjustment is required.

4   C   Bank interest is not taxed as trading profits, therefore deduct in full.

5   F   Add back the profit that would have been made had Adam paid the full selling price.

Test your understanding 4

Alphonse

Adjusted trading profit for 12 months ended 30 June 2023

Expenditure charged but not allowable

Most of the required adjustments will be under this heading.

Start at the top of the statement of profit or loss and work down considering the admissibility of each item in turn and reading any relevant notes.

Do not flit from item to item at random since this is a sure way to overlook something.

If you do not know for certain whether any particular item is allowable or not, do not waste time thinking too much about it – take an informed guess; more often than not you will guess right.

Remember the main rule of allowability – the expenditure must be 'incurred wholly and exclusively for the purposes of the trade', in this case the trade of a wine merchant.

The adjustments under this heading are as follows:

	£	Reason
Net profit per accounts	15,219	
Repairs to premises – floor alterations	1,460	Capital cost
Depreciation	4,150	Capital cost
Bad and doubtful debts		
General provision increase	3,350	An appropriation
Loan to ex-employee written off	400	Not wholly and exclusively
Sundry expenses		
Fine	250	Not wholly and exclusively
Salary – Alphonse	14,000	Appropriation

Note: It is assumed that Alphonse's wife's salary can be justified as a business expense.

Income credited but not taxable as trading income

It is fairly likely that all credit items will either be assessed as a type of non-trading income or will be capital items or will not be taxable.

The adjustment under this heading is as follows:

	£	Reason
Dividend income	300	Taxed as dividend income

Income not credited but assessable

An adjustment under this heading will normally arise because goods have been taken for the proprietor's own use. Legal precedent has established that this 'sale' is to be brought to account for tax purposes at full market price, i.e. (£455 × 100/65) = £700.

The £700 will be an addition to the profits per the accounts in calculating adjusted trading profits, i.e. an adjustment on the plus side of the computation.

Alphonse

Adjustment of profits for 12 months ended 30 June 2023

	+	–
	£	£
Net profit per accounts	15,219	
Repairs – alterations to flooring	1,460	
Depreciation	4,150	
Bad and doubtful debts		
General provision increase	3,350	
Loan to ex-employee written off	400	
Sundry expenses		
Fine	250	
Salary – Alphonse	14,000	
Dividends		300
Goods withdrawn by Alphonse (£455 × 100/65)	700	
	———	———
	39,529	300
	(300)	———
	———	
Adjusted trading profit (before capital allowances)	39,229	
	———	

Test your understanding 5

Georgina

The correct answer is D.

Explanation

D is the correct answer because the car attracts a WDA at 18%, proportionately reduced for the short 9-month accounting period and adjusted for private use, as follows:

9 months ended 31 May 2024	Private use car		Allowances
	£		£
Addition – no AIA	10,500		
WDA @ 18% × 9/12	(1,418)	× 30%	425
TWDV c/f	9,082		

Test your understanding 6

Ernest

Capital allowances computation – plant and machinery

	General pool	Private use asset	Allowances
	£	£	£
Year ended 31 March 2024			
TWDV b/f at 1 April 2023	24,000		
Additions: No AIA			
Cars			
15 April 2023	16,000		
16 July 2023	9,200		
17 August 2023		9,400	
Disposals			
30 April 2023	(3,200)		
	———		
	46,000		
WDA @ 18%	(8,280)	(1,692) × 70%	9,464
	———	———	
TWDV c/f	37,720	7,708	
			———
Total allowances			9,464
			———
Year ended 31 March 2025			
Disposals			
Car proceeds	(9,400)	(8,100)	
		———	
		(392)	
Balancing charge		392 × 70%	(274)
	———	———	
	28,320		
WDA @ 18%	(5,098)		5,098
	———		
TWDV at 31 March 2025	23,222		
	———		———
Total allowances			4,824
			———

Test your understanding 7

Etta

Capital allowances computation

	General pool	Private use asset	Allowances
	£	£	£
Year ended 31 March 2024			
Additions not qualifying for AIA			
11 May 2023	17,000		
21 June 2023	8,800		
16 September 2023		11,600	
	25,800		
WDA @ 18%	(4,644)		4,644
WDA @ 18% (Note 1)		(2,088)	1,462
TWDV c/f	21,156	9,512	
Total allowances			6,106
Year ended 31 March 2025			
Disposals	(10,000)	(9,700)	
	11,156	(188)	
Balancing charge (Note 2)		188	(132)
WDA @ 18%	(2,008)		2,008
TWDV c/f	9,148		
Total allowances			1,876

Notes:

(1) Business portion of WDA = (£2,088 × 70%) = £1,462

(2) Business portion of charge = (£188 × 70%) = £132

Test your understanding 8

Anjula

The correct answer is B.

Explanation

B is the correct answer because:

- the equipment attracts 100% AIA. As this accounting period is more than 12 months long the maximum AIA is £1,333,333 (£1,000,000 × 16/12). The expenditure is less than this so will be covered in full by the AIA.

- the car attracts a WDA of 18% multiplied by 16/12 as the first accounting period is 16 months long.

The calculation is therefore:

	£
AIA	2,500
WDA (£6,200 × 18% × 16/12)	1,488
	─────
Total allowances	3,988
	─────

Test your understanding 9

Raj

Capital allowances computation

	AIA	General pool	Private use asset	Allowances
	£	£	£	£
11 m/e 31 March 2024				
Additions not qualifying for AIA				
Car			16,000	
Additions qualifying for AIA				
Machinery	20,000			
Tool grinder	6,000			
	26,000			
AIA (Note 1)	(26,000)			26,000
		Nil		
WDA @ 6% × 11/12			(880) × 80%	704
TWDV c/f		Nil	15,120	
Total allowances				26,704
Year ended 31 March 2025				
Additions not qualifying for AIA				
Car		11,600		
		11,600		
WDA @ 18%		(2,088)		2,088
WDA @ 6%			(907) × 80%	726
TWDV c/f		9,512	14,213	
Total allowances				2,814

Notes:

(1) The maximum AIA available is £916,667 (£1,000,000 × 11/12).

(2) As the car has emissions of over 50g/km the WDA for Raj's car is 6% p.a.

Test your understanding 10

Hudson

Capital allowances computation

	AIA	General pool	Private use asset	Allowances
	£	£	£	£
Year ended 31 March 2024				
TWDV b/f		6,500		
Addition – No AIA			16,000	
Addition qualifying for AIA:				
– New plant	10,858			
– Second-hand plant	1,000			
	11,858			
AIA (Note 1)	(11,858)			11,858
		Nil		
WDA @ 18%		(1,170)	(2,880) × 75%	3,330
TWDV c/f		5,330	13,120	
Total allowances				15,188
7 months ended 31 Oct 2024				
Disposal proceeds		(2,450)	(14,000)	
Balancing allowance		2,880		2,880
Balancing charge			(880) × 75%	(660)
Total allowances				2,220

Notes:

(1)   The maximum AIA available is £1,000,000.

(2)   No WDAs are given in the final accounting period.

Test your understanding 11

Asha

Capital allowances computation

	General pool	Private use asset	Allowances
	£	£	£	£
18 m/e 30 April 2023				
Additions not qualifying for AIA				
Car			16,000	
Additions qualifying for AIA				
Machinery	40,000			
Plant	280,000			
		320,000			
AIA (Note)	(320,000)			320,000
		0		
WDA @ 6% × 18/12			(1,440) × 60%	864
TWDV c/f		0	14,560	
Total allowances				320,864

Note: The maximum AIA available is £1,500,000 (£1,000,000 × 18/12).

Test your understanding 12

Niamh

Structures and buildings allowances computation

	£
Year ended 31 March 2024	
Total cost	340,000
Less: Land	(140,000)
Qualifying cost	200,000
SBA @ 3% × 10/12	5,000

The SBA is only available once the office is brought into use.

Test your understanding 13

Meg

Trading income computation

	£
Tax year 2023/24	
Income	1,555
Less: Trading allowance	(1,000)
Taxable trading income	555

Meg should elect to use the trading allowance as her income is over £1,000 and the allowance exceeds her actual expenses.

Partnership profit allocation

Introduction

Some of the tasks in the assessment will relate to either a sole trader or a partnership (i.e. an unincorporated business).

Both are given the same tax treatment with one extra step for partnerships, the allocation of profits, which is covered in this chapter.

The allocation of profits will be tested in Task 3 of the assessment.

ASSESSMENT CRITERIA
Allocate profits between partners (1.3)

CONTENTS

1   Allocation of profits

2   Change in profit sharing arrangements

3   Partnership changes

1 Allocation of profits

1.1 Computation of taxable trade profits

There is no difference between a sole trader and a partnership when applying the rules for computing the tax adjusted trading profits.

A partnership is merely treated for tax purposes as a collection of sole traders.

Each partner is taxed individually on a share of partnership profits as if the partner were a sole trader earning those profits.

1.2 Division of profits between partners

Profits are allocated according to the profit sharing arrangements during the **accounting period** in which profits are earned.

 Example

Andrew and Bernard have been in business for many years, preparing their accounts to 31 December each year, and sharing profits in the ratio of 2:1.

The partnership's taxable trade profits for the year ended 31 December 2023 were £37,500.

Show how these profits are allocated to partners.

Solution

Year ended 31 December 2023	Andrew	Bernard	Total
Profits split (2:1)	£25,000	£12,500	£37,500

Test your understanding 1

John and Kyle began in partnership on 6 April 2023 and have taxable trading profits for the year to 5 April 2024 of £24,047.

They have agreed to share profits and losses in the ratio of 3:2.

Calculate each partner's share of the taxable profits for the year ended 5 April 2024.

Some partnership agreements specify that one or more partners will receive a salary to reflect their work in the partnership or interest on the capital they have invested in the partnership. These are ways of apportioning profits and must be allocated to the respective partners before the balance of profits. The example below considers this further:

 Example

Fatma, Caroline, Nathan and Gita started in business on 1 January 2023. They shared profits as follows:

Interest on fixed capital	10%

Salaries	
Fatma	£3,000 per annum
Caroline	£4,000 per annum
Nathan	£4,000 per annum
Gita	£3,000 per annum

Share of balance	
Fatma	50%
Caroline	20%
Nathan	10%
Gita	20%

Capital account balances were as follows:

Fatma	£10,000
Caroline	£5,000
Nathan	£5,000
Gita	£5,000

The taxable trade profits of the partnership for the year ended 31 December 2023 were £100,000.

Show how these profits are allocated to the partners.

Solution

Profits are allocated as follows:

	F	C	N	G	Total
	£	£	£	£	£
Interest on capital (10% × capital)	1,000	500	500	500	2,500
Salaries	3,000	4,000	4,000	3,000	14,000
Balance (50:20:10:20)	41,750	16,700	8,350	16,700	83,500
Total taxable profits	45,750	21,200	12,850	20,200	100,000

It is important to realise that the whole profit of £100,000 is classed as taxable trade profits.

Even though there is reference to salaries and interest, this is merely a means of allocation. For example, Fatma is now treated as having taxable trade profits of £45,750; she is not regarded as having received interest income or employment income.

2 Change in profit sharing arrangements

2.1 Principle of allocating profits

Where there is a change in the profit sharing arrangements during the accounting period, the period must be split into two or more parts (depending on the number of changes), with a separate division among the partners for each part.

Example

Riya, Fran and Gilly have been in business for many years.

During the year ended 31 December 2023, their taxable trade profits were £94,000. Profits were shared as follows:

	Riya	Fran	Gilly
To 30 June 2023			
Salary (per annum)	£10,000	£6,100	–
Balance	1	1	1
To 31 December 2023			
Salary (per annum)	£Nil	£Nil	£Nil
Balance	2	1	1

Show how the profits would be allocated between the partners.

Solution

Beware, the salaries are quoted per annum; if a change occurs during an accounting period the salary must be time apportioned.

Year ended 31 December 2023

	Riya £	Fran £	Gilly £	Total £
Period 1 January 2023 – 30 June 2023 (6/12)				
Salary	5,000	3,050		8,050
Balance (1:1:1)	12,983	12,983	12,984	38,950
				47,000
(£94,000 × 6/12)				
Period 1 July 2023 – 31 December 2023 (6/12)				
Balance (2:1:1)	23,500	11,750	11,750	47,000
Total	41,483	27,783	24,734	94,000

The profits are deemed to accrue evenly over time.

Each partner now has their own taxable trade profits for the accounting period.

Test your understanding 2

Read the following statements and state whether they are **true** or **false**.

1 A partnership pays tax on the partnership profits.

2 Brian and Mary trade in partnership sharing profits equally and preparing accounts to 31 December. If they want to change their profit shares to 1/3:2/3 on 1 July 2023 they need to prepare accounts to 30 June 2023.

3 Partners' salaries and interest on capital are deductible in computing adjusted trading profit.

Test your understanding 3

Bishal and Harold have traded in partnership for several years. Their accounts for the year ended 30 September 2023 show taxable trade profits of £16,500.

Bishal and Harold changed their profit-sharing ratio on 1 July 2023. The old profit-sharing ratio applies until 30 June 2023, and the new ratio applies from 1 July 2023.

	Bishal	Harold
Old ratio:		
Salaries p.a.	£3,000	£2,000
Share of balance	3/5	2/5
New ratio:		
Salaries p.a.	£6,000	£4,000
Share of balance	2/3	1/3

Show the allocation of the taxable trade profits between the partners for the year to 30 September 2023.

3 Partnership changes

3.1 Principle of allocating profits

Where there is a change in the partnership during the accounting period, the period must be split into two or more parts (depending on the number of changes), exactly as for a change in the profit share arrangement.

A change in the partnership may occur when a new partner is admitted.

 Example

Charbel and David began to trade in partnership with effect from 1 July 2020, preparing accounts to 30 June each year and sharing profits equally.

On 1 January 2022, Edward joined the partnership. Profits were then split in the ratio 2:2:1.

The tax adjusted trading profits of the partnership were as follows:

	£
Year ended 30 June 2021	70,000
Year ended 30 June 2022	73,200
Year ended 30 June 2023	74,000

Show the profit allocation for each partner for each accounting period.

Solution

Allocate accounting period profits to partners according to profit share, splitting the accounting period where appropriate.

	C £	D £	E £	Total £
Year ended 30 June 2021 (1:1)	35,000	35,000	–	70,000
Year ended 30 June 2022				
1 July 2021 – 31 Dec 2021 (1:1) 6/12	18,300	18,300	–	36,600
1 Jan 2022 – 30 June 2022 (2:2:1) 6/12	14,640	14,640	7,320	36,600
	32,940	32,940	7,320	73,200
Year ended 30 June 2023 (2:2:1)	29,600	29,600	14,800	74,000

A change in the partnership may also occur when a partner leaves the partnership or dies.

 Example

Fahd, George and Hussain began to trade in partnership with effect from 1 July 2019, preparing accounts to 30 June each year and sharing profits equally.

On 31 October 2022 George died. Profits and losses were then split in the ratio 3:2.

The tax adjusted trading profits of the partnership were as follows:

	£
Year ended 30 June 2020	60,000
Year ended 30 June 2021	85,200
Year ended 30 June 2022	75,000
Year ended 30 June 2023	75,600

Show the profit allocation for each partner for each accounting period.

Solution

Allocate accounting period profits to partners according to profit share, splitting the accounting period where appropriate.

	F £	G £	H £	Total £
Year ended 30 June 2020 (1:1:1)	20,000	20,000	20,000	60,000
Year ended 30 June 2021 (1:1:1)	28,400	28,400	28,400	85,200
Year ended 30 June 2022 (1:1:1)	25,000	25,000	25,000	75,000
Year ended 30 June 2023				
1 July 2022 – 31 Oct 2022 (1:1:1) 4/12	8,400	8,400	8,400	25,200
1 Nov 2022 – 30 June 2023 (3:2) 8/12	30,240	–	20,160	50,400
	38,640	8,400	28,560	75,600

The assessment could test changes to a partnership agreement and/or changes to the members of a partnership.

Test your understanding 4

Lindsay and Tricia have been in partnership for many years, running a dry cleaning business. They prepare their accounts to 31 March each year. Their profit sharing ratio has always been 3:2.

On 1 August 2023, Kate joined the partnership and the profit sharing ratio was changed to 4:3:2 for Lindsay, Tricia and Kate.

For the year ended 31 March 2024, the trading profit was £150,000.

The division of profit would be calculated as:

	Lindsay £	Tricia £	Kate £	Total £
Period to	2	3		1
Period to	5	6	7	4

Options

1	A	£150,000
	B	£75,000
	C	£50,000
	D	£100,000
2	A	£30,000
	B	£20,000
	C	£45,000
	D	£90,000
3	A	£30,000
	B	£20,000
	C	£60,000
	D	£40,000
4	A	£150,000
	B	£75,000
	C	£50,000
	D	£100,000
5	A	£33,333
	B	£22,222
	C	£66,667
	D	£44,445
6	A	£22,222
	B	£25,000
	C	£33,333
	D	£44,445
7	A	£16,667
	B	£22,222
	C	£33,333
	D	£44,445

Test your understanding 5

Michael and Nick started a business as printers on 1 October 2019, preparing accounts to 30 September each year and sharing profits equally.

On 1 January 2021, Liz was admitted to the partnership and profits continued to be shared equally.

On 30 June 2022, Nick retired. Profits continued to be shared equally.

On 31 December 2023 the partnership was dissolved.

The adjusted profits of the partnership, after deducting capital allowances, were as follows:

	£
Year ended 30 September 2020	30,000
Year ended 30 September 2021	36,000
Year ended 30 September 2022	42,500
Year ended 30 September 2023	40,000
Three months to 31 December 2023	17,500

Show the allocation of profits to each partner for all accounting periods.

 Test your understanding 6

Ariana and Betty have been in partnership for many years sharing profits equally.

On 30 June 2022, Betty resigned as a partner and was replaced on 1 July 2022 by Carlota. Diana was admitted as a partner on 1 April 2023. Profits were shared equally throughout.

The partnership's taxable trade profits are as follows:

	£
Year ended 31 December 2022	60,000
Year ended 31 December 2023	72,000

Show the allocation of the taxable trade profits between the partners for each of the years to 31 December 2022 and 2023.

4 Summary

The taxable trade profits of a partnership are apportioned between the partners in accordance with the profit sharing arrangements during the accounting period.

Where there are salaries and interest on capital these should be dealt with first, and then any balance shared out using the profit sharing ratio.

Test your understanding answers

◑ Test your understanding 1

John and Kyle

Year ending 5 April 2024	John £	Kyle £	Total £
Profits split (3:2)	14,428	9,619	24,047

◑ Test your understanding 2

1	False	The partnership is not a separate legal entity from the partners. It is the partners who pay tax on their share of the partnership profits.
2	False	The profits are time apportioned to the period before and after 30 June, and then allocated using the profit sharing ratio in each period.
3	False	Salaries and interest must be added back in calculating adjusted trading profit as they are not actually salaries and interest. They merely represent a method chosen by the partners of allocating profits between them.
		They are taken into account in apportioning the profit between the partners, but the partners are taxed on their total share of trading profits of the partnership as trading income.

Test your understanding 3

Bishal and Harold

Allocation of taxable trade profits

The profit-sharing ratio was changed on 1 July 2023 which is 9 months into the accounting period. The profits will therefore be time apportioned for allocation as follows:

Old ratio £16,500 × 9/12 = £12,375

New ratio £16,500 × 3/12 = £4,125

Allocation of taxable trade profits

	Bishal £	Harold £	Total £
1 Oct 2022 to 30 Jun 2023			
Salaries (9/12)	2,250	1,500	3,750
Balance (3:2)	5,175	3,450	8,625
	7,425	4,950	12,375
1 Jul 2023 to 30 Sep 2023			
Salaries (3/12)	1,500	1,000	2,500
Balance (2:1)	1,083	542	1,625
	2,583	1,542	4,125
Total allocation	10,008	6,492	16,500

Test your understanding 4

Lindsay, Tricia and Kate

The correct answers are as follows:

First period to: 31 July 2023

(1)   C

(2)   A

(3)   B

Second period to: 31 March 2024

(4)   D

(5)   D

(6)   C

(7)   B

Explanation:

The split of partnership profits will be as follows:

	Lindsay £	Tricia £	Kate £	Total £
Year ending 31 March 2024				
1 April 2023 – 31 July 2023 (4m)	30,000	20,000		50,000
1 Aug 2023 – 31 March 2024 (8m)	44,445	33,333	22,222	100,000
	74,445	53,333	22,222	150,000

Test your understanding 5

Michael, Nick and Liz

	Michael £	Nick £	Liz £	Total £
Year ended 30 September 2020	15,000	15,000		30,000
Year ended 30 September 2021				
1 October 2020 – 31 December 2020 (3/12)	4,500	4,500		9,000
1 January 2021 – 30 September 2021 (9/12)	9,000	9,000	9,000	27,000
	13,500	13,500	9,000	36,000
Year ended 30 September 2022				
1 October 2021 – 30 June 2022 (9/12)	10,625	10,625	10,625	31,875
1 July 2022 – 30 September 2022 (3/12)	5,313	–	5,312	10,625
	15,938	10,625	15,937	42,500
Year ended 30 September 2023	20,000		20,000	40,000
Period ending 31 December 2023	8,750		8,750	17,500

✸ Test your understanding 6

Ariana, Betty, Carlota and Diana

	Ariana £	Betty £	Carlota £	Diana £	Total £
Year ended 31 Dec 2022					
1 Jan 2022 – 30 Jun 2022					
6/12 × £60,000	15,000	15,000			30,000
1 Jul 2022 – 31 Dec 2022					
6/12 × £60,000	15,000		15,000		30,000
	30,000	15,000	15,000		60,000
Year ended 31 Dec 2023					
1 Jan 2023 – 31 Mar 2023					
3/12 × £72,000	9,000		9,000		18,000
1 Apr 2023 – 31 Dec 2023					
9/12 × £72,000	18,000		18,000	18,000	54,000
	27,000		27,000	18,000	72,000

Trading losses for individuals

Introduction

Just like companies, individuals can also make trading losses. This chapter discusses how a loss is calculated and how it can be relieved. Trading losses will be tested in Task 9 of the assessment, which will be partly manually marked.

ASSESSMENT CRITERIA

Options available to sole traders, partnerships and companies to utilise trading losses:

- opening years
- carry back
- current year
- carry forward
- terminal (6.1)

The best use of a trading loss for sole traders, partnerships and limited companies (6.1)

Calculate available loss relief using:

- carry back
- current year
- carry forward (6.1)

CONTENTS

1. Identification of a trading loss
2. Ongoing businesses
3. Opening years
4. Terminal loss relief
5. Partnership losses
6. Choice of loss relief

1   Identification of a trading loss

A trading loss is calculated in exactly the same way as a trading profit.

In other words, the accounting profit (or loss) is adjusted for tax purposes, and capital allowances are taken into account.

The adjusted loss is then identified with the tax year in which it arose.

In Task 9 of the assessment you will either be provided with figures for tax years, or the trader will have an accounting period ending on 31 March or 5 April which aligns with the tax year. This is illustrated in the examples that follow.

 Example

A trader has a net accounting profit of £9,000 for the year ended 31 March 2024 which includes £3,000 of disallowable expenses. Capital allowances of £14,000 are available.

Calculate the taxable trade profits assessed in 2023/24 and the trading loss available for relief.

Solution

Year ended 31 March 2024	£
Net profit	9,000
Add: Disallowable expenses	3,000
	12,000
Less: Capital allowances	(14,000)
Adjusted loss	(2,000)

In this situation when a loss has arisen, the 2023/24 trading profits assessment is determined as £Nil and there is a (£2,000) trading loss available for relief.

Example

A trader has a net accounting loss of £9,000 for the year ended 31 March 2024 which includes £3,000 of disallowable expenses. Capital allowances of £14,000 are available.

Calculate the taxable trade profits assessed in 2023/24 and the trading loss available for relief.

Solution

	£
Accounting loss	(9,000)
Add: Disallowable expenses	3,000
	———
	(6,000)
Less: Capital allowances	(14,000)
	———
Adjusted loss	(20,000)
	———

The assessment for 2023/24 is £Nil.

The trading loss available is £20,000.

It is easy to identify the wrong amount of loss available by not paying sufficient attention to the arithmetic.

Capital allowances, which normally reduce a profit, will increase a loss.

2 Ongoing businesses

2.1 Options available

There are two main ways of relieving a trading loss in an ongoing business:

- relief against total income of the current and/or the preceding tax year

- relief against future trading profits only.

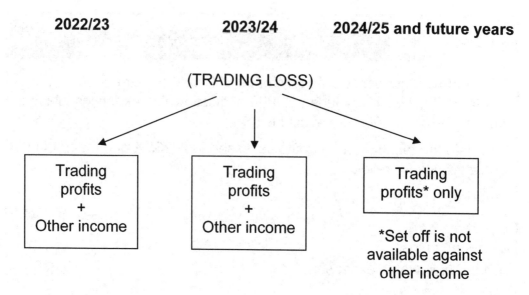

	2022/23	2023/24	2024/25 and future years

(TRADING LOSS)

Trading profits + Other income	Trading profits + Other income	Trading profits* only

*Set off is not available against other income

2.2 Set off of trading loss against total income

This relief allows the trading loss to be set **against total income** of:

(i)   the **tax year of the loss**, and/or

(ii) the **preceding tax year**.

A claim can be made to obtain relief in either year in isolation, or in both years, in either order.

For a 2023/24 loss the claim must be made by 31 January 2026.

If the individual wants relief as early as possible then the losses should be carried back against the previous tax year. This will generate a repayment of tax which will benefit cash flow.

When applying the loss relief it cannot be restricted to preserve the personal allowance. The personal allowance is deducted from income after loss relief has been deducted.

The personal allowance for 2023/24 is £12,570. This means that if a trader has total income of £12,570 or less, it is not worth claiming loss relief against total income for that year as the income will be covered by the personal allowance.

Any excess loss over and above total income is available for relief by carrying forward.

Reference material

Some information about current year and carry back options can be found in the 'Trading losses' section of the reference material provided in the real assessment, so you do not need to learn it.

Why not look up the correct part of the reference material in the introduction to this text book now?

 Example

Beryl has a trading loss in her accounting year ended 31 March 2024 of £18,000.

Her other income is as follows:

	2022/23 £	2023/24 £
Taxable trade profits	14,000	Nil
Other income	2,000	6,000

State the alternative claims Beryl could make to obtain loss relief against her total income.

Solution

The loss for the year ended 31 March 2024 is identified with the tax year 2023/24.

As a result the taxable trade profits for 2023/24 are £Nil.

The loss could be offset against her total income in that year (2023/24) and/or the previous tax year (2022/23) as follows:

- set off £6,000 in 2023/24 and relieve the balance of £12,000 in 2022/23, or

- set off £6,000 in 2023/24 and make no claim for 2022/23, or

- set off £16,000 in 2022/23 and relieve the balance of £2,000 in 2023/24, or

- set off £16,000 in 2022/23 and make no claim for 2023/24.

It is important to identify all of the available options before deciding the course of action you will take.

2.3 Future relief for trading losses

The individual taxpayer does not *have* to claim relief for the loss against total income as described in section 2.2. If no such claim is made, all of the loss will be carried forward for relief in the future.

Alternatively, a claim may have been made for loss relief against total income, but as it can only be used in the same tax year as the loss and/or the previous year, there may be an amount of trading loss still unrelieved after this relief. This remaining amount will be available to carry forward.

Whatever the reason, any trading loss **not** relieved in the same or previous tax year is automatically carried forward.

The trading loss carried forward must be relieved against the **first available** taxable **trading profits** from the **same trade**.

The set off cannot be restricted. If there are sufficient losses, future taxable trade profits will be reduced to £Nil.

Trading losses carried forward cannot be set against other sources of income.

 Reference material

Some information about carry forward relief can be found in the 'Trading losses' section of the reference material provided in the real assessment, so you do not need to learn it.

Why not look up the correct part of the reference material in the introduction to this text book now?

 Test your understanding 1

Sole trader losses

Which one of the following statements is correct with regard to a sole trader's losses?

A   A loss can only be relieved against trading profits made in the same tax year

B   A loss can be relieved in the preceding tax year, but only after a claim for relief has been made in the current tax year

C   A carried forward loss must be relieved against profits from the same trade in future years

D   A loss can be relieved against total income arising in future years

Test your understanding 2

Belinda has been trading for many years and incurred a tax adjusted trading loss for the period ended 5 April 2024.

Which one of the following statements is correct with regard to the use of the trading loss?

A   The trading loss may be carried forward and set against trading income for 2023/24 arising from the same trade

B   The trading loss can be set against total income for 2023/24, but only after the loss is set against total income for 2022/23

C   The trading loss can be set against total income for 2022/23, irrespective of whether the loss has been set against total income for 2023/24

D   The trading loss can be set against total income for 2022/23, but only after the loss is set against total income for 2023/24

 Example

Dong has been trading for some time preparing accounts to 31 March.

His recent adjusted trading results are as follows:

		£
Year ended 31 March 2021	Profit	18,000
Year ended 31 March 2022	Loss	43,200
Year ended 31 March 2023	Profit	13,000
Year ended 31 March 2024	Profit	15,000

Dong's other income in each year is £12,000.

Show Dong's net income after loss relief for all tax years affected by the above results assuming:

(a)   no claim is made against total income for the trading loss

(b)   full claims are made to obtain relief against total income as early as possible.

Solution

(a)   If no claim is made against total income

The trading loss of 2021/22 is carried forward against future trading profits.

	2020/21 £	2021/22 £	2022/23 £	2023/24 £
Taxable trade profits	18,000	Nil	13,000	15,000
Less: Loss relief b/f			(13,000)	(15,000)
	18,000	Nil	Nil	Nil
Other income	12,000	12,000	12,000	12,000
Net income after reliefs	30,000	12,000	12,000	12,000

Loss memorandum

	£
Year ended 31 March 2022 – Loss	43,200
Less: Utilised – 2022/23	(13,000)
– 2023/24	(15,000)
Loss left to carry forward to 2024/25	15,200

(b)   Full claims made against total income

Claims against total income can only be made for 2021/22 and/or 2020/21, and any balance is carried forward for relief against future trading profits.

	2020/21 £	2021/22 £	2022/23 £	2023/24 £
Taxable trade profits	18,000	Nil	13,000	15,000
Less: Loss relief b/f			(1,200)	–
			11,800	15,000
Other income	12,000	12,000	12,000	12,000
	30,000	12,000	23,800	27,000
Less: Loss relief				
– current year		(12,000)		
– preceding year	(30,000)			
Net income after reliefs	Nil	Nil	23,800	27,000

Loss memorandum

		£
Year ended 31 March 2022 – Loss		43,200
Less: Relief against total income – 2020/21		(30,000)
– 2021/22		(12,000)
		─────
		1,200
Less: Utilised in 2022/23		(1,200)
		─────
Loss left to carry forward		Nil
		─────

 Test your understanding 3

Caroline has been in business as a gourmet caterer since 1 October 2020.

She prepares accounts for tax years and her adjusted trading results were as follows:

	£
Six months ended 31 March 2021	4,900
Year ended 31 March 2022	10,500
Year ended 31 March 2023	(45,000)
Year ended 31 March 2024	350

Caroline also receives a salary of £12,000 per annum from part-time secretarial work.

She has also received interest as follows:

2021/22 £220
2022/23 £8,715
2023/24 £8,700

Required:

Calculate Caroline's net income after reliefs (but before the personal allowance) for the years 2021/22 to 2023/24 inclusive, assuming reliefs for losses are claimed as early as possible.

3 Opening years

3.1 Options in opening years

The options available in the opening years of trade are exactly the same as those available to an ongoing business except that an extra option of special opening years loss relief is available.

3.2 Special opening year loss relief

A special loss relief is available for a loss arising in any of the **first four tax years** of trade.

The loss can be carried back for **three tax years** on a **first in, first out (FIFO) basis**, against **total income**.

For example, a loss made in 2023/24 would be offset against total income in the following tax years:

1   2020/21

2   2021/22

3   2022/23

One claim applies to all three years and may generate a refund of income tax.

The relief is all or nothing: it cannot be restricted to preserve the personal allowance.

For a 2023/24 loss, a claim for special opening years relief must be made by 31 January 2026.

If a trading loss arises in the opening years, the trader has to decide whether to claim normal relief against total income, special opening year loss relief or carry forward the loss.

Reference material

Some information about special opening years relief can be found in the 'Trading losses' section of the reference material provided in the real assessment, so you do not need to learn it.

Why not look up the correct part of the reference material in the introduction to this text book now?

4 Terminal loss relief

4.1 Options in closing years

The options available in the closing years of trade are exactly the same as those available to an ongoing business, except that:

- the option to carry forward losses is not available as there will be no further trading profits once the trade ceases

- an extra option of terminal loss relief is available.

4.2 Terminal loss relief

A loss made in the **final 12 months** to the cessation of trade is described as a 'terminal loss'.

A terminal loss relief claim can be made to set the terminal loss against **trading profit** of the **previous three tax years** on a **last in, first out (LIFO)** basis.

For example, if trade ceased in 2023/24 the terminal loss would be offset against trading profits in the following tax years:

1   2022/23

2   2021/22

3   2020/21

One claim applies to all three years and may generate a refund of income tax.

The relief is all or nothing: it cannot be restricted to preserve the personal allowance.

A claim for terminal loss relief must be made within four years from the end of the final tax year of trade; so if trade ceased in 2023/24, a claim for terminal loss relief must be made by 5 April 2028.

If a trading loss arises in the closing years, the trader has to decide whether to claim relief against total income or claim terminal loss relief against trading profits.

Reference material

Some information about terminal loss relief can be found in the 'Trading losses' section of the reference material provided in the real assessment, so you do not need to learn it.

Why not look up the correct part of the reference material in the introduction to this text book now?

5 Partnership losses

5.1 Reliefs available to partners

Partners are allocated losses in the same way as profits. Each partner is then entitled to decide independently on how to use the share of the loss they have been allocated.

An ongoing partner could use the loss against total income in the current and/or preceding tax year or carry the loss forward against trading profits. A new partner could make an opening year loss relief claim, and a partner ceasing to trade could make a terminal loss relief claim.

 Test your understanding 4

Read the following statements and state whether they are **true** or **false**.

1   A sole trader can restrict the amount of loss relief claimed against total income in the current year so that the personal allowance is not lost.

2   Kate has been trading for many years. A trading loss for the year to 31 March 2024 can be relieved by set off against total income of 2022/23 and/or 2023/24 (in any order). Any balance unrelieved will be carried forward and set against future trading profits of the same trade.

3   If a partnership makes a loss, all partners must claim loss relief in the same way.

Test your understanding 5

Diane, Lynne and John are in partnership preparing their accounts to 5 April. During the tax year 2023/24, John left the partnership and Helen joined in his place.

For the year ended 5 April 2024, the partnership made a tax adjusted trading loss of £40,000.

State the loss relief claims that are available to the partners.

6 Choice of loss relief

6.1 Utilising loss relief

When planning relief for trading losses, careful consideration needs to be given to the personal circumstances of the individual.

Tax advice should aim to satisfy the following goals of a taxpayer:

- Obtain tax relief in the tax year in which income is taxed at the highest rate.
- Obtain relief as soon as possible.
- Ensure the taxpayer's personal allowance is not wasted, if possible.

It may not be possible to satisfy all of these aims, for example:

- In order to get a higher rate of relief, the taxpayer's personal allowance may have to be wasted.
- Carrying losses forward may give a higher rate of relief, but the cash flow implications of claiming relief now rather than waiting for relief, may be more important to the taxpayer.

The specific circumstances faced by the taxpayer will help to determine which of these is most important.

 Reference material

Some information about the personal allowance and rates of income tax can be found in the 'Income tax' section of the reference material provided in the real assessment, so you do not need to learn it.

Why not look up the correct part of the reference material in the introduction to this text book now?

6.2 Factors to consider

In understanding the position of the taxpayer, it is important to understand the comparative features of the various reliefs.

Income relieved	Timing of relief	Flexibility
Total income – normal claim	Current and/or previous tax year	Either, neither or both tax years (in either order). All or nothing.
Total income – special opening years claim	Preceding three tax years on a FIFO basis	Only in opening years. All or nothing. Can be used with a normal claim against total income.
Future trading profit	As soon as possible in future	None.
Trading profit – terminal loss claim	Current and then preceding three tax years on a LIFO basis	Only on cessation. All or nothing. Can be used with a normal claim against total income.

Test your understanding 6

Bourbon has been trading as a self-employed biscuit maker for many years. His taxable trade profits or losses are given below.

		£
Year to 5 April 2023	Profit	12,200
Year to 5 April 2024	Loss	(24,050)
Year to 5 April 2025	Profit	12,750

Details of Bourbon's other income is as follows:

	2022/23 £	2023/24 £	2024/25 £
Building society interest received	7,250	17,170	5,250

Required:

(a) Set out the options to an established business continuing to trade for relief of the loss.

(b) Advise Bourbon, with calculations, as to the best method of obtaining loss relief.

7 Summary

The loss reliefs available to individuals are summarised below.

For an ongoing business:

* Relief against total income – current and/or preceding tax year.

* Carry forward against future profits of the same trade.

Special opening year loss relief can be claimed for losses made in the first four tax years of trade:

* Relief against total income of the previous three tax years on a FIFO basis

Terminal loss relief is available for losses made in the final 12 months of trade:

* Relief against trading profits of the previous three tax years on a LIFO basis

Test your understanding answers

 ### Test your understanding 1

Sole trader losses

The correct answer is C.

Explanation

Once a loss has been carried forward it must be set against future profits of the same trade. It cannot be set against total income in the future.

The taxpayer can choose whether to offset a trading loss against total income in the current tax year and/or the preceding year. It is not necessary to make these claims in any particular order.

 ### Test your understanding 2

Belinda

The correct answer is C.

Explanation

The trading loss can be carried forward and set against future trading profits, but the loss is incurred in 2023/24 and will therefore be available to carry forward to 2024/25, not 2023/24.

The trading loss can be set against total income of 2023/24 and/or 2022/23. There is no need for the claim for 2022/23 to be made before that of 2023/24 or vice versa.

Test your understanding 3

Caroline

Income tax computations

	2021/22 £	2022/23 £	2023/24 £
Taxable trade profits	10,500	Nil	350
Less: Loss relief b/f	–	–	(350)[3]
	10,500	Nil	Nil
Employment income	12,000	12,000	12,000
Interest	220	8,715	8,700
Total income	22,720	20,715	20,700
Less: Loss relief			
– preceding year	(22,720)[1]		
– current year		(20,715)[2]	
Net income after reliefs	Nil	Nil	20,700

Notes:

1   Relief against total income can be in any order.

2   The question says offset the loss as early as possible, therefore the claim is made against 2021/22 first, then 2022/23.

3   The remaining loss is then carried forward to 2023/24 and set against the first available trading profits.

Loss memorandum

		£
Loss in 2022/23 – year ended 31 March 2023		45,000
Less: Claim 2021/22 (preceding year)	(1)	(22,720)
		22,280
Less: Claim 2022/23 (year of loss)	(2)	(20,715)
		1,565
Less: Carry forward claim 2023/24	(3)	(350)
Loss carried forward		1,215

Test your understanding 4

1   False   Loss relief claims cannot be restricted to preserve the personal allowance.

2   True

3   False   Each partner can choose independently what loss relief to claim.

Test your understanding 5

Diane, Lynne and John

All the partners are entitled to relief against total income in the current and/or previous tax year.

All the partners except John are entitled to carry forward loss relief.

John is entitled to terminal loss relief since he has ceased trading.

Helen is entitled to claim special opening years relief since she has recently started trading.

Diane and Lynne are not entitled to terminal loss relief or special opening year loss relief.

Test your understanding 6

Bourbon

(a)   Alternative means of loss relief

(i)   Carry forward for set off against the next available taxable trading income from the same trade until the loss is fully relieved.

(ii)   Claim against the total income of:

–   the tax year of loss; and/or

–   the preceding tax year.

(b) Advice on relief

From the following computations it can be determined that the best method of obtaining relief is for Bourbon to claim relief against total income for 2022/23 to obtain relief as early as possible.

A claim against total income should also be made in 2023/24 for the balance of the loss, as there will still be enough income remaining after the loss claim to use up the personal allowance of £12,570.

	2022/23 £	2023/24 £	2024/25 £
Trading profits	12,200	Nil	12,750
Less: Loss relief b/f	–	–	–
	12,200	Nil	12,750
Interest	7,250	17,170	5,250
	19,450	17,170	18,000
Less: Loss relief			
– Current year		(4,600)	
– Carry back	(19,450)		
Net income after reliefs	Nil	12,570	18,000

Payment and administration – individuals

11

Introduction

This chapter covers tax returns and amendments, the payment of tax and compliance checks for individuals. Payment and administration will be tested in Task 7 of the assessment.

At the end of each section you will find a summary showing which information from that section is provided in the AAT reference material, and which information is not provided and therefore needs to be learnt.

ASSESSMENT CRITERIA

Tax return filing deadlines for sole traders, partnerships and companies (4.1)

Tax payment dates for sole traders, partners and companies (4.1)

Time limits for notifying chargeability to tax (4.1)

The enquiry window (4.1)

The time period within which amendments to a tax return can be made (4.1)

What records need to be maintained and for what time period (4.1)

Penalties for:

–   late filing

–   late payment

–   failing to notify chargeability

–   errors in tax returns

–   not providing records in an enquiry

–   not retaining records.

Calculate penalties and interest for non-compliance (4.2)

CONTENTS

1   Introduction to the self-assessment return

2   Payment of income tax and capital gains tax

3   Interest and penalties on payments of tax

4   HM Revenue and Customs' compliance checks

5   Penalties for incorrect returns

1 Introduction to the self-assessment return

1.1 The self-assessment return

Certain individuals are required to complete a return for every tax year.

Amongst other things the return covers trading income and capital gains and, in some cases, a calculation of the tax payable.

The key details to grasp concerning the return are the filing dates.

The taxpayer has the choice of filing a paper return or filing electronically online. The date by which a return must be filed depends on the method used.

All completed and signed paper returns must be filed by:

- 31 October following the end of the tax year.

All online electronic returns must be filed by:

- 31 January following the end of the tax year.

The relevant dates for a 2023/24 return are therefore 31 October 2024 for a paper return and 31 January 2025 for an electronic return.

Where a taxpayer submits a paper return HMRC will calculate the tax due. If a taxpayer chooses to file online then the tax will be calculated automatically.

HMRC normally issue an individual with a notice to complete a tax return in April/May following the end of the tax year.

However, where HMRC issue a notice to complete a tax return late, the taxpayer has until the later of the filing dates mentioned above and 3 months after the notice is issued in which to file their return.

An individual who receives a notice to file a 2023/24 tax return from HMRC on 15 August 2024 therefore has until 15 November 2024 to file a paper return or until 31 January 2025 to file the return electronically.

31 January following the end of the tax year is known as the 'filing date', regardless of whether the return is filed on paper or electronically. This must be distinguished from the date on which the return is filed/submitted to HMRC (known as the 'actual' filing date).

The return consists of an eight page summary form with six supplementary pages for self-employed individuals.

Where a notice to file a tax return is not issued, an individual is required to notify HMRC by **5 October** following the tax year where there is chargeable income (i.e. new sources of income) or gains arising.

Notification is not required where there are no taxable gains or where the income is either covered by allowances or the full tax liability has been deducted at source.

Failure to notify may result in a penalty. The penalty is calculated in broadly the same way as penalties for incorrect returns (see section 5) and is a maximum of 100% of the tax outstanding.

The taxpayer is permitted to correct or 'repair' their self-assessment return within 12 months of the filing date (i.e. by 31 January 2026 for a 2023/24 return). HMRC can correct 'obvious errors' and anything else which they believe to be incorrect by reference to the information they hold in the period of nine months from actual filing.

Where an assessment is excessive due to an error or mistake in a return, the taxpayer can claim overpayment relief. The claim must be made within four years of the end of the tax year concerned.

 Reference material

Some information about dates, time limits and penalties can be found in the 'Payment and administration' section of the reference material provided in the real assessment, so you do not need to learn it.

Why not look up the correct part of the reference material in the introduction to this text book now?

1.2 Records

An individual must retain certain records to support the completed tax return, to assist with providing evidence to support information given to HMRC.

Self-employed people (i.e. sole traders and partners in a partnership) must keep records for five years after the filing date (i.e. until 31 January 2030 for 2023/24 information).

Examples of records to be kept include the following:

- accounts
- supporting documentation such as receipts and invoices
- dividend vouchers.

Failure to keep records can lead to a penalty of up to £3,000 per tax year.

1.3 Penalties for late filing

Failure to submit a return by 31 January following a tax year will result in a penalty.

The system operates as follows:

Immediate penalty	£100
Delay of more than three months	an additional £10 per day (maximum 90 days = £900)
Delay of more than six months	an additional 5% of tax due
Delay of more than 12 months where:	the penalties above, plus:
No deliberate withholding of information	5% of tax due
Deliberate withholding of information	70% of tax due
Deliberate withholding of information with concealment	100% of tax due

The penalties based on the tax due are each subject to a minimum of £300.

A penalty will not be charged if the taxpayer has a reasonable excuse for the late filing, for example a serious illness. A lack of knowledge of the tax system is not a reasonable excuse.

 Test your understanding 1

Bob understands that he has responsibilities under the self-assessment system and is required to meet a number of deadlines. In particular, he needs confirmation of the deadlines for the following actions.

1   Notifying HMRC that he started receiving rent for the first time on 1 January 2024.

2   Filing a paper return for 2023/24.

3   Filing his 2023/24 return electronically.

4   Amending his 2023/24 tax return.

Match each of Bob's responsibilities with the correct deadline:

A   5 October 2024

B   31 January 2025

C   31 October 2024

D   31 January 2026

1.4   Summary of reference material

Item	Included in reference material	Not included in reference material
Paper and online filing deadlines	✓	
Extension to deadline where notice to file given late		✓
Deadline to notify chargeability	✓	
Penalties for failure to notify chargeability		✓
Deadline for taxpayer to amend return	✓	
Deadline for HMRC to amend return		✓
Deadline to claim overpayment relief		✓
Deadline for keeping records	✓	
Examples of records to keep		✓
Penalty for failure to keep appropriate records for required period	✓	
Penalties for late filing	✓	

2 Payment of income tax and capital gains tax

2.1 The instalment system

As well as submitting a tax return certain individuals will also need to make payments of tax.

Self-employed individuals are required to pay their tax liability in instalments.

The instalment system operates as follows:

• 31 January in the tax year:	first payment on account (POA).
• 31 July *following* the tax year:	second payment on account (POA).
• 31 January *following* the tax year:	final payment.

For example, for 2023/24 the following dates are relevant:

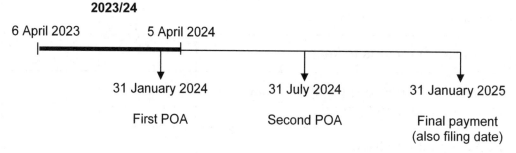

The payments on account are estimated, in that they are based on the previous year's income tax and class 4 national insurance contributions (NICs) payable. Note that the tax payable figure used in the payments on account calculation is net of any tax deducted under PAYE.

The taxpayer can claim to make reduced payments on account where this year's income tax payable is expected to be less than that of last year. The taxpayer will be charged a penalty if the claim to make reduced payments on account was made either fraudulently or negligently.

In the assessment a detailed understanding of the payments on account system is expected, including when payments are due and how to pay them.

Example

Roderic is self-employed. His only source of income is from his trade. The income tax payable for 2022/23 was £5,100.

His income tax payable for 2023/24 based on his taxable trade profits for the year ended 31 March 2024 is £7,032.

Ignoring NICs, state Roderic's payments in respect of his 2023/24 income tax liability.

Solution

Step 1: Determine the relevant dates

31 January 2024	–	first payment on account
31 July 2024	–	second payment on account
31 January 2025	–	final payment

Step 2: Determine the amounts due

- The amounts due for the 'payments on account' are based on an equal division of the previous year's tax payable, hence £2,550 (£5,100 ÷ 2).

- The final payment will be based on the final liability for 2023/24 less the payments on account already made.

	£
2023/24 IT liability	7,032
Payments on account (2 × £2,550)	(5,100)
	———
Final payment	1,932
	———

Step 3: Prepare a final summary

	£
31 January 2024	2,550
31 July 2024	2,550
31 January 2025	1,932

The amount due on 31 January following the end of the tax year consists of the final payment for the year just ended and the first payment on account for the new tax year.

In Roderic's case this means that on 31 January 2025 he will start the instalment option all over again, by making the first payment on account of his 2024/25 liability based on 2023/24 tax payable.

Hence his 31 January 2025 payment is £5,448 ((£7,032 × 1/2) + £1,932).

The class 4 national insurance contributions payable by a self-employed person are also paid by the instalment system (see Chapter 12).

 Test your understanding 2

Kazuo is required to pay tax in instalments.

For 2022/23, his income tax liability was £18,700, of which £2,000 was collected via PAYE. He estimates that his income tax payable for 2023/24 will be £22,000.

What is the amount of the first payment on account that Kazuo should make on 31 January 2024 in respect of his income tax liability for 2023/24?

Ignore national insurance.

A   £8,350

B   £9,350

C   £10,000

D   £11,000

2.2   No requirement for payments on account

Payments on account are not required in the following circumstances:

- The income tax and class 4 NICs payable for the previous tax year by self-assessment is less than £1,000, or

- More than 80% of the income tax liability for the previous tax year was met through tax deducted at source.

2.3   Class 2 NICs

Class 2 NICs (see Chapter 12) are payable on 31 January following the end of the tax year, together with the final payment of income tax. They are not subject to payments on account.

2.4 Capital gains tax

The capital gains tax due for a tax year (see Chapter 15) is payable on 31 January following the end of the tax year, together with the final payment of income tax.

CGT is therefore paid in one instalment on 31 January following the tax year regardless of whether there was a CGT liability for the previous year.

The CGT liability is not taken into account when determining the payments on account for income tax.

Payments on account of capital gains tax are never required.

 Test your understanding 3

State the appropriate dates in respect of the following payments.

1　First instalment for tax year – 2023/24

2　Second instalment for tax year – 2023/24

3　Final instalment for tax year – 2023/24

4　Payment date for capital gains tax for tax year – 2023/24

 Test your understanding 4

(a)　State the latest date by which the 2023/24 tax return should be submitted if the taxpayer:

　　(i)　wishes to file the return online, or

　　(ii)　wishes to file a paper return.

(b)　State:

　　(i)　the normal dates of payment of income tax and class 4 NICs for a sole trader in respect of the tax year 2023/24, and

　　(ii)　how the amounts of these payments are calculated.

(c)　State:

　　(i)　the penalties that can be charged where a tax return is submitted within six months after the due date, and

　　(ii)　the penalties that can be charged where a tax return is submitted more than six months late.

2.5 Recovery of overpaid tax

Taxpayers who believe that they have paid too much income tax or capital gains tax can submit a claim in order to have the excess tax repaid. The claim must be submitted within four years of the end of the relevant tax year.

2.6 Summary of reference material

Item	Included in reference material	Not included in reference material
Due dates for payments on account and balancing payment	✓	
Instances where payments on account are not required	✓	
Class 2 NIC due date	✓	
Capital gains tax due date	✓	
Recovery of overpaid tax		✓

3 Interest and penalties on payments of tax

3.1 Interest

Taxpayers that fail to make payments, whether payments on account (POA) or final payments, by the due date will be charged interest.

Interest is not perceived as being a penalty but merely as commercial compensation for late payment. It is not a deductible expense when computing taxable income.

Interest is charged from the day the tax is due until the day it is paid.

In addition to the interest charge there is also a penalty where tax is paid late.

An individual who receives a tax repayment may receive interest in respect of the amount repaid. This interest income is not taxable.

The tax treatment of interest on underpayments/overpayments of corporation tax paid by or to companies is different from that for individuals and is covered in Chapter 7.

Example

Rodney was due to make the following payments of tax for 2023/24.

		Actual date of payment
31 January 2024	£2,100	29 February 2024
31 July 2024	£2,100	31 August 2024
31 January 2025	£1,000	31 March 2025

For what periods will interest be charged?

Solution

On first POA	31 January 2024 – 29 February 2024	1 month
On second POA	31 July 2024 – 31 August 2024	1 month
On final payment	31 January 2025 – 31 March 2025	2 months

3.2 Penalty for late payment of tax

A penalty will be charged where there is income tax or capital gains tax outstanding after the day on which the final payment of tax is due (31 January after the end of the tax year). This penalty is in addition to any interest that is charged.

- More than 30 days late   5% of tax overdue
- More than 6 months late   further 5% of tax overdue
- More than 12 months late   further 5% of tax overdue

A late payment penalty may be mitigated (i.e. reduced) where the taxpayer can provide a reasonable excuse, for example a serious illness.

Insufficiency of funds or lack of knowledge of self-assessment are not reasonable excuses.

No penalties are due in respect of late payments on account.

Example

Star made the final payment in respect of their 2022/23 self-assessment return on 31 August 2024.

What penalties will be charged in respect of the late payment of the tax?

Solution

The final payment in respect of the 2022/23 self-assessment return was due on 31 January 2024. The payment is more than 6 months but less than 12 months late.

Because the payment is more than 6 months late there will be a total penalty of 10% of the tax outstanding, i.e. 5% for being 30 days late and an additional 5% for being 6 months late.

(Note that Star will also be charged interest on the late paid tax from 31 January 2024 to 31 August 2024. However, the question only asked for the penalties.)

 Test your understanding 5

Read the following statements and state whether they are true or false.

1   An individual must retain tax records for 2023/24 until 5 April 2029.

2   If an individual is two months late in submitting their tax return for 2023/24, they will receive a penalty of £100.

3   Penalties for errors made by individuals in their tax returns vary from 30% to 100%.

4   Late payment penalties can be imposed on balancing payments made late.

3.3 Summary of reference material

Item	Included in reference material	Not included in reference material
Interest on tax paid late/overpaid tax	✓	
Dates between which interest will be charged		✓
Penalties on late paid tax	✓	
Details of which payments penalties are charged on		✓
Mitigation of penalties where there is a reasonable excuse		✓

4 HM Revenue and Customs' compliance checks

4.1 Introduction

HMRC have the right to enquire into an individual's tax return (similar to the system on corporation tax returns) under their compliance check powers. This may be a random check or because they have reason to believe that income or expenses have been misstated in the tax return.

Normally, HMRC must make their compliance check (enquiry) within 12 months of the date the return was filed.

4.2 Compliance check (enquiry) procedure

Once the compliance check notice is given, an Officer can request relevant documents and written particulars. If the individual fails to produce enquiry documents, a penalty of £300, plus up to £60 a day, may be imposed.

At the end of the compliance check a closure notice is issued stating the outcome of the enquiry, for example, no amendment made or business profits increased by a particular amount.

In more complex cases, if the compliance check covers several different aspects, then a partial closure notice (PCN) may be issued to bring one particular part of the compliance check to an end ahead of the final closure notice.

The taxpayer has 30 days from completion to ask for their case to be reviewed.

4.3 Discovery assessments

Although HMRC usually only have 12 months from the date a return is filed to open a compliance check (enquiry), they can replace a self-assessment at a later date by making a discovery assessment.

A discovery assessment can be made where tax has been lost perhaps because of insufficient information in the tax return.

The taxpayer can appeal to the Tax Tribunal against a discovery assessment.

4.4 Appeals procedure

The taxpayer can request an informal review of a disputed decision.

Alternatively, a formal appeal may be made to the Tax Tribunal.

Appeals from the Tax Tribunal on a point of law (but not on a point of fact) may be made to the Court of Appeal and from there to the Supreme Court.

The Tax Tribunal is independent of HMRC.

4.5 Summary of reference material

Item	Included in reference material	Not included in reference material
Reasons why HMRC may open an enquiry		✓
Deadline for HMRC to open an enquiry	✓	
Penalty for failure to produce enquiry documents	✓	
Details of closure notice/partial closure notice		✓
Discovery assessments		✓
Appeals		✓

5 Penalties for incorrect returns

5.1 Penalties for incorrect returns

The common penalty regime described in Chapter 7 applies to income tax returns as well as corporation tax returns.

The penalties are the same for individuals in that a penalty will be charged where an inaccurate return is submitted to HMRC or where the individual fails to notify HMRC where an under assessment of tax is made by them.

 Example

State the maximum and minimum penalties that may be levied on each of the following individuals who have submitted incorrect tax returns.

Lars   Deliberately understated his tax liability and attempted to conceal the incorrect information that he had provided. HMRC have identified the understatement and Lars is helping them with their enquiries.

Sven   Accidentally provided an incorrect figure even though he checked his tax return carefully. He realised his mistake a few days later and notified HMRC.

Jo   Completed his tax return too quickly and made a number of errors. The day after he had submitted the tax return he decided to check it thoroughly and immediately provided HMRC with the information necessary to identify the errors.

Solution

Penalties for incorrect tax returns are a percentage of the under declared tax.

Lars   The maximum percentage for a deliberate understatement with concealment is 100%. The minimum percentage for prompted disclosure of information (where the taxpayer provides information in response to HMRC identifying the error) in respect of deliberate understatement with concealment is 50%.

Sven   No penalty is charged where a taxpayer has been careful and has made a genuine mistake.

Jo   The maximum percentage for failing to take reasonable care is 30%. The minimum percentage for unprompted disclosure is nil.

Test your understanding 6

1   James started his own business in February 2024.

    If he does not receive a notice to complete a tax return for 2023/24, by what date should he notify HMRC that he is chargeable to tax for 2023/24?

2   Isabel made her second payment on account of tax for 2023/24 on 15 September 2024.

    What are the consequences?

3   Mike filed his 2023/24 tax return on 18 January 2025.

    What is the latest date for HMRC to open a compliance check (enquiry)?

 Test your understanding 7

Clark is a new client who has come to you for information about the self-assessment system.

Explain to Clark:

(a)   The latest date by which income tax returns for the year 2023/24 should be submitted to HM Revenue and Customs (HMRC).

(b)   The date by which Clark should notify HMRC that they have received income in the year 2023/24 which is liable to income tax where no notice to complete an income tax return has been issued.

(c)   The potential penalties for the late submission of income tax returns and when they apply.

(d)   The penalty for the submission of an incorrect income tax return.

(e)   The penalty for failing to maintain or retain adequate records to back up an income tax return.

5.2   Summary of reference material

Item	Included in reference material	Not included in reference material
Penalties for incorrect returns	✓	

6 Summary

This chapter covers a core topic – self-assessment.

Traders have to self-assess their tax liability and pay any tax due because they receive trading income gross, i.e. without deduction of tax at source.

Payment dates

31 January 2024

- Balance of income tax and class 4 NICs payable for 2022/23.

- CGT liability for 2022/23.

- First POA for 2023/24 (based on previous year's liability).

31 July 2024

- Second POA for 2023/24.

31 January 2025

- Balance of income tax and class 4 NICs payable for 2023/24.

- CGT liability for 2023/24.

- First POA for 2024/25 (based on liability for 2023/24).

Filing returns (2023/24 return)

Paper return   –   31 October 2024

Electronic return   –   31 January 2025 (the 'filing date')

Main penalties

Late filing – an immediate £100 penalty with further penalties if the return is more than three, six or 12 months late.

Incorrect returns – same as Corporation tax (see Chapter 7).

Tax unpaid 30 days after 31 January – 5% penalty with further 5% penalties if the tax remains outstanding after six and 12 months.

If no compliance check (enquiry) notice issued by the anniversary of the date the return is filed, the taxpayer can assume it is 'final'.

However, if HMRC are able to show they had insufficient information supplied in the tax return, they can make a 'discovery' assessment.

Test your understanding answers

Test your understanding 1

1   A
2   C
3   B
4   D

Test your understanding 2

Kazuo

The correct answer is A.

Explanation

The payment on account is calculated as follows:

	£
2022/23 income tax liability	18,700
Less: PAYE	(2,000)
Income tax payable under self-assessment	16,700
First payment on account for 2023/24 (£16,700 ÷ 2)	8,350

Test your understanding 3

Payments on account

1   31 January 2024
2   31 July 2024
3   31 January 2025
4   31 January 2025

Test your understanding 4

Self-assessment

(a) (i)   31 January following the tax year to which the return relates (i.e. 31 January 2025 for 2023/24).

(ii) 31 October following the tax year to which the return relates (i.e. 31 October 2024 for 2023/24).

(b) (i)   (1)   31 January in the tax year (i.e. 31 January 2024).

(2)   31 July following the tax year (i.e. 31 July 2024).

(3)   31 January following the tax year (i.e. 31 January 2025).

(ii) Payments (1) and (2) are equal amounts each amounting to half the income tax and class 4 NIC payable in respect of the preceding tax year.

Payment (3) is the balancing figure (i.e. it is the amount of the final income tax and class 4 NIC liability for the year, less any tax deducted at source, less payments (1) and (2)).

(c) (i)   There will be an immediate penalty of £100.

A further penalty of £10 per day for a maximum of 90 days can be charged once the return is more than three months late.

(ii) As well as the penalties listed above, there will be a further penalty of 5% of the tax due (minimum £300) once the return is more than six months late.

Once the return is more than 12 months late there will be a further penalty equal to a percentage of the tax due (minimum £300). The percentage is determined by the reason for the delay.

No deliberate withholding of information	5%
Deliberate withholding	70%
Deliberate withholding with concealment	100%

Test your understanding 5

Period of assessment

1	False	The records must be retained until 31 January 2030.
2	True	
3	False	The penalties start at 0% for a genuine mistake.
4	True	

Test your understanding 6

1   James must notify HMRC by 5 October 2024.

2   Isabel will be charged interest from the due date of 31 July 2024 until 15 September 2024, the day of payment.

3   The latest date for opening a compliance check (enquiry) is 18 January 2026; one year after Mike filed the return.

Test your understanding 7

Clark

(a) The date by which a return must be filed depends on the filing method used.

A paper return must be filed by 31 October 2024 for the tax year 2023/24 (i.e. 31 October following the end of the tax year).

An electronic return must be filed by 31 January 2025 for the tax year 2023/24 (i.e. 31 January following the end of the tax year).

(b) Notification is due by 5 October 2024 if a new income source arises in 2023/24 and a tax notice to complete a tax return has not been issued.

(c) If a tax return is submitted late, a £100 fixed penalty is charged.

If it is still outstanding after 3 months, a further £10 per day can be charged for a maximum of 90 days.

If it is still outstanding after 6 months, a further penalty equal to 5% of the tax due is charged.

If the return is still outstanding after 12 months, a penalty of up to 100% of the tax outstanding is charged.

(d) The penalty for submitting an incorrect tax return is a percentage of the revenue lost.

The percentage ranges from 0% (where the taxpayer has simply made a mistake) to 100% (where the taxpayer has deliberately understated the return and concealed the error).

(e) The penalty for failing to maintain adequate records is up to £3,000.

National insurance contributions

Introduction

A self-employed individual has personal national insurance contributions to pay, but may also have to pay contributions as an employer.

The calculation of national insurance contributions will be tested in Task 3 of the assessment.

ASSESSMENT CRITERIA
What income Class 2 and Class 4 NICs are payable on (1.4)
Calculate NICs:
– Class 2
– Class 4 (1.4)

CONTENTS

1 Contributions as an employer

2 Contributions as a sole trader

3 Effect of partnerships

1 Contributions as an employer

1.1 Class 1 secondary and class 1A contributions

A sole trader or partnership may employ staff.

As an employer, they may be liable to class 1 secondary and class 1A contributions in relation to the remuneration paid to their employees.

The calculation of employer's contributions is outside the syllabus for business tax, but the rates may be used in tax planning discussions as part of Task 8 (see Chapter 16).

2 Contributions as a sole trader

2.1 Class 4 NICs

A self-employed person, whether operating as a sole trader or as a partner, pays two types of national insurance contributions:

- class 2 and
- class 4.

Class 4 NICs are calculated by applying a fixed percentage (currently 9%) to the amount by which the taxpayer's 'profits' (or share of 'profits', where the taxpayer is a member of a partnership) exceed a lower limit (£12,570 for 2023/24).

> ### Example
>
> If Nicholas has 'profits' of £15,775 for 2023/24, he will be liable to pay class 4 NICs calculated as follows:
>
> | | £ |
> | --- | --- |
> | 'Profits' | 15,775 |
> | Less: Lower limit | (12,570) |
> | Excess | 3,205 |
> | Class 4 NICs (9% × £3,205) | 288.45 |

The 9% rate only applies up to an upper limit of profits (£50,270 for 2023/24).

Where a taxpayer's 'profits' exceed the upper limit, the excess profit is liable to class 4 NICs at 2%.

For example, if taxable trading profits are £54,500 for 2023/24 the taxpayer is liable to class 4 NICs of £3,477.60 calculated as follows:

	£
(£50,270 – £12,570) × 9%	3,393.00
(£54,500 – £50,270) × 2%	84.60
	————
	3,477.60
	————

Note that where a taxpayer's 'profits' do not exceed the lower limit (i.e. £12,570 for 2023/24) there is no liability to class 4 NICs.

2.2　Profits

The 'profits' to be used in the calculation of the taxpayer's liability to class 4 NICs are:

	£
Taxable trade profits	X
Less: Trading losses brought forward	(X)
	—
Profits for class 4 NICs	X
	—

2.3　Payments of class 4 NICs

Class 4 NICs are payable under self-assessment at the same time as the related income tax liability (i.e. two payments on account and a balancing payment).

Interest will be charged on late payments.

Class 4 NICs are not payable if the taxpayer is:

- of state pension age or over at the beginning of the tax year

- aged under 16 at the beginning of the tax year.

In 2020 the state pension age was 66 for both men and women, and this is gradually increasing. It would be clear in the assessment that someone had reached state pension age.

2.4   Class 2 NICs

In addition to class 4 NICs, a trader is also liable for class 2 NICs which are payable at a fixed rate of £3.45 per week. The liability relates to the individual trader, such that it does not increase where an individual has more than one trade.

There is no liability if the 'profits' are below the lower profits threshold of £12,570.

'Profits' for class 2 NIC purposes are the same as for class 4 purposes (i.e. tax adjusted trading profits less losses brought forward).

Class 2 NICs are payable under the self-assessment system. They are reported on the tax return and payable on 31 January following the end of the tax year (i.e. 31 January 2025 for 2023/24). There are no payments on account for class 2 NICs.

A taxpayer does not have to pay class 2 NICs in respect of any week in which they are:

* aged under 16, or

* of state pension age or over.

 Reference material

Some information about class 2 and 4 NICs can be found in the 'National insurance (NI)' section of the reference material provided in the real assessment, so you do not need to learn it.

Why not look up the correct part of the reference material in the introduction to this text book now?

 Test your understanding 1

Naomi, aged 45, has been self-employed for many years.

State the national insurance contributions payable by Naomi for 2023/24, assuming her taxable trade profits are:

(a)   £10,600

(b)   £24,600

(c)   £51,300

Test your understanding 2

Wei's tax liability for 2022/23 was as follows:

	£
Income tax liability	9,400
Less: PAYE	(2,100)
Income tax payable	7,300
Class 2 NICs	164
Class 4 NICs	700
CGT	5,000
	13,164

What will each of the payments on account be for 2023/24?

A   £6,582

B   £4,082

C   £4,000

D   £3,650

3 Effect of partnerships

3.1 Each partner is treated as a separate sole trader

Each partner is taxed individually and must pay class 2 and class 4 contributions.

Both class 2 and class 4 contributions are based on the partner's allocated share of profits, as assessed to income tax for the tax year.

Test your understanding 3

1   A taxpayer has self-employed income of £81,750 for the tax year 2023/24. The amount of income which will be chargeable to class 4 NICs at 2% is   £

2   A taxpayer has self-employed income of £30,000. The amount of class 4 NICs payable would be   £

3   Anne has tax adjusted trading profits for 2023/24 of £6,900.

Her accounts show a net profit of £12,900 for the year to 31 March 2024.

- What class 4 NICs are due?   £

- What class 2 NICs are due?   £

4   Which one of the following statements is correct?

A   Self-employed taxpayers pay either class 2 or class 4 NICs, but not both

B   Every self-employed taxpayer must pay class 2 NICs, regardless of the level of their profits

C   Class 4 NICs are based on the amount of income a taxpayer withdraws from the business

D   In a partnership, each partner is responsible for his, her or their own NICs

4 Summary

Sole traders and partners may have to pay the following contributions:

- class 2, and
- class 4.

Test your understanding answers

Test your understanding 1

Naomi

Naomi must pay class 2 NICs of £3.45 per week if her taxable profits exceed £12,570. Her profits do not exceed this amount in (a) and therefore no class 2 NICs are payable. In all other cases her taxable profits exceed the lower profits threshold of £12,570.

She is liable to pay class 4 NICs as follows:

		£
(a)	Profits do not exceed lower limit, no class 4 NIC	Nil
(b)	Class 4 NICs (£24,600 – £12,570) × 9%	1,082.70
(c)	Class 4 NICs (£50,270 – £12,570) × 9% + (£51,300 – £50,270) × 2%	3,413.60

Test your understanding 2

Wei

The correct answer is C.

Explanation

The relevant amount for income tax is   £7,300
The relevant amount for class 4 NIC is   £700

Payments on account will be due for 2023/24 as follows:

	£
31 January 2024 ((£7,300 + £700) = £8,000 × 1/2)	4,000
31 July 2024	4,000

No payments on account of class 2 NICs or capital gains tax are required.

Test your understanding 3

1 £31,480   (£81,750 − £50,270)

2 £1,568.70   (£30,000 − £12,570) × 9%

3 Anne's NICs for 2023/24 are:

- class 4 – £Nil, taxable profits less than £12,570

- class 2 – £Nil, taxable profits less than £12,570.

4 The correct answer is D.

Explanation

Taxpayers are required to pay class 2 and class 4 NICs if their taxable profits for the tax year exceed £12,570, so they can be liable to both classes 2 and 4.

NICs are based on the taxable trading profits, **not** the net profit in the trader's accounts or the amount of income a taxpayer withdraws from the business.

Chargeable gains for companies

13

Introduction

Both individuals and companies pay tax on chargeable gains.

Individuals pay capital gains tax on their chargeable gains.

Companies include chargeable gains in their taxable total profits and therefore pay corporation tax on them.

This chapter covers the calculation of gains and losses for companies and the relief that exists to defer a gain when a replacement asset is acquired.

Chargeable gains and allowable losses for companies will be tested in Task 4 of the assessment.

ASSESSMENT CRITERIA	CONTENTS
Calculate: – chargeable gains and allowable losses – rollover relief – indexation allowance (3.1)	1 Principle of a chargeable gain 2 Pro forma computation 3 The chargeable gain computation 4 Enhancement expenditure 5 Rollover relief

1 Principle of a chargeable gain

1.1 The three essential elements

In order for a chargeable gain to be calculated there are three essential requirements.

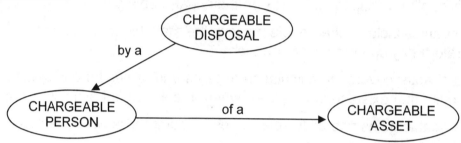

1.2 Chargeable disposal

A chargeable disposal includes:

*   a sale of an asset (whole or part of an asset)

*   a gift of an asset

*   an exchange of an asset

*   the loss or destruction of an asset.

Where a gift is made the sale proceeds are deemed to be the asset's market value.

Where an asset is lost or destroyed the sale proceeds are likely to be £Nil or insurance proceeds.

The following occasions are exempt disposals and so no CGT computation is required:

*   the sale is a trading disposal (badges of trade – Chapter 8)

*   on a gift to a charity.

In the assessment it will be obvious whether the disposal is of:

*   stock/inventory, therefore dealt with as trading income, or

*   a capital item (for example land), therefore calculate a gain.

1.3 Chargeable person

Chargeable gains will be calculated on disposals by:

- Individuals
- Partners in partnership ⎱ — pay capital gains tax (Chapter 15)
- Companies — pay corporation tax on chargeable gains (see Chapter 5 pro forma)

1.4 Chargeable asset

All assets are chargeable unless they are classified specifically as exempt assets. For example, cars are exempt assets.

You will not have to identify exempt assets in your assessment.

2 Pro forma computation

2.1 The pro forma computation (for corporation tax)

Gains and losses are calculated for accounting periods.

Once you have calculated all the individual chargeable gains and allowable capital losses for an accounting period, summarise them as follows:

	£
Chargeable gain (1)	X
Chargeable gain (2)	X
Allowable loss (3)	(X)
	X
Less: Capital losses brought forward	(X)
Net chargeable gains	X

The net chargeable gains are then put into the computation of taxable total profits and the corporation tax liability is calculated in the normal way.

If there is an overall capital loss, net chargeable gains for the accounting period are £Nil. The loss is carried forward and set against future chargeable gains. It cannot be relieved against other income.

Example

Alpha Ltd made three disposals in its year ended 31 March 2024, giving the following results:

Asset	Gain/(loss)
	£
1	20,000
2	5,000
3	(8,000)

Calculate the net chargeable gains shown on the corporation tax computation.

Solution

Included within taxable total profits will be net chargeable gains of £17,000 (£20,000 + £5,000 – £8,000).

If the loss on asset 3 had been £28,000, the corporation tax computation would show net chargeable gains of £Nil.

A net loss of £3,000 (£20,000 + £5,000 – £28,000) would then be carried forward to offset against the next available net chargeable gains.

 Test your understanding 1

Bubbles Ltd disposed of two assets during its accounting period to 31 March 2024, realising a chargeable gain of £13,000 and an allowable loss of £4,000.

It had allowable capital losses brought forward of £2,000.

How much will be included in taxable total profits for the year to 31 March 2024?

The remainder of this chapter considers how to calculate the gains and losses on each chargeable disposal made by a company.

3 The chargeable gain computation

3.1 The standard pro forma

The following pro forma should be used:

	Notes	£
Gross sale proceeds	1	X
Less: Selling costs	2	(X)
Net sale proceeds (NSP)		X
Less: Allowable cost	3	(X)
Unindexed gain	4	X
Less: Indexation allowance (IA) = Cost × 0.XXX	5	(X)
Chargeable gain		X

Notes to the pro forma

1 The sale proceeds are usually given in the question.

   However, where a disposal is not a sale at arm's length (e.g. a gift) then **market value** will be substituted for sale proceeds in the computation.

2 The selling costs incurred on the disposal of an asset are an allowable deduction.

   Examples of such allowable costs include valuation fees, advertising costs, legal fees, auctioneer's fees.

3 The purchase price of an asset is the main allowable cost, but this will also include any incidental purchase expenses, including legal fees, stamp duty, etc.

4 The gain after deducting the costs above is known as an unindexed gain.

5 An indexation allowance (IA) may then be available to reduce that gain.

   The indexation allowance is intended to give relief for inflation and is based upon the movement in the retail prices index (RPI).

3.2   The indexation allowance (IA)

The IA is relief for inflation covering the period since the asset was purchased up to the date of disposal.

The indexation allowance generally runs:

- from the month of the purchase (i.e. when the cost was incurred)
- to the month of disposal.

It is computed by multiplying the acquisition cost by an indexation factor.

The formula for calculating the indexation factor is:

$$\frac{\text{RPI for month of disposal} - \text{RPI for month of acquisition}}{\text{RPI for month of acquisition}}$$

This produces a decimal figure which must be rounded to three decimal places.

In the assessment you will be given the indexation factor or the amount of the indexation allowance.

Companies do not get the benefit of indexation allowance beyond 31 December 2017.

Therefore, if an asset acquired before 1 January 2018 is sold on/after 1 January 2018 then the December 2017 RPI should be used as the RPI at disposal.

If an asset is both acquired and disposed of on/after 1 January 2018 then no indexation allowance will be available.

 Example

Eli Ltd sells a chargeable asset on 31 March 2024 for £24,600 after deducting auctioneer's fees of £400. The asset was acquired on 1 May 2005 for £10,000.

Calculate the chargeable gain. Assume that the indexation factor for May 2005 to December 2017 is 0.448.

Solution

	£
Gross sales proceeds (March 2024)	25,000
Less: Selling costs	(400)
Net sale proceeds	24,600
Less: Allowable cost (May 2005)	(10,000)
Unindexed gain	14,600
Less: Indexation allowance (£10,000 × 0.448)	(4,480)
Chargeable gain	10,120

Be careful to ensure that you **index the allowable cost** and **not** the **unindexed gain** – a very easy mistake to make!

Note also that the indexation allowance:

- cannot be used to turn a gain into a loss
- is not available where there is an unindexed loss.

💡 Example

JNN Ltd is considering selling a field at auction in August 2023. It acquired the field in August 1995 for £10,000 and the sale proceeds are likely to be one of three results.

(a) £25,000

(b) £12,000

(c) £8,000

Calculate the chargeable gain or loss under each of these alternatives.

Assume the indexation factor from August 1995 to December 2017 is 0.855.

Solution

	(a)	(b)	(c)
	£	£	£
Sale proceeds	25,000	12,000	8,000
Less: Cost	(10,000)	(10,000)	(10,000)
Unindexed gain or (loss)	15,000	2,000	(2,000)
Less: Indexation allowance (0.855 × £10,000) = £8,550	(8,550)	(2,000)*	Nil**
Chargeable gain/(allowable loss)	6,450	Nil	(2,000)

Notes:

* Restricted, because indexation cannot create a loss.

** No indexation because indexation cannot increase a loss.

 Test your understanding 2

JHN Ltd made the following disposals in the year ended 31 March 2024.

1   On 9 June 2023 it sold a machine for £15,000. The machine was bought in October 1999 for £8,000.

2   On 5 September 2023 it sold a building which had been purchased for £27,500 in November 2000. Sale proceeds were £26,500.

3   Also on 3 March 2024, it sold some land which was purchased in April 1993 for £15,000. The land was sold for £25,000.

Calculate the chargeable gain on each of the above transactions and the net chargeable gains for the year ended 31 March 2024.

You should use the following indexation factors.

April 1993 – December 2017	0.978
Oct 1999 – December 2017	0.670
Nov 2000 – December 2017	0.616

Approach to the question

It is important that the chargeable gain or allowable loss on each transaction is **separately** computed.

Finally, prepare a summary adding gains and losses together to arrive at one overall net chargeable gains figure.

Test your understanding 3

RBQ Ltd made the following disposals in the year ended 31 March 2024.

(1) On 11 August 2023, it sold a shop for £15,000. The shop was bought in May 2003 for £8,000.

(2) On 16 October 2023, it sold a painting which had been purchased for £30,000 in November 2000. Sale proceeds were £25,000.

(3) On 3 January 2024, it sold a piece of land for £29,000. It had cost £6,000 in May 2001.

Calculate the total net chargeable gains on the above transactions in the year ended 31 March 2024.

You should use the following indexation factors, where relevant:

November 2000 – December 2017   0.616

May 2001 – December 2017   0.596

May 2003 – December 2017   0.532

 4 **Enhancement expenditure**

4.1 Enhancement expenditure

The main allowable cost in computing an unindexed gain is the purchase cost (including incidental acquisition costs).

Any additional capital expenditure incurred at a later date on the asset is also an allowable cost. This normally takes the form of improvement (i.e. enhancement) expenditure.

As the additional expenditure is incurred later than the original expenditure, there will be an impact on the calculation of the indexation allowance.

Indexation allowance can only be calculated from the actual date of expenditure; therefore, where there is cost plus enhancement expenditure incurred before 31 December 2017, **two** indexation allowance calculations will be required.

Example

RMY Ltd bought a shop in November 1997 for £13,200. The company spent £3,800 on improvements in May 2000. The shop was sold for £49,000 in October 2023.

The indexation factor from November 1997 to December 2017 is 0.742 and from May 2000 to December 2017 is 0.629.

Calculate the chargeable gain on the sale of the shop.

Solution

	£
Sale proceeds (October 2023)	49,000
Less: Cost (November 1997)	(13,200)
Enhancement (May 2000)	(3,800)
Unindexed gain	32,000
Less: Indexation allowance	
Cost (£13,200 × 0.742)	(9,794)
Enhancement (£3,800 × 0.629)	(2,390)
Chargeable gain	19,816

 Test your understanding 4

On 15 February 2024, Lindham Ltd sold a factory building for £420,000.

The factory had been purchased on 14 October 2004 for £194,000, and was extended at a cost of £58,000 during March 2006.

During May 2008, the roof of the factory was repaired at a cost of £12,000 following damage in a fire.

Lindham Ltd had incurred legal fees of £3,600 in connection with the original purchase of the factory, and £6,200 in connection with the disposal.

What is the chargeable gain on the disposal?

A £24,116

B £39,632

C £41,342

D £158,200

You should use the following indexation factors, where relevant.

October 2004 – December 2017	0.475
March 2006 – December 2017	0.426
May 2008 – December 2017	0.293

 Test your understanding 5

During the year to 30 September 2023, Jackson Ltd had the following capital transactions:

(a) In October 2022 it sold land for £27,000. It bought the land in February 1998 for £14,000.

(b) It also sold a factory unit in December 2022 for £100,000. Out of that the company had to pay legal fees of £1,200. It had originally bought the factory unit in March 1997 for £10,500, extended it in April 2001 for £3,000 and extended it again in June 2004 for £4,600.

Calculate the chargeable gain on each of the above transactions in the year ended 30 September 2023.

Use the following indexation factors, where relevant:

March 1997 – December 2017	0.790
February 1998 – December 2017	0.735
April 2001 – December 2017	0.607
June 2004 – December 2017	0.489

5 Rollover relief

5.1 Principle of rollover relief

Rollover relief (or 'replacement of business assets relief') allows a company to defer a chargeable gain, provided certain conditions are met.

This relief is also available for unincorporated businesses (sole traders and partnerships, which are covered in Chapter 15) but it is only examinable in relation to companies.

In order to qualify for relief, the company must reinvest the proceeds from the sale of a qualifying business asset into another qualifying business asset.

Any gain on the disposal of the first asset is then 'rolled over' against the capital gains cost of the new asset. Therefore, rollover relief simply **defers** the gain on the sale of the asset until the later disposal of the replacement asset.

A typical situation can be depicted as follows.

A company sells a building and then buys a new bigger building.

		£
Building (1)	Sale proceeds	100,000
	Less: Cost and indexation allowance	(40,000)
	Indexed gain	60,000
	Less: Rollover relief	(60,000)
	Chargeable gain	Nil
Building (2)	Purchase price	150,000
	Less: 'Rolled over gain'	(60,000)
	Base cost	90,000

The gain on building (1) has been deferred against the base cost of building (2).

Provided that **at least** an amount equal to the proceeds received is reinvested, then **full** deferral applies.

On the sale of the second building, a higher gain will result as the building's allowable cost has been reduced by the rolled over gain from the first building. This higher gain represents both the gain on the second asset and the deferred gain from the first.

	If no rollover relief claimed on building (1) £		If rollover relief is claimed on building (1) £
Sale of building (2) Sale proceeds, say	200,000	Sale proceeds	200,000
Less: Original cost	(150,000)	Less: Base cost	(90,000)
Unindexed gain	50,000	Unindexed gain	110,000

The benefit of rollover relief is that tax which would otherwise be payable now is deferred, possibly for many years.

5.2 Conditions for relief

Now that we have considered the mechanics, it is necessary to look at the conditions which apply.

There must be a disposal of and reinvestment in:

- a qualifying business asset
- within a qualifying time period.

Qualifying business assets

The assets must be used in a **trade**. Where they are only partly used in a trade then only the gain on the trade portion is eligible.

The main qualifying assets are:

- land and buildings (freehold and leasehold)
- fixed plant and machinery

The following assets are **not** qualifying assets:

- shares in a company

- buildings rented out to tenants.

Note that the replacement asset does not have to be the same type as the asset sold. A company could sell a factory and reinvest in fixed plant and still claim the relief.

Qualifying time period

The qualifying period for reinvestment in the replacement asset is up to 12 months before the sale to within 36 months after the sale.

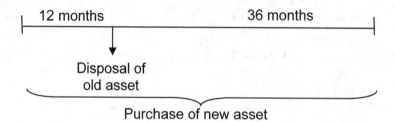

Claims

A claim for rollover relief must be made within four years from the later of the end of the accounting period in which:

- the disposal takes place or

- the replacement asset is purchased.

Therefore, for a disposal and replacement in the year ended 31 December 2023, the election must be made by 31 December 2027.

Note that it is not possible to make a partial claim for rollover relief. If a claim is made then the whole of the eligible gain must be rolled over.

5.3 Partial reinvestment

Rollover relief may still be available even where only part of the proceeds is reinvested. However, it will be restricted, as there is some cash retained which is available to settle tax liabilities. This is logical as the main purpose of the relief is not to charge tax where cash has been reinvested in the business.

The amount which is chargeable now is the lower of:

- the proceeds not reinvested

- the chargeable gain.

This amount cannot be rolled over (i.e. cannot be deferred).

The following example will demonstrate where full relief is available, partial relief is available and no relief is available.

Reference material

Some information about rollover relief can be found in the 'Chargeable gains – Reliefs' section of the reference material provided in the real assessment, so you do not need to learn it.

Why not look up the correct part of the reference material in the introduction to this text book now?

Example

AB Ltd sold an office block for £500,000 in December 2023. The office block had been acquired for £200,000 and was used throughout AB Ltd's ownership for trade purposes. The indexation allowance on the disposal was £213,100. A replacement office block was acquired in February 2023.

Assuming rollover relief is claimed where possible, calculate the gain taxable on AB Ltd and the base cost of the replacement office block if it cost:

(a) £610,000

(b) £448,000

(c) £345,000

Solution

Gain on sale of old office block.

	£
Proceeds	500,000
Less: Cost	(200,000)
Unindexed gain	300,000
Less: Indexation allowance	(213,100)
Chargeable gain before reliefs	86,900

(a) New asset cost £610,000

As all the proceeds have been reinvested, the full gain is rolled over and no gain is immediately chargeable.

	£
Chargeable gain before reliefs	86,900
Less: Rollover relief	(86,900)
Chargeable gain	Nil
Base cost of new asset	
Cost	610,000
Less: Gain rolled over	(86,900)
Base cost	523,100

Note that it is not possible to elect to rollover less than £86,900 i.e. a partial claim cannot be made.

(b) New asset cost £448,000

As not all of the proceeds have been reinvested, a gain arises when the old office block is sold as follows:

Gain chargeable now = lower of

(i)	Proceeds not reinvested	
	(£500,000 – £448,000)	£52,000
(ii)	The whole of the chargeable gain	£86,900

	£
Chargeable gain before reliefs	86,900
Less: Rollover relief (£86,900 – £52,000)	(34,900)
Chargeable gain now	52,000
Base cost of new asset	
Cost	448,000
Less: Gain rolled over	(34,900)
Base cost	413,100

(c) **New asset cost £345,000**

As not all of the proceeds have been reinvested, a gain arises immediately.

Gain chargeable now = lower of

(i)	Proceeds not reinvested	
	(£500,000 – £345,000)	£155,000
(ii)	The whole of the chargeable gain	£86,900

	£
Chargeable gain before reliefs	86,900
Less: Rollover relief (balance)	(Nil)
Chargeable gain now	86,900

As the proceeds not reinvested exceed the gain, the full gain of £86,900 is chargeable and no rollover relief is available.

Base cost of new asset	£345,000

Test your understanding 6

An office building was sold by Spares Ltd on 30 April 2023. Spares Ltd has a year end of 31 December.

The dates during which the proceeds must be reinvested are:

From:

A   30 April 2022

B   30 April 2023

C   31 December 2022

D   31 December 2023

To:

A   30 April 2026

B   30 April 2027

C   31 December 2026

D   31 December 2027

Test your understanding 7

DRV Ltd prepares accounts to 31 March annually.

The company sold the freehold of a factory on 3 March 2024 for £325,000, having previously purchased it as a replacement freehold factory for £200,000 in October 1995.

The factory which it replaced was acquired in May 1991 for £65,000 and sold in December 1995 for £140,000.

Calculate the chargeable gains, assuming all available reliefs are claimed. The indexation factors are:

May 1991 – December 1995	0.129
October 1995 – December 2017	0.856

 Test your understanding 8

DRV Ltd prepares accounts to 31 March annually.

The company sold the freehold of a factory on 3 March 2024 for £325,000, having previously purchased it as a replacement freehold factory for £115,000 in October 1995.

The factory which it replaced was acquired in May 1991 for £65,000 and sold in December 1995 for £140,000.

Calculate the chargeable gains, assuming all available reliefs are claimed.

The indexation factors are:

May 1991 – December 1995	0.129
October 1995 – December 2017	0.856

Test your understanding 9

Astute Ltd sold a factory on 15 February 2024 for £320,000. The factory was purchased on 24 October 2006 for £164,000, and was extended at a cost of £37,000 during March 2008.

Astute Ltd incurred legal fees of £3,600 in connection with the purchase of the factory, and legal fees of £6,200 in connection with the disposal.

Astute Ltd is considering the following alternative ways of reinvesting the proceeds from the sale of its factory.

(1)   A freehold warehouse can be purchased for £340,000.

(2)   A freehold factory building can be purchased for £300,000.

  The reinvestment will take place during May 2024. All of the above buildings have been, or will be, used for business purposes.

(a)   State the conditions that must be met in order that rollover relief can be claimed.

  You are not expected to list the categories of asset that qualify for rollover relief.

(b)   Before taking account of any available rollover relief, calculate Astute Ltd's chargeable gain in respect of the disposal of the factory.

(c)   Advise Astute Ltd of the rollover relief that will be available in respect of EACH of the two alternative reinvestments.

  Your answer should include details of the base cost of the replacement asset for each alternative.

Indexation factors are as follows:

October 2006 to December 2017   0.388
March 2008 to December 2017   0.311

6 Summary

There is a pro forma computation for the calculation of gains and losses on individual asset disposals.

The gains and losses of the accounting period are netted off to give the net chargeable gains to include in the company's corporation tax computation.

Companies receive an indexation allowance. Original and improvement costs are indexed from the month the cost is incurred to the month of disposal (or to December 2017 if disposal is after 31 December 2017).

If a replacement asset is purchased, rollover relief may be available to defer the gain on the original asset.

Test your understanding answers

Test your understanding 1

Bubbles Ltd

The amount to include in taxable total profits will be £7,000 (£13,000 – £4,000 – £2,000 b/f).

Test your understanding 2

JHN Ltd

Chargeable gains

	£
Machine (W1)	1,640
Building (W2)	(1,000)
Land (W3)	Nil
Net chargeable gains	640

Workings

(W1) Machine

	£
Proceeds	15,000
Less: Cost	(8,000)
Unindexed gain	7,000
Less: Indexation allowance (£8,000 × 0.670)	(5,360)
Chargeable gain	1,640

(W2) Building

	£
Proceeds	26,500
Less: Cost	(27,500)
Allowable loss	(1,000)

No indexation is available to increase the loss.

(W3) Land

	£
Proceeds	25,000
Less: Cost	(15,000)
Unindexed gain	10,000
Less: Indexation allowance (£15,000 × 0.978) (restricted)	(10,000)
	Nil

The IA is restricted because indexation cannot create an allowable loss.

Test your understanding 3

RBQ Ltd

	£
Shop (W1)	2,744
Painting (W2)	(5,000)
Land (W3)	19,424
Total net chargeable gains	17,168

Workings

(W1) Shop

	£
Proceeds	15,000
Less: Cost	(8,000)
Unindexed gain	7,000
Less: Indexation allowance (£8,000 × 0.532)	(4,256)
Chargeable gain	2,744

(W2) Painting

	£
Proceeds	25,000
Less: Cost	(30,000)
Allowable loss	(5,000)

No indexation is available to increase the loss

(W3) Land

	£
Proceeds	29,000
Less: Cost	(6,000)
Unindexed gain	23,000
Less: Indexation allowance (£6,000 × 0.596)	(3,576)
Chargeable gain	19,424

✎ Test your understanding 4

Lindham Ltd

The correct answer is B.

Explanation

The gain is calculated as shown below.

	£	£
Disposal proceeds		420,000
Less: Incidental costs of disposal		(6,200)
		———
Net proceeds		413,800
Less: Acquisition cost	194,000	
Incidental costs of acquisition	3,600	
	———	(197,600)
Enhancement expenditure		(58,000)
		———
		158,200
Less: Indexation allowance		
Cost (£197,600 × 0.475)		(93,860)
Extension (£58,000 × 0.426)		(24,708)
		———
Chargeable gain		39,632
		———

The expenditure incurred in May 2008 for repairing the roof does not enhance the value of the factory and is therefore not an allowable deduction in the gain computation.

The repair is a revenue expense which is allowable against the company's trading profits.

Test your understanding 5

Jackson Ltd

		£	£
(a)	**Land**		
	Sale proceeds	27,000	
	Less: Cost	(14,000)	
	Unindexed gain	13,000	
	Less: Indexation allowance		
	(£14,000 × 0.735)	(10,290)	
	Chargeable gain		2,710

		£
(b)	**Factory**	
	Sale proceeds	100,000
	Less: Legal fees	(1,200)
		98,800
	Less: Cost (March 1997)	(10,500)
	Extension (April 2001)	(3,000)
	Extension (June 2004)	(4,600)
	Unindexed gain	80,700
	Less: Indexation allowance	
	Cost (£10,500 × 0.790)	(8,295)
	Extension (£3,000 × 0.607)	(1,821)
	Extension (£4,600 × 0.489)	(2,249)
	Chargeable gain	68,335

Test your understanding 6

Spares Ltd

The correct answers are both A.

Explanation

A company has from 12 months before the disposal to 3 years after the disposal to reinvest the proceeds.

Test your understanding 7

DRV Ltd (1)

Sale of original freehold factory (purchased May 1991)

	£
Sale proceeds (December 1995)	140,000
Less: Cost	(65,000)
Unindexed gain	75,000
Less: Indexation allowance	
(May 1991 – December 1995) (0.129 × £65,000)	(8,385)
Chargeable gain before relief	66,615
Less: Rollover relief upon purchase of replacement factory in October 1995	(66,615)
Chargeable gain – year ended 31 March 1996	Nil

Sale of replacement factory

	£	£
Sale proceeds (March 2024)		325,000
Cost (October 1995)	200,000	
Less: Rolled over gain	(66,615)	
		(133,385)
Unindexed gain		191,615
Less: Indexation allowance		
(October 1995 – December 2017) (0.856 × £133,385)		(114,178)
Chargeable gain (Note)		77,437

Note: DRV Ltd may be able to roll this gain over if it makes a further qualifying purchase in the qualifying time period.

No indexation allowance is permitted after 31 December 2017.

Test your understanding 8

DRV Ltd (2)

Sale of original freehold factory (purchased May 1991)

	£
Sale proceeds (December 1995)	140,000
Less: Cost	(65,000)
	———
Unindexed gain	75,000
Less: Indexation allowance	
(May 1991 – December 1995) (0.129 × £65,000)	(8,385)
	———
Indexed gain (as above)	66,615
Less: Rollover relief (balancing figure)	(41,615)
	———
Chargeable gain – year ended 31 March 1996 (Note)	25,000
	———

Note: Not all of the sale proceeds are reinvested.

Therefore, the chargeable gain arising now is the sale proceeds not reinvested = £25,000 (£140,000 – £115,000).

Sale of replacement factory

	£	£
Sale proceeds (March 2024)		325,000
Cost	115,000	
Less: Rolled over gain	(41,615)	
	———	
		(73,385)
		———
Unindexed gain		251,615
Less: Indexation allowance		
(October 1995 – December 2017) (0.856 × £73,385)		(62,818)
		———
Chargeable gain		188,797
		———

Test your understanding 9

Astute Ltd

(a) Conditions for rollover relief

(i) The reinvestment must be within the period starting 12 months before the disposal and ending 36 months after the date of disposal of the original asset.

(ii) The original asset and the replacement asset must be qualifying business assets used for a trading purpose by the taxpayer.

(iii) The replacement asset must be brought into use by the taxpayer for a trading purpose on acquisition.

(b) Disposal of the factory – 15 February 2024

	£
Proceeds (£320,000 – £6,200)	313,800
Less Cost (October 2006)	(164,000)
Legal fees of purchase	(3,600)
Extension (March 2008)	(37,000)
Unindexed gain	109,200
Less Indexation allowance	
On cost: (£164,000 + £3,600) × 0.388	(65,029)
On extension: (£37,000 × 0.311)	(11,507)
Chargeable gain	32,664

(c) Alternative reinvestments

(1) Freehold warehouse costing £340,000

As the full sale proceeds will have been reinvested, the company can claim to rollover the gain in full.

The base cost of the warehouse will be £307,336 (£340,000 – £32,664).

(2) **Freehold factory building costing £300,000**

As less than the full proceeds will have been reinvested, only part of the gain can be rolled over.

The proceeds not reinvested of £20,000 (£320,000 – £300,000) results in a gain of £20,000 remaining chargeable (see notes).

The balance of £12,664 (£32,664 – £20,000) is rolled over.

The base cost of the factory building becomes £287,336 (£300,000 – £12,664).

Note: HMRC allow the 'proceeds not reinvested' to be calculated as the difference between the **net** sale proceeds (i.e. after selling costs) and the purchase cost (including purchase expenses) of the replacement asset.

In (c) (2) this would mean only £13,800 (£313,800 – £300,000) of the gain remaining chargeable. However, you are not expected to know this and would not be penalised either way.

Shares and securities – disposals by companies

Introduction

A company may hold another company's shares as an investment. Special rules apply to the calculation of chargeable gains on the disposal of shares.

The calculation of gains and losses for a company disposal of shares will be tested in Task 5 of the assessment. This task will be manually marked.

ASSESSMENT CRITERIA
Apply matching rules for companies (3.2)
Account for:
– bonus issues
– rights issues
– indexation allowance (3.2)

CONTENTS
1 The matching rules
2 Bonus issues and rights issues
3 Approach to assessment questions

1 The matching rules

1.1 Disposal of shares and securities

What distinguishes a share disposal from other asset disposals is the need for matching rules.

Before considering what these matching rules are, it helps to understand why we need them.

1.2 Principle of matching rules

Suppose that a company makes the following purchases of shares in another company, A plc:

1 September 1995	800 shares for	£2,000
3 February 1998	300 shares for	£1,000
1 July 2004	500 shares for	£1,000

On 1 November 2023, 400 of these shares are sold – but which 400?

- It could be the 300 acquired in 1998 and 100 acquired in 1995.

- It could be 400 out of the 500 acquired in 2004.

- It could be based on 400 out of the total 1,600 with costs being averaged.

We need matching rules so that we can establish **which** shares have been sold, and consequently what allowable costs and indexation allowances can be deducted from the sale proceeds.

The matching rules dictate the order in which the shares disposed of are matched with purchases.

1.3 The matching rules for companies

Shares of the same type in the same company (for example Lionel Ltd ordinary shares) are matched as follows:

(1) first, with shares bought on the same day, then

(2) second, with shares bought in the previous nine days (on a first in first out basis), then

(3) third, with shares in the 'share pool' (sometimes referred to as the s104 pool or the FA1985 pool).

The 'share pool' is considered in detail below. For companies, shares are pooled together from 10 days after purchase.

Note that the matching rules for individuals are different and are not examinable in the Business Tax assessment.

 Example

Minnie Ltd has sold 3,000 shares in Mickey plc for £15,000 on 2 February 2024. The shares in Mickey plc were purchased as follows:

Date	Number	Cost
		£
1 July 1997	1,000	2,000
1 September 2007	1,000	2,500
27 January 2024	500	1,200
2 February 2024	1,500	6,000

Explain which shares Minnie Ltd is deemed to have sold.

Solution

Using the matching rules, the 3,000 shares sold are as follows:

	Number
2 February 2024 (same day purchase)	1,500
27 January 2024 (in previous 9 days)	500
	─────
	2,000

Share pool:
All other shares were purchased more than 9 days ago, therefore must be in the pool.

1 July 1997	1,000	
1 September 2007	1,000	
	─────	
Total number of shares in pool	2,000	
	─────	
Out of the pool (1,000 out of 2,000)		1,000
		─────
Shares disposed of		3,000
		─────

Note: When dealing with the pool we do not identify which 1,000 shares are sold.

1.4 Calculation of gains on same day and previous 9 day purchases

If a disposal is matched with the first two rules (i.e. matching against a same day purchase or purchases in the previous 9 days), there will be no indexation allowance available (even in the unlikely event of the relevant dates occurring before 1 January 2018).

Hence, the gain is calculated as:

	£
Sale proceeds	X
Less: Allowable cost	(X)
Chargeable gain	X

Example

For Minnie Ltd in the previous example, calculate the gains on the shares purchased:

(1)   on the same day, and

(2)   in the previous 9 days.

Solution

Step 1: Calculate the gain on the same day purchase (1,500 shares)

3,000 shares are sold for £15,000.

	£
Sale proceeds (1,500/3,000 × £15,000)	7,500
Less: Allowable cost	(6,000)
Chargeable gain	1,500

Step 2: Calculate the gain on the previous 9 days purchase (500 shares)

	£
Sale proceeds (500/3,000 × £15,000)	2,500
Less: Allowable cost	(1,200)
Chargeable gain	1,300

1.5 The operation of a share pool

Any purchases from 1 April 1982 are 'pooled' in the 'share pool'.

Purchases before 1 April 1982 are not in the syllabus.

Indexation will apply to the pool from the date of acquisition to the date of disposal or December 2017, whichever is earlier.

To enable the correct indexation to be calculated, a separate working is needed to identify the amount available. The working is also used to find the average cost of a partial disposal.

The pool is initially set up with three columns as follows:

	Number	Cost £	Indexed cost £
Purchases (say) June 1991	1,000	2,000	2,000

Then every time there is an 'operative event' (an event involving cash – i.e. a sale or a purchase), two steps must be performed.

Step 1: An indexation update.

In the indexed cost column, add in indexation from the last operative event until this one.

This is calculated by multiplying the balance in the indexed cost column by the increase in the RPI since the last operative event.

Step 2: Deal with the operative event.

– for a purchase add in the new shares. The cost must be added in to both the cost and indexed cost columns.

– for a sale eliminate some shares. The amounts to be deducted from the cost and indexed cost columns are calculated in proportion to the number of shares being removed from the pool.

The following working should be produced:

Pro forma for the share pool

	Number	Cost	Indexed cost
		£	£
Purchase	X	X	X
Index to next event			X
Record next event (e.g. purchase)	X	X	X
	X	X	X
Index to next event			X
	X	X	X
Record next event (e.g. sale)	(X)	(X) (W1)	(X) (W2)
Pool carried forward	X	X	X

Note: For the 'indexed rises' the indexation factor is **not** rounded in practice. This is the only situation where a non-rounded factor is ever used.

However, in the assessment you will always to be given a rounded indexation factor, therefore use the factor given.

Workings:

(W1) Total cost × (number of shares sold/number of shares in pool)

(W2) Total indexed cost × (number of shares sold/number of shares in pool)

The purpose of the share pool working is to find:

- the average pool cost of shares disposed of = working 1 (W1)

- the **indexation** of shares disposed of = (working 2 – working 1).

The gain on the shares is then calculated as normal:

	£
Sale proceeds	X
Less: Cost (W1)	(X)
Unindexed gain	X
Less: Indexation allowance (W2 – W1)	(X)
Chargeable gain	X

The indexation factor is **always** applied to the total on the indexed cost column (**not** cost).

A partial disposal from a share pool uses straight line apportionment of cost and indexation.

In your assessment you will be provided with a grid to enter your calculations (section 3).

💡 Example

For Minnie Ltd in the previous example, calculate the gain on the disposal from the share pool.

The indexation factors to use are as follows:

July 1997 – September 2007	0.321
September 2007 – December 2017	0.337

Solution

Step 1:   Calculate cost and indexed cost from the share pool.

	Number	Cost	Indexed cost
		£	£
July 1997 purchase	1,000	2,000	2,000
Index to next event			
(July 1997 to September 2007)			
Indexed cost × 0.321			
(£2,000 × 0.321)			642
September 2007 purchase	1,000	2,500	2,500
	2,000	4,500	5,142
Index to next event			
(September 2007 to December 2017)			
(£5,142 × 0.337)			1,733
	2,000	4,500	6,875
February 2024 sale (half)	(1,000)	(2,250)	(3,438)
Pool carried forward	1,000	2,250	3,437

Step 2: **Calculate the gain on share pool shares.**

	£
Sale proceeds (1,000/3,000 × £15,000)	5,000
Less: Allowable cost	(2,250)
Unindexed gain	2,750
Less: Indexation allowance	
(£3,438 – £2,250)	(1,188)
Chargeable gain	1,562

Step 3: **Calculate total chargeable gains on the disposal of all 3,000 shares in Minnie Ltd**

The total chargeable gains
= (£1,500 + £1,300 + £1,562) = £4,362

 Test your understanding 1

FDC Ltd has purchased shares in DCC Ltd. The share pool information of the shares in DCC Ltd is given below.

		Cost £
1 June 1993	4,000 shares for	8,000
30 July 2002	1,800 shares for	9,750

FDC Ltd disposed of 2,000 of its shares in DCC Ltd for £20,571 in March 2024.

The indexation factors to use are as follows:

June 1993 – July 2002	0.248
July 2002 – December 2017	0.581

Calculate the chargeable gain on the share pool shares.

Test your understanding 2

Jester Ltd sold ordinary 25p shares in Blue plc as follows:

	Number of shares	Proceeds
September 1999	2,000	£9,000
March 2024	2,000	£14,500

At 1 July 1995, Jester Ltd had 4,100 shares in the share pool, with an indexed cost of £10,744 and a cost of £8,200.

Purchases were made as follows:

	Number of shares	Cost
January 2001	200	£450

Compute the gains arising on all of the above transactions in quoted securities.

Use the following indexation factors as appropriate:

July 1995 – September 1999	0.115
September 1999 – January 2001	0.029
January 2001 – December 2017	0.625

2 Bonus issues and rights issues

2.1 Principle of bonus issues and rights issues

A bonus issue is the distribution of free shares to shareholders based on existing shareholdings.

A rights issue involves shareholders paying for new shares, usually at a rate below market price and in proportions based on existing shareholdings.

Matching

In both cases, therefore, the shareholder is making a new acquisition of shares. However, for **matching** purposes, such acquisitions arise out of the original holdings.

Bonus and rights issues therefore attach to the original shareholdings for the purposes of the identification rules.

Example

Alma Ltd acquired shares in S plc, a quoted company, as follows.

- 2,000 shares acquired in June 1994 for £11,500.
- In October 1995 there was a 1 for 2 bonus issue.
- In December 2001 there was a 1 for 4 rights issue at £3 per share.

Alma Ltd sold 2,600 shares in December 2023 for £30,000.

Calculate the number of shares in the share pool.

Solution

	Number
June 1994 purchase	2,000
October 1995 bonus issue (1 for 2)	
1/2 × 2,000	1,000
	———
December 2001 rights issue (1 for 4)	3,000
1/4 × 3,000	750
	———
	3,750
December 2023 sale	(2,600)
	———
Balance in pool c/f	1,150
	———

2.2 Bonus issue

A bonus issue is the issue of free shares (i.e. no cost is involved). As there is no expenditure involved it is not an operative event and therefore no indexation is calculated before recording the event.

Simply add the number of bonus issue shares received to the pool.

When the next event occurs (a sale, purchase or rights issue), index from the operative event prior to the bonus issue.

Example

For Alma Ltd in the previous example, set up the share pool and deal with events up to and including the bonus issue.

Solution

Share pool	Number	Cost	Indexed cost
		£	£
Purchase June 1994	2,000	11,500	11,500
Bonus issue October 1995			
(1 for 2) 1/2 × 2,000	1,000	Nil	Nil
	3,000	11,500	11,500

Note: We have NOT indexed the pool before recording the bonus issue (as no cost is involved).

Therefore, next time there is an operative event we will index from June 1994 (the last operative event involving cost).

2.3 Rights issue

A rights issue involves a payment for new shares. Accordingly, it is treated simply as a purchase of shares (usually at a price below the market rate).

Hence, it should be treated in the same way as a purchase in the share pool:

- index up to the rights issue, then
- add in the number and cost of new shares.

 Example

For Alma Ltd in the previous example, you are required to calculate the gain on disposal.

Assume that the indexation factor from June 1994 to December 2001 is 0.198 and from December 2001 to December 2017 is 0.604.

Solution

Share pool	Number	Cost £	Indexed cost £
Purchase June 1994	2,000	11,500	11,500
Bonus issue October 1995 (1 for 2)	1,000	Nil	Nil
	3,000	11,500	11,500
Indexed rise to December 2001 (£11,500 × 0.198)			2,277
	3,000	11,500	13,777
Rights issue (1 for 4) at £3	750	2,250	2,250
	3,750	13,750	16,027
Indexed rise to December 2017 (£16,027 × 0.604)			9,680
	3,750	13,750	25,707
Disposal December 2023	(2,600)		
Allocate costs (2,600/3,750) × £13,750/£25,707		(9,533)	(17,824)
Balance c/f	1,150	4,217	7,883

Computation of gain – share pool

	£
Proceeds	30,000
Less: Cost	(9,533)
Unindexed gain	20,467
Less: Indexation (£17,824 – £9,533)	(8,291)
Chargeable gain	12,176

Note that the indexed cost is updated prior to the rights issue, because there is a purchase which involves additional cost.

Following the disposal there are 1,150 shares in the pool with a cost of £4,217 and an indexed cost of £7,883. This will be used as the starting point when dealing with the next operative event.

In the assessment you may be given details of brought forward amounts, rather than the complete history of the share pool.

Test your understanding 3

On 20 September 2023, Scarlet Ltd sold 1,500 ordinary shares in Red plc for £4,725. The company's previous transactions were as follows.

Balance on the share pool at 5 May 2004 is 2,500 shares with a qualifying cost of £3,900 and an indexed cost of £4,385.

Transactions from 5 May 2004 were as follows:

4 April 2005	Took up 1 for 2 bonus issue
19 January 2006	Took up 1 for 3 rights issue at 140p per share

The indexed rise from May 2004 to January 2006 is 0.037 and from January 2006 to December 2017 is 0.438.

Calculate Scarlet Ltd's chargeable gain on the disposal on 20 September 2023.

 Test your understanding 4

Chrome Ltd sold all of its ordinary shares in Copper plc for £17,760 on 1 October 2023.

Chrome Ltd acquired its shares in Copper plc as follows:

10 May 2007	Purchased 3,200 shares for £9,600
9 June 2011	Took up 1 for 4 rights issue at 260p per share
20 January 2013	Purchased 2,100 shares for £4,400

Indexation factors were:

May 2007 to June 2011	0.141
June 2011 to January 2013	0.045
January 2013 to December 2017	0.131

Calculate Chrome Ltd's chargeable gain on the disposal on 1 October 2023.

Test your understanding 5

On 8 August 2023, Purple Ltd sold 5,000 ordinary shares in Indigo plc for £15,000. The company's previous transactions were as follows.

Balance on share pool at 9 June 1998, 3,000 shares with a qualifying cost of £4,000 and an indexed cost of £5,010.

Transactions from 9 June 1998 were as follows:

12 August 2003   Took up 1 for 3 bonus issue

7 May 2008   Took up 1 for 2 rights issue at 150p per share

4 August 2023   500 shares purchased for £1,410

The indexation factor from June 1998 to May 2008 is 0.316 and from May 2008 to December 2017 is 0.293.

Calculate Purple Ltd's chargeable gain on the disposal on 8 August 2023.

3   Approach to assessment questions

In Task 5 of the assessment you will be asked to calculate a gain or loss on shares. This question will be manually marked, so it is important that you enter your answer into the table supplied correctly and show your workings.

You may be given the column headings for the share pool and then be asked to calculate the chargeable gain or allowable loss as a separate working.

This should allow you to enter your answer in the same layout as used throughout this chapter although with a little less detail. For example, you do not need to include lines marking totals and subtotals.

Example

Mag Ltd bought 1,000 shares in Elswick plc for £4.40 each in December 2006.

In July 2014 it received a 1 for 5 rights issue at £4.80 each.

In May 2023 it sold 400 shares for £35,000.

The indexation factor from December 2006 to July 2014 is 0.263 and from July 2014 to December 2017 is 0.086.

(a) Complete the share pool and show the balance of shares carried forward.

(b) Calculate the chargeable gain or allowable loss on the disposal of the Elswick plc shares by Mag Ltd.

Solution

(a) Share pool

Description	Number of shares	Cost £	Indexed cost £
December 2006 Purchase	1,000	4,400	4,400
Index to July 2014 (£4,400 × 0.263)			1,157
July 2014 Rights issue (1,000/5 × £4.80)	200	960	960
Total	1,200	5,360	6,517
Index to December 2017 (£6,517 × 0.086)			560
Total	1,200	5,360	7,077
May 2023 Sale (400/1,200) × £5,360 / £7,077	(400)	(1,787)	(2,359)
Balance c/f	800	3,573	4,718

(b) Gain on disposal

	£
Proceeds	35,000
Less cost (pool)	(1,787)
	33,213
Indexation (£2,359 – £1,787)	(572)
Gain	32,641

4 Summary

When disposing of shares we apply matching rules to identify which shares have been disposed of.

These rules are needed so that we can deduct the appropriate acquisition costs from the disposal proceeds.

The matching rules for companies generally match disposals with shares held in the share pool.

Bonus and rights issues attach themselves to the original shareholdings.

Test your understanding answers

Test your understanding 1

FDC Ltd

Share pool working	Note	Number	Cost	Indexed cost
			£	£
Purchase 1 June 1993	1	4,000	8,000	8,000
Indexed rise to July 2002	2			
£8,000 × 0.248				1,984
Purchase – July 2002		1,800	9,750	9,750
		5,800	17,750	19,734
Indexed rise to December 2017	3			
£19,734 × 0.581				11,465
		5,800	17,750	31,199
Sale of 2,000 shares	4	(2,000)		
$\frac{2,000}{5,800}$ × £17,750/£31,199			(6,121)	(10,758)
Carried forward		3,800	11,629	20,441

Notes:

(1) Any entry in the cost column must also be made in the indexed cost column.

(2) Indexation must be added before the purchase in July 2002 is added to the pool.

(3) No indexation is given after 31 December 2017.

(4) Use apportionment to allocate cost and indexed cost.

Gain on share pool shares

	£
Sale proceeds	20,571
Less: Cost	(6,121)
Unindexed gain	14,450
Less: Indexation allowance (£10,758 – £6,121)	(4,637)
Chargeable gain	9,813

Note: If the proceeds exceed the indexed cost then it is an acceptable short cut to just deduct the indexed cost from the proceeds in calculating the gain on the pool shares.

Test your understanding 2

Jester Ltd

	£
Disposal – September 1999	
Proceeds	9,000
Less: Cost (W)	(4,000)
Unindexed gain	5,000
Less: Indexation (£5,844 – £4,000)	(1,844)
Chargeable gain	3,156
Disposal – March 2024	
Proceeds	14,500
Less: Cost (W)	(4,043)
Unindexed gain	10,457
Less: Indexation (£9,558 – £4,043)	(5,515)
Chargeable gain	4,942

Share pool working

	Number of shares	Cost £	Indexed cost £
Balance at 1 July 1995	4,100	8,200	10,744
Indexed rise to September 1999			
(0.115 × £10,744)			1,236
			11,980
September 1999 Sale			
(2,000/4,100) × £8,200 and £11,980	(2,000)	(4,000)	(5,844)
	2,100	4,200	6,136
Indexed rise to January 2001			
(0.029 × £6,136)			178
January 2001 Acquisition	200	450	450
	2,300	4,650	6,764
Indexed rise to December 2017			
(0.625 × £6,764)			4,228
			10,992
March 2024 Sale			
(2,000/2,300) × £4,650 and £10,992	(2,000)	(4,043)	(9,558)
	300	607	1,434

Test your understanding 3

Scarlet Ltd

Share pool	Number of shares	Cost	Indexed cost
		£	£
Balance at 5 May 2004	2,500	3,900	4,385
4 April 2005 Bonus issue (1 for 2)	1,250	–	–
	3,750	3,900	4,385
Indexed rise to January 2006 £4,385 × 0.037			162
19 January 2006			4,547
Rights issue (1 for 3) × 140p	1,250	1,750	1,750
	5,000	5,650	6,297
Indexed rise to December 2017 £6,297 × 0.438			2,758
	5,000	5,650	9,055
Cost of sale $\frac{1,500}{5,000} \times$ £5,650/£9,055	(1,500)	(1,695)	(2,717)
Pool balance c/f	3,500	3,955	6,338

Gain on the disposal of shares

	£
Proceeds	4,725
Less: Cost	(1,695)
Unindexed gain	3,030
Less: Indexation allowance (£2,717 – £1,695)	(1,022)
Chargeable gain	2,008

Test your understanding 4

Chrome Ltd

	£
Disposal – October 2023	
Proceeds	17,760
Less: Cost (W)	(16,080)
Unindexed gain	1,680
Less: Indexation (£20,382 – £16,080)	
Restricted, indexation allowance cannot create a loss	(1,680)
Chargeable gain	Nil

Share pool working

	Number of shares	Cost	Indexed cost
		£	£
Purchase May 2007	3,200	9,600	9,600
Indexed rise to June 2011			
(0.141 × £9,600)			1,354
9 June 2011 Rights issue (1 for 4)			
(3,200/4 × £2.60)	800	2,080	2,080
	4,000	11,680	13,034
Indexed rise to January 2013			
(0.045 × £13,034)			587
20 January 2013 Purchase	2,100	4,400	4,400
	6,100	16,080	18,021
Indexed rise to December 2017			
(0.131 × £18,021)			2,361
			20,382
1 October 2023 Sale	(6,100)	(16,080)	(20,382)
	Nil	Nil	Nil

☀ Test your understanding 5

Purple Ltd

Disposal – 8 August 2023

(Sale of 500 shares purchased in previous 9 days)

	£
Sale proceeds (500/5,000 × £15,000)	1,500
Less: Cost	(1,410)
	————
Unindexed gain	90
Less: Indexation allowance	Nil
	————
Chargeable gain	90
	————

Disposal – 8 August 2023 (Sale of 4,500 shares from the pool)

	£
Sale proceeds (£15,000 – £1,500)	13,500
Less: Cost	(5,250)
	————
Unindexed gain	8,250
Less: Indexation allowance (£9,303 – £5,250)	(4,053)
	————
Chargeable gain	4,197
	————

Total gains (£90 + £4,197) = £4,287

Share pool working

	Number of shares	Cost	Indexed cost
		£	£
Balance at 9 June 1998	3,000	4,000	5,010
12 August 2003			
Bonus issue (1 for 3)	1,000	Nil	Nil
	4,000	4,000	5,010
Indexed rise to May 2008			
(£5,010 × 0.316)			1,583
7 May 2008 Rights issue			
(1 for 2 × 150p)	2,000	3,000	3,000
	6,000	7,000	9,593
Indexed rise to December 2017			
(£9,593 × 0.293)			2,811
			12,404
8 August 2023 Sale			
$\frac{4,500}{6,000}$ × £7,000/£12,404	(4,500)	(5,250)	(9,303)
Pool c/f	1,500	1,750	3,101

Business disposals

15

Introduction

This chapter considers the tax implications for an individual disposing of an unincorporated business or shares in a personal company and the capital gains tax reliefs that may be available.

It begins with an introduction to the calculation of gains and losses and capital gains tax payable for individuals.

Business disposals will be tested in Task 10 of the assessment.

ASSESSMENT CRITERIA
The income tax and capital gains tax implications of disposing of an unincorporated business (5.1)
The capital gains tax reliefs (gift relief, business asset disposal relief) available on the disposal of:
– an unincorporated business
– shares in a personal company (5.1)
Calculate capital gains on disposal of:
– trade and assets
– shares in a personal company
– capital gains tax reliefs available on disposal of:
– trade and assets
– shares in a personal company (5.1)
– post-tax proceeds following a business disposal (5.1)

CONTENTS

1 Gains and losses for individuals

2 Business asset disposal relief

3 Gift relief (holdover relief)

4 Disposal of an unincorporated business

1 Gains and losses for individuals

1.1 Calculation of individual gains and losses

The standard pro forma used to calculate a gain or loss on disposal of an asset is essentially the same as for companies except that individuals are not entitled to an indexation allowance.

	£
Gross sale proceeds	X
Less: Selling costs	(X)
Net sale proceeds (NSP)	X
Less: Allowable cost	(X)
Incidental costs of acquisition	(X)
Enhancement expenditure	(X)
Chargeable gain/(allowable loss)	X/(X)

1.2 Capital gains tax

Individuals pay capital gains tax (CGT) on their taxable gains for the tax year (e.g. 2023/24).

Individuals are entitled to an annual exempt amount (AEA) for each tax year (£6,000 in 2023/24).

The AEA is deducted from the total net chargeable gains of the year to give the taxable gains.

	£
Capital gains	X
Less: Capital losses	(X)
Net chargeable gains	X
Less: AEA	(6,000)
Taxable gains	X

1.3 Calculating the tax payable

Taxable gains are treated as an additional amount of income in order to determine the rates of CGT. However, the gains must not be included in the income tax computation.

Where the taxable gains fall within any remaining basic rate band (after income has been taxed) they are taxed at 10%. For 2023/24 the basic rate band is £37,700.

The balance of the taxable gains is taxed at 20%.

 Reference material

Some information about the annual exempt amount and the rates of capital gains tax can be found in the 'Capital gains tax' section of the reference material provided in the real assessment, so you do not need to learn it. The basic rate band is also provided, in the 'Income tax' section.

Why not look up the correct part of the reference material in the introduction to this text book now?

 Example

Carl sold some assets in 2023/24 and made chargeable gains of £31,700 and a capital loss of £5,800.

Carl's taxable income for the year, after deducting the personal allowance, is £35,715.

What is Carl's CGT liability for 2023/24?

Solution

	Total £
Chargeable gains for the year	31,700
Less: Capital loss	(5,800)
Net chargeable gains for the year	25,900
Less: AEA	(6,000)
Taxable gains	19,900

CGT	
£1,985 (£37,700 − £35,715) × 10%	199
£17,915 (£19,900 − £1,985) × 20%	3,583
	———
Capital gains tax liability	3,782
	———

 **Test your understanding 1**

Misha sold two assets in 2023/24 and made two chargeable gains of £17,300 and £11,700. Her taxable income for the year, after deducting the personal allowance, is £24,900.

What is Misha's capital gains tax liability for 2023/24?

---

2 Business asset disposal relief

The disposal of a business could give rise to a large gain. If all of the gain was subject to tax at normal rates, it would make it difficult for business assets to be sold if the owner could not afford the tax due.

Business asset disposal relief (BADR) reduces the capital gains tax payable by an individual on qualifying business disposals; for example, where all or part of an unincorporated business is sold by an individual.

2.1 The relief

The relief operates as follows:

- Gains on 'qualifying business disposals' of up to £1 million are taxed at a lower rate of 10%.

- Any gains above the £1 million limit are taxed at the normal rates of 10% and 20%.

- The limit is a lifetime limit that is diminished each time a claim for the relief is made.

- In order to maximise tax savings, the annual exempt amount (AEA) should be deducted from gains on disposals of assets that do not qualify for BADR wherever possible.

- The amount of qualifying gains that is taxed at 10% must be deducted from the remaining basic rate band when determining the rate of tax to be paid on non-qualifying gains (which will therefore usually be 20%).

The relief must be claimed within 12 months of the 31 January following the end of the tax year in which the disposal is made.

For 2023/24 disposals, the relief must be claimed by 31 January 2026.

The relief is not available to companies.

2.2 Qualifying business disposals

The relief applies to the disposal of:

- the whole or part of a business carried on by the individual either alone or in partnership

- assets of the individual's or partnership's trading business that has **now ceased**

- shares, provided:

    - the shares are in the individual's 'personal trading company', and

    - the individual is an employee of the company (part time or full time).

An individual's 'personal trading company' is one in which the individual:

- owns at least 5% of the ordinary shares

- which carry at least 5% of the voting rights, entitlement to distributable profits and entitlement to net assets.

Note in particular that:

- the disposal of an individual business asset used for the purposes of a **continuing trade** does not qualify. There must be a disposal of the whole or part of the trading business; the sale of an asset in isolation does not qualify.

2.3 Qualifying ownership period

In the case of the disposal of a business it must have been owned by the individual making the disposal in the 24 months prior to the disposal.

Where the disposal is of an asset of the individual's or partnership's trading business that has now ceased the individual must have owned the business for 24 months prior to the date of cessation and the disposal of the asset must also take place within three years of the cessation of trade.

In the case of shares the individual must have been an employee of the company and the company must have been the individual's personal trading company for at least 24 months prior to the disposal.

Reference material

Some information about business asset disposal relief can be found in the 'Chargeable gains - Reliefs' section of the reference material provided in the real assessment, so you do not need to learn it.

Why not look up the correct part of the reference material in the introduction to this text book now?

Test your understanding 2

Which of the following statements is correct?

A   The maximum business asset disposal relief available is £1,000,000 per business disposal.

B   Business asset disposal relief is not available in respect of a gain on a sale of shares.

C   Where a gain qualifies for business asset disposal relief the relief is given automatically.

D   Gains qualifying for business asset disposal relief are taxed at 10% even if the vendor is a higher rate taxpayer.

2.4 Applying the relief

When a qualifying disposal is made:

- Calculate the qualifying gains arising on the disposal of the individual assets as normal.

- Add the individual gains arising on the qualifying disposals together.

- Deduct the AEA from gains that do **not** qualify for the relief (if any).

- Deduct any remaining AEA from the gains qualifying for the relief.

- The taxable qualifying gains are taxed at 10% (subject to the £1 million lifetime limit).

- The non-qualifying gains are taxed at 10%/20% depending on the amount of basic rate band (currently £37,700) available.

Example

In July 2023, Katie sold her unincorporated trading business which she set up in 1997. The following gains arose on the disposal of the business:

	£
Factory	275,000
Goodwill	330,000
Warehouse	100,000

In August 2023 Katie also realised a gain of £20,300 on the sale of a painting.

Calculate the capital gains tax payable by Katie in respect of 2023/24.

Solution

	Qualifying for BADR £	Non-qualifying gains £
Business:		
Factory	275,000	
Goodwill	330,000	
Warehouse	100,000	
Painting		20,300
Less: AEA		(6,000)
Taxable gains	705,000	14,300

CGT payable:

£705,000 × 10%	70,500
£14,300 × 20%	2,860
	———
Capital gains tax payable	73,360
	———

Note: The gain on the painting is taxed at 20% because the gains qualifying for BADR are deemed to use up any basic rate band available.

 Test your understanding 3

On 1 July 2023 Hamza, a higher rate taxpayer, sold his 25% shareholding in Osprey Ltd, a trading company for which he had worked for the last five years. Hamza acquired his shares in the company in May 2014 for £20,000. He sold the shares for £500,000. This was his only disposal in the year.

Calculate the capital gains tax payable by Hamza for 2023/24.

3 Gift relief (holdover relief)

3.1 Principle of gift relief

When a gift is made by an individual, the capital gains tax rules require any gain to be calculated as if the disposal had been a sale at full market value.

The legislation allows a claim to defer the gain where the asset is a qualifying 'business asset' as defined for 'gift relief' purposes.

The broad purpose of gift relief is to enable sole traders and shareholders of family companies to pass on their business or shares to the next generation. Note that this relief is not available for gifts by companies.

Gift relief works by 'deducting' the gain (often described as 'holding over' the gain) from the base cost to the donee (i.e. the person receiving the asset).

	Donor		Donee
	£		£
Market value	50,000	Deemed cost	50,000
Less: Cost	(10,000)		
	————		
	40,000		
Less: Gift relief	(40,000)	Less: Held over gain	(40,000)
	————		————
Chargeable gain	Nil	CGT base cost	10,000
	————		————

In effect, the donee 'takes over' the responsibility for the donor's gain until such time as the donee makes a disposal of the asset.

3.2 Conditions for relief

There are various conditions which must be considered before applying gift relief. We deal with them under the following headings:

- assets which qualify for the relief
- administration of the election.

Assets which qualify for the relief include the following:

- assets used in a trade by the donor or by the donor's personal trading company
- shares in an unquoted trading company (regardless of how many shares are owned)
- shares in the donor's personal trading company (quoted or unquoted).

A 'personal company' is one in which the donor holds at least 5% of the voting rights.

There is no requirement for the taxpayer to be an employee of the company.

Note that relief is therefore only available for quoted company shares if the donor holds at least a 5% interest in the company.

Administration of the election

Gift relief requires a joint election by the donor and the donee.

This must be made within four years of the end of the tax year in which the gift takes place. Therefore, for a gift in 2023/24, the election must be made by 5 April 2028.

It is not possible to specify the amount of the gain to holdover in a claim. All of the gain qualifying is held over if a claim is made.

Reference material

Some information about qualifying assets for gift relief can be found in the 'Chargeable gains – Reliefs' section of the reference material provided in the real assessment, so you do not need to learn it.

Why not look up the correct part of the reference material in the introduction to this text book now?

 Example

Jonas, aged 48, gave the factory that he used in his business to his son on 16 June 2023 when it was valued at £600,000. The factory cost him £150,000 on 16 October 2004.

Calculate the chargeable gain arising and show the base cost of the factory for Jonas' son, assuming gift relief is claimed.

Solution

Step 1: Calculate the gain on the gift using market value

	£
Proceeds (use market value)	600,000
Less: Cost	(150,000)
	————
Chargeable gain before reliefs	450,000
	————

Step 2: Consider whether the gift relief conditions are satisfied

- Asset used in Jonas' trade.
- Factory is a qualifying asset.

Step 3: Hold over the gain against the base cost of the factory

	£
Chargeable gain before reliefs	450,000
Less: Gift relief	(450,000)
	————
Chargeable now	Nil
	————
Base cost of factory for Jonas' son.	
Market value of factory	600,000
Less: Gain held over	(450,000)
	————
Base cost	150,000
	————

Test your understanding 4

Which one of the following statements is FALSE?

A   Gift relief is available on the gift of quoted shares in a trading company provided the individual holds at least 5% of the voting rights in the company.

B   Gift relief is available on the gift of unquoted shares in a trading company regardless of the number of shares held by the individual.

C   Gift relief is only available on the assets of a trade when the trade is disposed of as a whole or after it has ceased.

D   Gift relief is available on any assets used in a trade by the donor or by the donor's personal trading company.

 Test your understanding 5

On 5 June 2023 Jonald, aged 49, gifted his 80% shareholding in Jonald Limited (with a market value of £5 million) to his son Reg.

The resulting gain for the purposes of capital gains tax was £900,000.

Assuming gift relief is claimed, compute:

(a)   the amount chargeable on Jonald in 2023/24

(b)   Reg's base cost in respect of the shares gifted.

 Test your understanding 6

In September 2023 Roy gave his business premises to his son Colin.

At that time the premises had a market value of £500,000 and had been purchased by Roy in September 1991 for £100,000.

Roy and Colin made a joint claim for any capital gain to be held over.

Calculate the gain taxable on Roy for 2023/24, before deduction of the annual exempt amount, and the cost which will be available to Colin when computing the gain on a future disposal of the premises.

4 Disposal of an unincorporated business

The disposal of an unincorporated business by a sole trader or a partner in a partnership has implications for two key taxes:

*   income tax, and

*   capital gains tax.

There will be income tax implications on the cessation of trade, and the disposal of assets could have capital gains tax and/or income tax implications, depending on the type of asset.

4.1 Income tax on cessation of trade

When a business is disposed of, the trade of the sole trader or partner disposing of the business will cease.

As we have seen, on cessation, the calculation of taxable trading profits will require the calculation of capital allowances for the final accounting period (Chapter 4).

4.2 Disposal of assets

Capital gains/losses

The sale or gift of a business will represent a disposal for capital gains tax purposes.

Separate gains or losses will be calculated for each chargeable asset of the business, using market value as the proceeds where assets are gifted rather than sold.

Typical examples of chargeable assets are:

*   goodwill, and

*   land and buildings.

As we have seen, reliefs may be available to reduce the tax payable on disposal (business asset disposal relief), or to defer the gains when assets are given away (gift relief).

Trading profits/losses

If inventory is disposed of as part of a business disposal, the resulting profit or loss will be a trading profit/loss, not a capital gain/loss. This will be subject to income tax.

The disposal of plant and machinery will be subject to capital allowances.

There will either be a balancing allowance or a balancing charge on the disposal of plant and machinery, calculated as follows.

Capital allowances	£
TWDV b/f	X
Less: Proceeds	(X)
Balancing allowance/(balancing charge)	X/(X)

A balancing allowance will be deducted in the adjustment of profits, so will decrease the trading profit, whereas a balancing charge will increase the trading profit.

There is no allowable capital loss on the disposal of plant and machinery, as capital allowances are given instead (although it is possible for a chargeable gain to arise if plant and machinery is sold for more than its cost).

4.3 Calculating proceeds after tax

In the assessment, you may be asked to calculate the after tax proceeds following a business disposal.

This will be the sale proceeds received less the capital gains tax payable.

 Example

After trading for 15 years, Lyuba sold her business in 2023/24 for £320,000 and made chargeable gains of £140,000 on her business assets.

Lyuba is a higher rate taxpayer.

What are Lyuba's proceeds after tax from the sale of her business?

Solution

Capital gains tax

	Qualifying for BADR £
Chargeable gains for the year	140,000
Less: AEA	(6,000)
Taxable gains	134,000
CGT (£134,000 × 10%)	13,400

Proceeds after tax

	£
Sale proceeds	320,000
Less: CGT	(13,400)
Proceeds after tax	306,600

 Test your understanding 7

On 1 August 2023 Aya sold the trade and assets of her business for £13,000,000.

The only assets of the business chargeable to capital gains tax were goodwill and a factory. The goodwill and the factory were acquired in June 2010 for £10,000 and £1,300,000 respectively.

The proceeds received on the sale of the business included £5,500,000 for goodwill and £6,000,000 for the factory.

Aya is a higher rate taxpayer and made no other disposals in 2023/24.

Calculate the capital gains tax payable by Aya for 2023/24 and the after tax proceeds from the sale of her business on the assumption that all beneficial claims are made.

5 Summary

The main differences between calculating gains for individuals and those for companies are:

- individuals are not entitled to the indexation allowance

- individuals are entitled to an AEA which is deducted from chargeable gains in arriving at taxable gains

- individuals pay capital gains tax on the taxable gains arising in a tax year at 10% and 20% depending on the level of their taxable income and gains.

On the disposal of an unincorporated business or shares in a personal company:

- business asset disposal relief may be available and reduces the rate of tax to 10%

- if the disposal is a gift, gift relief may be claimed to defer the gain.

Test your understanding answers

Test your understanding 1

Misha

The correct answer is £3,320.

	£
Chargeable gains (£17,300 + £11,700)	29,000
Less: AEA	(6,000)
Taxable gains	23,000
£12,800 (£37,700 – £24,900) × 10%	1,280
£10,200 (£23,000 – £12,800) × 20%	2,040
Capital gains tax liability	3,320

Test your understanding 2

Business asset disposal relief

The correct answer is D.

Explanation

The maximum business asset disposal relief is £1,000,000 per lifetime not per disposal.

Business asset disposal relief is available on the disposal of shares in the individual's personal trading company.

The relief must be claimed within 12 months of the 31 January following the end of the tax year in which the disposal occurs.

Test your understanding 3

Hamza

	Qualifying for BADR £
Shares	
Proceeds	500,000
Less: Cost	(20,000)
Chargeable gain	480,000
Less: AEA	(6,000)
Taxable gains	474,000
Capital gains tax payable (£474,000 × 10%)	47,400

 Test your understanding 4

Gift relief

The correct answer is C.

Explanation

C is the correct answer because gift relief is available on:

- quoted shares in a trading company provided the individual holds at least 5% of the voting rights in the company

- unquoted shares regardless of the number of shares held, and

- any assets used in a trade by the donor or by the donor's personal trading company.

It is business asset disposal relief that is only available on the assets of a trade when the trade is disposed of as a whole or after it has ceased.

Test your understanding 5

Jonald

(a) **Amount chargeable on Jonald in 2023/24**

Gain eligible to be held over = £900,000

The gain assessable in 2023/24 is therefore £Nil.

(b) **Reg's base cost for shares gifted**

Market value at date of gift less gain held over
= (£5,000,000 – £900,000) = £4,100,000

 Test your understanding 6

Roy and Colin
Roy

	£
Deemed disposal proceeds	500,000
Less: Cost	(100,000)
Chargeable gain before reliefs	400,000

If a joint claim for gift relief is made, there will be no chargeable gain arising on Roy in 2023/24.

Colin

The cost available to Colin when computing the gain on a future disposal of the building is (£500,000 – £400,000) = £100,000.

Test your understanding 7

Aya

Capital gains tax

	£	£
Goodwill		
Proceeds	5,500,000	
Less: Cost	(10,000)	
		5,490,000
Factory		
Proceeds	6,000,000	
Less: Cost	(1,300,000)	
		4,700,000
Total chargeable gains		10,190,000
Less: AEA		(6,000)
		10,184,000
Qualifying gains (£1,000,000 × 10%)		100,000
Remaining gains (£9,184,000 × 20%)		1,836,800
Capital gains tax payable		1,936,800

Proceeds after tax

	£
Sale proceeds (total)	13,000,000
Less: CGT payable	(1,936,800)
Proceeds after tax	11,063,200

Tax planning for businesses

16

Introduction

The way that a business is set up, either as an unincorporated business or as a company, will determine how it is taxed.

This chapter considers the different rates of tax that apply to different types of business and the implications of these rates for tax planning purposes.

In addition, there are tax planning opportunities for married couples or civil partnerships.

Tax planning will be tested in Task 8 of the assessment. This task will be manually marked.

ASSESSMENT CRITERIA	CONTENTS
The tax rates which apply: – to sole traders – to companies – on extraction of profits from companies (6.3) Implications of different business structures on tax planning (6.3) Impact on tax when using different methods of extracting profits, including salary and dividends (6.3) Tax planning opportunities to ensure taxable income is optimally allocated between spouses/civil partners (6.3)	1 Rates of tax for unincorporated businesses 2 Extraction of profits from companies 3 Choice of business structure 4 Tax planning for couples

1 Rates of tax for unincorporated businesses

Sole traders and partners in a partnership pay income tax on their total taxable trading profits for a tax year, regardless of the level of drawings.

For the purposes of the assessment you will not be asked to calculate income tax, although you need to understand the rates of tax that apply. However, some calculations have been included in this chapter to aid your understanding.

1.1 Personal allowance

All individuals are entitled to a personal allowance of £12,570 for the tax year 2023/24.

The personal allowance is deducted from the individual's income in arriving at taxable income.

The personal allowance can only be relieved against income of the current tax year. Any unused amount cannot be carried forward or carried back, nor can it be offset against capital gains.

The personal allowance is restricted if an individual's income exceeds £100,000. However, you will not have to calculate this restriction in your assessment.

1.2 Income tax

Any trading income in excess of the personal allowance is taxable at the basic, higher and additional rates.

The basic rate of 20% is charged on the first £37,700 of taxable income.

The higher rate of 40% is charged on taxable income between £37,700 and £125,140.

The additional rate of 45% is charged on taxable income in excess of £125,140.

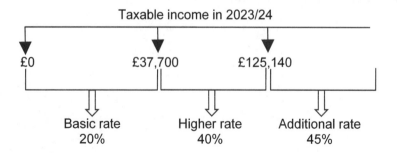

Taxable income in 2023/24

£0	£37,700	£125,140
Basic rate 20%	Higher rate 40%	Additional rate 45%

Example

Isla has taxable trading profits of £62,000 in the tax year 2023/24 and no other income.

Calculate her taxable income and income tax liability for the tax year 2023/24.

Solution

	£
Trading profit	62,000
Less: Personal allowance	(12,570)
Taxable income	49,430

Isla's income tax liability is:

£			£
37,700	× 20%		7,540
11,730	× 40%		4,692
49,430			12,232

 Reference material

Some information about the personal allowance and income tax rates can be found in the 'Income tax' section of the reference material provided in the real assessment, so you do not need to learn it.

Why not look up the correct part of the reference material in the introduction to this text book now?

1.3 National insurance contributions

In addition to paying income tax, sole traders and partners are also subject to class 2 and class 4 national insurance contributions based on their trading profits, as we saw in Chapter 12.

2 Extraction of profits from companies

If an individual decides to set up a limited company, rather than trading as a sole trader, the tax position for the individual becomes more complex.

The individual will be a shareholder in the company and also (probably) a director of the company.

This means that the individual can either withdraw funds from the company as salary or as dividends. Both of these are taxable, but are taxed in different ways.

Again, the personal allowance of £12,570 is available before applying the appropriate income tax rates to any excess.

In Task 8 of the assessment, you may have to advise on the tax implications and rates of tax which apply on the extraction of profits from companies.

2.1 Income tax on salary

Salary is subject to income tax at the same basic, higher and additional rates as trading profits, i.e. 20%/40%/45%.

2.2 National insurance contributions on salary

In addition, salary is subject to class 1 NICs for both the employee and the employer (the company).

The employee contributions payable are calculated as:

- 12% on gross annual earnings between £12,570 and £50,270

- 2% on gross annual earnings in excess of £50,270.

The employer contributions, payable by the company are calculated as:

- 13.8% on all gross annual earnings above £9,100.

You will not have to calculate class 1 NICs in the assessment. However, calculations are included here to aid your understanding.

Example

Millie is employed by Blue Forge Ltd and is paid an annual salary of £54,000.

Calculate Millie's and Blue Forge Ltd's class 1 NIC liability due for the tax year 2023/24.

Solution

	£
Millie's class 1 employee NICs	
(£50,270 – £12,570) × 12%	4524.00
(£54,000 – £50,270) × 2%	74.60
	4,598.60
Blue Forge Ltd's class 1 employer NICs	
(£54,000 – £9,100) × 13.8%	6,196.20

Employers are able to claim up to £5,000 relief each year from their total class 1 employer's NIC payments for the business. This means

- if the total class 1 employer's NICs liability does not exceed £5,000 the amount due for this will be £Nil; and

- if the total class 1 employer's liability is more than £5,000 this amount can be deducted from the liability.

The allowance is not available to companies where a director is the only employee.

2.3 Income tax on dividends

A dividend allowance applies to the first £1,000 of dividend income. The dividend allowance will not be tested in the Business Tax assessment but is included here to aid your understanding.

Any remaining dividend income is taxed at the dividend rates set out below.

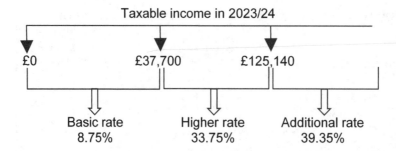

Taxable income in 2023/24

£0	£37,700	£125,140
Basic rate 8.75%	Higher rate 33.75%	Additional rate 39.35%

If an individual has other income such as salary as well as dividends, the salary uses the personal allowance and basic rate band before the dividends.

There are no NICs payable on dividends by the individual or the company.

Example

During the tax year 2023/24, Aage withdraws a salary of £15,000 and a dividend of £50,000 from his company.

Calculate Aage's income tax liability.

	Salary £	Dividends £	Total £
Salary	15,000		15,000
Dividends		50,000	50,000
Net income	15,000	50,000	65,000
Less: Personal allowance	(12,570)		(12,570)
Taxable income	2,430	50,000	52,430

	£		£
Salary – basic rate	2,430	× 20%	486
Dividend allowance	1,000	× 0%	0
Dividends – basic rate	34,270	× 8.75%	2,999
	37,700		
Dividends – higher rate	14,730	× 33.75%	4,971
	52,430		
Income tax liability			8,456

2.4 Impact on the company

As we have already seen, a company must pay corporation tax on its taxable profits.

If the company pays salary, it will have to pay employer's NICs (as set out in section 2.2). However, both the salary and the employer's NICs will be allowable deductions from the trading profits of the company, and will reduce the corporation tax payable.

Dividends are not subject to NICs, but they are paid out of profits after tax and are not an allowable deduction from trading profits.

2.5 Extraction of profits – summary

The table below summarises the tax implications for the individual and the company for the extraction of profits as either salary or dividend.

	Salary	Dividend
Rates of income tax	20%/40%/45%.	8.75%/33.75%/ 39.35%.
NICs paid by individual	Individual must pay class 1 NICs on the salary at 12% or 2%.	No NICs payable on dividends.
NICs paid by company	Employer must pay class 1 NICs on the salary at 13.8%. Note that the £5,000 NIC employment allowance is not available where the director is the sole employee.	No NICs payable on dividends.
Corporation tax implications for company	The salary paid to the employee and the NICs paid by the company are treated as staff costs. This reduces the trading profit of the company and the corporation tax payable.	None – not an allowable deduction in the corporation tax computation.

Reference material

Some information about the rates of income tax applicable to salary and dividends and employer and employee NICs can be found in the 'Income tax' and 'National insurance' sections of the reference material provided in the real assessment, so you do not need to learn it.

Why not look up the correct part of the reference material in the introduction to this text book now?

Test your understanding 1

Mark the following statements as true or false.

		True	False
1	A sole trader with trading profits of £18,000 must pay NICs at 12% on profits above £12,570.		
2	If a company pays a dividend of £10,000 to a shareholder the dividend cannot be deducted from the company's taxable trading profits.		
3	If a company pays a salary of £60,000 to an employee the company must pay NICs at 13.8% on part of this salary.		
4	If a taxpayer has no taxable income for the tax year 2023/24 the benefit of the unused personal allowance for that tax year can be carried forward to the tax year 2024/25.		

3 Choice of business structure

When an individual decides to start a business, one of the most important factors to consider is how to own it.

Direct ownership will be as a sole trader, or if there is more than one person involved, a partnership.

The alternative is to set up a limited company, and own the assets through the company. This will involve more administration and adherence to company law. The individuals involved will then be shareholders and (probably) directors of the company.

As we have seen, each method has its own tax implications.

The main areas that need to be considered are:

- What amounts does the individual pay tax on?

- Is there a liability to NIC?

- When is any tax payable?

3.1 Summary of differences

The main differences between operating as an unincorporated business or as a company can broadly be summarised as follows:

	Sole trader/partnership	Company
Taxation of profits	Trading profit taxed on a tax year basis under income tax rules.	Corporation tax on TTP – after the individual has been paid a salary.
	Adjustments for private use when calculating trading profit.	No adjustments for private use when calculating trading profit – instead the individual is taxed on benefits received.
	Capital allowances with private use adjustments.	Capital allowances in full (no private use adjustments).
	Personal allowance.	No personal allowance for the company (although the individual will have a personal allowance to set against income extracted from the company).
	Income tax at: 20%/40%/45%.	Corporation tax at: • 25% if profits exceed £250,000. • 19% if profits are no more than £50,000. • 25% less marginal relief if profits are between £50,000 and £250,000.
	Class 4 NICs = 9% of profits (£12,570 to £50,270) and 2% thereafter.	
	Class 2 NICs = £3.45 per week.	

	Sole trader/partnership	Company
Relief for losses	Relief available against total income of individual. Opening years relief – loss in any of first four tax years, set against total income of three preceding tax years (FIFO). Relief against total income of current/previous tax year. Carry forward against trading profit of same trade.	Loss relieved against company's total profits (income and gains) only. No opening years relief available. Current year – set against total profits (income and gains) of current AP. Prior year – set against total profits (income and gains) of previous 12 months. Carry forward – against future total profits (income and gains).
Withdrawal of funds	No tax implications – all profits taxable on the individual as trading profit since drawings by the business owner are not allowable deductions.	Salary • Income tax at 20%/40%/45%. • Allowable deduction for the company. • Employee class 1 NICs. • Employer's class 1 NICs for company (allowable deduction). Dividend • Taxed as top slice of income. • Income tax at 8.75%/33.75%/39.35%. • No NICs. • Dividends not an allowable deduction from trading profit for a company. • Company must have distributable profit.

	Sole trader/partnership	Company
Payment of tax	Payments on account of income tax : • 31 January during tax year • 31 July following end of tax year • balancing payment 31 January following end of tax year	Corporation tax payable • 9 months and 1 day after end of accounting period • Large companies pay in quarterly instalments

3.2 Considerations when choosing the relevant structure

Intention to withdraw profits:

* A sole trader is required to pay tax on the profits made, not the amount drawn out of the business.

* Where it is not intended to withdraw all the profits, it will probably be more advantageous to operate as a company. If profits are below the standard lower limit, the company pays tax at 19% on all the profits allowing the retained profits to be taxed at the lower rate (although the future extraction of funds will potentially have further tax consequences).

Initial losses

* If the business will start with losses it may be preferable to structure it initially as a sole trade, allowing the losses to be used against the owner's total income and take advantage of opening years loss relief, which is only available to individuals, not companies.

* Once the business becomes profitable, it may be incorporated if a company is the preferred structure.

Liability

* Where liability is an issue, a company will probably be preferred as a corporate structure will limit the individual's potential liability.

Test your understanding 2

Mark the following statements as true or false.

		True	False
1	A company can deduct salaries and employer's NICs from its taxable trading profits.		
2	If a sole trader with total taxable trading profits of £200,000 withdraws £30,000 of this profit, the trader will only be taxed on the £30,000 withdrawn.		
3	Losses made in the first tax year of trade by a sole trader can be set against total income of the previous three tax years.		
4	If a shareholder who is a higher rate taxpayer is paid a dividend, the shareholder must pay income tax on the dividend at 33.75%.		

4 Tax planning for couples

4.1 Married couples and civil partnerships

Married couples and civil partners can arrange their assets and income between them in order to minimise the total income tax and capital gains tax they pay as a couple.

4.2 Transfer of assets

The transfer of an asset between spouses or civil partners takes place at no gain, no loss (NGNL).

This means that any actual proceeds received from the transfer of the asset are ignored. Instead, the transferor is deemed to dispose of the asset at its original acquisition cost.

Example

David purchased some jewellery in August 2002 for £50,000. In July 2023 he gave it to his wife Victoria when it was worth £200,000.

Calculate the deemed sale proceeds of David's disposal and state Victoria's deemed acquisition cost.

Solution

David is deemed to have transferred the asset at its acquisition cost so that no gain or loss arises on the transfer.

The deemed proceeds are therefore £50,000 and Victoria's deemed acquisition cost is the same as David's deemed proceeds (i.e. £50,000).

When the transferee subsequently sells the asset to a third party, the deemed acquisition cost will be the original cost to the first spouse or civil partner.

The effect of this is that when the asset is eventually sold to a third party, the gain will be taxed as if the transferee has always owned the asset.

Example

Following on from the above example, Victoria then sells the jewellery to a third party in December 2023 for £220,000.

Calculate the chargeable gain on Victoria's disposal in December 2023.

Solution

Victoria's chargeable gain	£
Sale proceeds	220,000
Less: Deemed acquisition cost	(50,000)
	———
Chargeable gain	170,000
	———

4.3   Capital gains tax planning opportunities

The NGNL rules can be used to transfer assets between spouses or civil partners before disposal to a third party, to effectively 'choose' which spouse or civil partner will be taxed on the capital gain arising on the subsequent disposal.

They can transfer assets between them to maximise the use of:

- each individual's AEA
- each individual's basic rate band, and
- capital losses.

4.4   Income tax planning opportunities

Income generating assets can be transferred from one spouse or civil partner to the other (NGNL, as previously explained) in order for the income to be taxed on the one who is now holding the assets.

This tax planning can be used to maximise the use of each individual's:

- dividend allowance
- lower tax bands
- personal allowance.

 Test your understanding 3

Lin earns an annual salary of £18,600 and has no other income.

His husband Joe earns an annual salary of £73,000 and receives property income of £4,000 each year in respect of a rental property (taxable at the same rates as salary).

How much income tax could be saved each year if Joe were to give the rental property to his husband?

5 Summary

If a business is set up as an unincorporated business, the sole trader or partner will pay income tax on trading profits at 20%/40%/45% and class 2 and class 4 NICs.

If a business is set up as a company, profits can be extracted as salary or dividends.

- Salary is subject to income tax at 20%/40%/45% and class 1 NICs for both the employee and the company.

- Dividends are subject to income tax at 8.75%/33.75%/39.35% but are not subject to NICs.

There are tax planning opportunities for married couples or civil partnerships.

Test your understanding answers

Test your understanding 1

1   **False** – a sole trader must pay class 4 NICs at 9% on profits above £12,570, and class 2 NICs at £3.45 per week.

2   **True**

3   **True**

4   **False** – the personal allowance cannot be carried forward.

Test your understanding 2

1   **True**

2   **False** – a sole trader is taxed on total trading profits, not just the amount withdrawn

3   **True**

4   **True**

Test your understanding 3

Joe's taxable income would be reduced by £4,000, such that his income tax liability would be reduced by £1,600 (£4,000 × 40%).

Lin would have additional taxable income of £4,000. He is a basic rate taxpayer and therefore his income tax liability on the additional income would be £800 (£4,000 × 20%).

The total tax saved would be £800 (£1,600 – £800).

Note that the transfer of the property from Joe to Lin would be at no gain, no loss for capital gains tax purposes.

MOCK ASSESSMENT

1 Mock Assessment Questions

You have **2 hours** to complete this mock assessment.

- This assessment contains **10 tasks** and you should attempt to complete **every** task.

- Each task is independent. You will not need to refer to your answers to previous tasks.

- The total number of marks for this assessment is 100.

- Read every task carefully to make sure you understand what is required.

- Where the date is relevant, it is given in the task data.

- Both minus signs and brackets can be used to indicate negative numbers **unless** task instructions state otherwise.

- You must use a full stop to indicate a decimal point. For example, write 100.57 **not** 100,57 or 100 57

- You may use a comma to indicate a number in the thousands, but you don't have to. For example, 10000 and 10,000 are both acceptable.

- If your answer requires rounding, normal mathematical rounding rules should be applied **unless** the task instructions say otherwise.

Task 1 (8 marks)

This task is about adjusting accounting profits and losses for tax purposes.

(a) **For each statement, tick whether the items are capital or revenue expenditure for tax purposes for a trading company.**

(2 marks)

	Capital	Revenue
Legal costs on the purchase of a second-hand building		
Repairs to the building to make it useable		

John runs a small shed building business and made accounting profits of £190,000. The accounts showed a depreciation charge of £1,410. He had taken drawings of £25,000 for himself and paid his husband a salary of £10,000 for working part time as a receptionist (this is a market rate for this work).

During the year, John had a shed installed at his house for £700, the resale value was £1,300. John reflected this work in the accounts at cost. John also provided gifts of wine to customers at a total cost of £420 (the cost per customer was £25).

Capital allowances for the year have been calculated as £7,300.

(b) **Calculate the taxable trading profit for John's business by entering adjustments to accounting profit below. If no adjustment is needed, you should enter a zero. If any adjustments are deducted from accounting profits, these should be shown as a negative figure (for example, a deduction of 3,000 should be shown as -3,000 or (3,000))**

(6 marks)

	£
Accounting profit	190,000
Depreciation	
Drawings	
Husband's salary	
John's shed	
Gifts	
Capital allowances	
Taxable profit	AUTOSUM

Task 2 (12 marks)

This task is about capital allowances.

Beach Ltd built a factory for use in its business and incurred the following expenditure.

Description	Cost £
Land acquisition including stamp duty and legal fees	201,000
Site preparation	17,500
Construction (including £10,000 for moveable partitioning)	300,000

(a) **Calculate how much of the expenditure will be eligible for structures and buildings allowance.** (2 marks)

£ _____

Armin is a sole trader who has prepared annual accounts to 31 March in the past. He decides to change his year end and prepares accounts for the period to 31 May 2024. His capital allowance information is as follows:

£

Tax written down value at 1 April 2023

General pool	74,000
Armin's car	8,200

Armin's car originally cost £14,000, has CO$_2$ emissions of 40g/km and 60% business use.

During the period ended 31 May 2024, Armin makes the following additions and disposals.

Additions: £

1 April 2023	Car for employee – CO$_2$ emissions 0g/km (private use 40%)	12,000
1 June 2023	Plant and machinery	37,000
15 June 2023	New car for Armin – CO$_2$ emissions 110g/km and 60% business use	22,000

Disposals:

13 June 2023	Armin's old car	10,000

(b) **Complete the capital allowances computation for the period ended 31 May 2024. The brought forward figures have already been entered.**

You should ensure that:

– **any additions qualifying for AIA or FYA are included in the appropriate column**

– **all allowances are included in the total allowances column**

– **the total allowances for the period are clearly shown**

– **carried forward balances are clearly shown.**

Any columns that are not required should be left blank.

(10 marks)

	AIA	FYA	General pool	Special rate pool	Private use asset (1)	Private use asset (2)	Total allowances
	£	£	£	£	£	£	£
TWDV b/f			74,000		8,200		

Task 3 (8 marks)

This task is about analysing profits and losses of a partnership and calculating NICs.

David, George and Nick are in partnership sharing profits equally, after allocation of a salary of £18,000 per annum to David.

On 1 August 2023 they changed their profit sharing arrangements so that David received an annual salary of £24,000. The balance of profits was to be shared 2:3:1 for David, George and Nick.

For the year ended 31 March 2024, their tax adjusted trading profit was £180,000.

(a) **Show the division of profit between the partners.** (6 marks)

	David	George	Nick	Total
	£	£	£	£
Period to 31 July				
Salary				AUTOSUM
Profit share				
Total	AUTOSUM	AUTOSUM	AUTOSUM	AUTOSUM
Period to 31 March				
Salary				AUTOSUM
Profit share				
Total	AUTOSUM	AUTOSUM	AUTOSUM	AUTOSUM
Total for year	AUTOSUM	AUTOSUM	AUTOSUM	AUTOSUM

Jane has taxable profits of £57,514 for the tax year 2023/24.

(b) (i) **Calculate Jane's class 2 and class 4 national Insurance contributions. State your answer to the nearest penny.**

(2 marks)

National insurance	£
Class 2	
Class 4	

Task 4 (8 marks)

This task is about chargeable gains and allowable losses of companies.

On 12 December 2023 Lotus Ltd sold a factory used in its trade for £550,000, making an indexed gain of £370,000. It had purchased an office block for use in its trade on 1 July 2023 for £400,000.

(a) **Identify whether the following statements are true or false.**

(2 marks)

Statement	True	False
Lotus Ltd will be not be able to make a rollover relief claim for the gain on the factory as the reinvestment in the office is not a qualifying reinvestment.		
Assuming Lotus Ltd reinvests £400,000 in qualifying assets and claims rollover relief, £220,000 of the indexed gain on the factory will be rolled over.		

Obscure Ltd purchased a factory in December 2010 for £120,000. In June 2012 the company spent £5,000 to repair the roof, and in September 2014 spent £70,000 building an extension on the factory. On 15 March 2024 it sold the factory for £280,000 incurring £3,420 of legal costs.

The indexation factors are:

December 2010 – December 2017	0.218
June 2012 – December 2017	0.150
September 2014 – December 2017	0.080

(b) **Complete the following computation for the sale of the factory by Obscure Ltd. Any amounts to be deducted in calculating the gain should be shown as a negative figure (for example, a deduction of 5,000 should be shown as -5000 or -5,000). All entries should be stated to the nearest pound.** **(6 marks)**

	£
Proceeds	
Selling expenses	
Cost	
Enhancement expenditure	
Unindexed gain	
Indexation allowance (cost)	
Indexation allowance (enhancement)	
Indexed gain/loss	

Task 5 (9 marks)

This task is about calculating chargeable gains and allowable losses in company disposal of shares.

Immense plc bought 40,000 shares in Smith plc for £2.20 each in August 2010. There was a bonus issue of 1 for 1 in February 2013 and a rights issue of 1 for 4 at £2.11 each in September 2015. Immense plc took up all its rights. Immense plc sold 75,000 shares in February 2024 for £350,000.

Indexation factors were:

August 2010 – February 2013	0.103
August 2010 – September 2015	0.156
February 2013 – September 2015	0.048
September 2015 – December 2017	0.071

(a) Complete the share pool. The purchase in August 2010 has already been included. Show the balance of shares carried forward. Show your answers to the nearest pound. **(6 marks)**

Description	Number of shares	Cost £	Indexed cost £
Aug 2010 – purchase	40,000	88,000	88,000

(b) Calculate the chargeable gain or allowable loss on the disposal of the shares in Smith Plc in February 2024. Show your answer to the nearest pound. You have been given more space than you will need. **(3 marks)**

Task 6 (10 marks)

This task is about calculating taxable profits and corporation tax payable.

Sirtis Ltd prepared accounts for the 16 months to 30 June 2024.

The company made a tax adjusted trading profit of £1,728,000 for the period. It had also earned rental profits of £192,000.

Sirtis Ltd made a chargeable gain of £21,200 on 15 December 2023 and a qualifying charitable donation (QCD) of £6,500 on 21 April 2024.

(a) **Calculate the taxable profits for each period in the table below. Any amounts decreasing taxable profits should be shown with a negative figure (for example, a deduction of £5,000 should be shown as -5000 or -5,000).** **(6 marks)**

Show all answers to the nearest pound. Leave boxes blank where not required.

	First period £	Second period £
Trading profit		
Property income		
Chargeable gains		
QCDs		
Taxable profits	AUTOSUM	AUTOSUM

Urban Ltd has taxable total profits of £27,500 for the year ended 31 March 2024. Urban Ltd has three associated companies.

(b) **Calculate the corporation tax payable for the year ended 31 March 2024.** **(3 marks)**

£ _____

Saints Ltd has taxable total profits of £330,000 for the year ended 31 March 2024. Saints Ltd has no associated companies.

(c) **Calculate the corporation tax payable for the year ended 31 March 2024.** **(1 mark)**

£ _____

Task 7 (15 marks)

This task is about the administrative requirements for UK tax law.

Cherry has a painting and decorating business and has prepared self-assessment tax returns for many years. Cherry's income tax and class 4 national insurance liability for each year is as follows:

Year	£
2021/22	750
2022/23	1,100
2023/24	1,900

(a) **State how much income tax and class 4 NICs will be due on the following dates assuming Cherry pays all of her tax by self-assessment.** (4 marks)

Date	Amount £
31 July 2023	
31 January 2024	
31 July 2024	
31 January 2025	

Cherry filed her tax return for 2023/24 on 20 January 2025. She has asked for some further information about self-assessment.

(b) **Are the following statements true or false?** (4 marks)

Statement	True	False
Cherry must keep her records supporting her 2023/24 tax return until 5 April 2024.		
If Cherry discovers an error in her 2023/24 tax return she has until 20 October 2025 to correct it.		
If HMRC discover an obvious error in Cherry's tax return they have until 20 October 2025 to correct it.		
If HMRC wish to enter into a compliance check on Cherry's 2023/24 tax return they will usually issue notice of this by 20 January 2026.		

Maximus wishes to complete a paper-based self-assessment tax return for the 2023/24 tax year.

(c) **By which date should he submit?** **(1 mark)**

[ ]

Gina did not pay her balancing payment of income tax of £10,800 for the 2023/24 tax year until 20 March 2025, although she filed her tax return on time.

(d) **Calculate the penalty that Gina will have to pay for the late payment of the income tax. Show your answer in whole pounds only.** **(2 marks)**

£ [ ]

Bonkers Ltd prepared its accounts to 30 November 2023 and has a liability of £29,870.

(e) **Identify which one of the following statements is true.** **(1 mark)**

Bonkers Ltd must file its tax return by 30 November 2024 [ ]

Bonkers Ltd must file its tax return by 31 January 2024 [ ]

Bonkers Ltd must file its tax return by 1 September 2024 [ ]

Bonkers Ltd must file its tax return by 5 April 2024 [ ]

Khalid started to trade selling music memorabilia from 1 February 2023.

(f) **Khalid needs to inform HMRC that he has income chargeable to tax by:** **(1 mark)**

[ ]

(g) **Identify whether the following statements are true or false**

(2 marks)

Statement	True	False
Donald submitted his tax return on 31 January 2024 but found an error on 28 February. Donald decided to tell HMRC. This is an unprompted disclosure of an error.		
Grasmere Ltd made an error in its tax return which was corrected after being identified by HMRC. This is an unprompted disclosure of an error.		

Task 8 (12 marks)

This task is about tax planning and the responsibilities of the business and agent.

Zahera is a client of your firm. She is the director and only shareholder of Lakeside Ltd, a company making profits of £340,000. Zahera plans to take £60,000 out of Lakeside Ltd each year. Her only other income is her existing salary from Lakeside Ltd which uses her personal allowance each year, and dividends of £3,000.

She would like your advice as to the tax implications of taking this money out either as a salary, or dividends.

(a) **Explain the tax implications for Zahera of taking out a salary or dividend. Calculations are not required.** (5 marks)

(b) **Explain the tax implications for Lakeside Ltd of making the payment as either a salary or dividend.** **(4 marks)**

(c) **Explain the terms tax planning, tax avoidance and tax evasion.**

(3 marks)

Task 9   (8 marks)

This task is about trading losses.

Holly has run a profit-making tree cutting business for many years but due to customer issues she made a loss in the tax year 2023/24.

Her recent trading results are shown below:

Year ended	Profits/(losses)
	£
5 April 2023	22,000
5 April 2024	(24,000)
5 April 2025 (projected)	10,000

Holly also has property income of £8,000 per annum.

(a) **Explain the loss options available to Holly. You do not need to include detailed calculations but should use numbers to illustrate your answer. You should also make a recommendation as to the most appropriate option for Holly.**

                                                                          (5 marks)

(b) **Identify whether the following statements are true or false.**

(3 marks)

Statement	True	False
Keswick Ltd is able to offset its current period trading losses against its total profits before QCDs.		
Lina ceases trading on 31 March 2024. She has four years from 5 April 2024 to make a terminal loss claim.		
Savvas has made a trading loss in one of his first four tax years of trade. That loss can be carried back two years against total income.		

Task 10

(10 marks)

This task is about business disposals.

Chad has been a sole trader for many years but now wishes to retire and gift his business to his daughter.

On the date of retirement (31 January 2024) the following assets were valued:

Asset	Market value £	Original cost £
Factory	998,000	320,000
Goodwill	300,000	0
Inventory	145,000	200,000

(a) **Select the correct option to show the capital gains tax impact. Assume that no reliefs are claimed.** (3 marks)

Asset	Capital gain/(loss)
Factory	Gain/loss/nil
Goodwill	Gain/loss/nil
Inventory	Gain/loss/nil

Chad and his daughter will make an election to claim gift relief on the transfer of the factory.

Assume that the building is worth £998,000 at the date of transfer and was purchased by Chad for £320,000. Chad also added an extension costing £102,000 and spent £7,000 on repairs.

(b) Calculate the chargeable gain made by Chad and the new base cost to his daughter. Any amounts to be deducted in calculating the gain should be shown as a negative figure (for example, a deduction of 5,000 should be shown as -5000 or -5,000). All entries should be stated to the nearest pound.

(5 marks)

Gain to Chad	£
Sale proceeds	
Less: Cost	
Less: Enhancement expenditure	
Less: Gift relief	
Gain	

Cost to daughter	£
Cost	
Less: Gift relief	
Base cost	

(c) Which of the following statements about business asset disposal relief is correct? Select one answer only. **(2 marks)**

A   The first £1 million of gains on each qualifying disposal is charged at 10%.

B   Manuel has owned 10% of the shares in ABC Ltd, a trading company, for 20 years. He does not work for the company. If he sells his shares in ABC Ltd he will be able to claim business asset disposal relief.

C   Jonah bought a sole trader business, ran it for nine months and then sold it making a gain of £500,000. Jonah will be able to claim business asset disposal relief on this disposal.

D   Abigail bought a sole trader business which she ran successfully for 10 years. Due to illness she ceased to trade in June 2023. She was unable to sell her business until July 2024. Abigail will be able to claim business asset disposal relief on this disposal.

2 Mock Assessment Answers

Task 1

(a) Capital or revenue

	Capital	Revenue
Legal costs on the purchase of a second-hand building	✓	
Repairs to the building to make it usable	✓	

Although ongoing repairs are classed as revenue, the initial repairs to a building to make it usable are treated as if they are part of the purchase price and thus capital in nature.

(b) Treatment in adjustment of profits computation

	£
Accounting profit	190,000
Depreciation	1,410
Drawings	25,000
Husband's salary	0
John's shed (£1,300 – £700)	600
Gifts	420
Capital allowances	(7,300)
Taxable profit	210,130

Drawings are appropriations of profits and need adding back. No adjustment needs making for the husband's salary as this appears to be reasonable remuneration.

The installation of a shed at John's house represents goods taken for John's own use. Goods for own use should be recorded at market value. If recorded at cost, the difference between this and market value needs adding to the taxable profits.

Gifts to customers are not allowable as they are gifts of drink (gifts are only allowable if they are not food, drink, tobacco or vouchers; cost no more than £50 per recipient and contain advertising).

Task 2

(a) **Structures and buildings allowance**

The answer is £307,500.

Structures and buildings allowance is available on qualifying costs of construction. The cost of purchasing land is not allowed, but site preparation is a qualifying cost. The cost of moveable partitioning will qualify for capital allowances, not structures and buildings allowances. Therefore, the qualifying cost is calculated as:

	£
Site preparation	17,500
Construction	300,000
Less: Moveable partitioning	(10,000)
	307,500

(b) **Capital allowances computation – period ended 31 May 2024**

	AIA	FYA	General pool	Private use asset (1)		Private use asset (2)		Total allowances
	£	£	£	£		£		£
TWDV b/f			74,000	8,200				
Additions: No AIA or FYA						22,000		
Addition: FYA		12,000						
FYA 100%		(12,000)						12,000
Additions: AIA	37,000							
AIA	(37,000)							37,000
			0					
Disposals				(10,000)				
				(1,800)				
BC				1,800	× 60%			(1,080)
			74,000	0		22,000		
WDA 18% × 14/12			(15,540)					15,540
WDA 6% × 14/12						(1,540)	× 60%	924
TWDV c/f			58,460	0		20,460		
								64,384

Note: In the assessment you do not need to enter lines marking totals and subtotals.

Task 3

(a) **Division of profits between partners**

	David	George	Nick	Total
	£	£	£	£
Period to 31 July (4/12 × £180,000 = £60,000)				
Salary (4/12 × £18,000)	6,000	0	0	6,000
Profit Share (1:1:1) (£60,000 – £6,000 = £54,000)	18,000	18,000	18,000	54,000
Total	24,000	18,000	18,000	60,000
Period to 31 March (8/12 × £180,000 = £120,000)				
Salary (8/12 × £24,000)	16,000	0	0	16,000
Profit Share (2:3:1) (£120,000 – £16,000 = £104,000)	34,667	52,000	17,333	104,000
Total	50,667	52,000	17,333	120,000
Total for year	74,667	70,000	35,333	180,000

When a change in the profit sharing agreement occurs the accounting period should be split into two periods for allocation of profits.

(b) **Jane's NICs**

National insurance	£
Class 2	179.40
Class 4	3,537.88

As Jane's profits exceed £12,570 she pays class 2 NICs at a flat £3.45 per week.

52 × £3.45 = £179.40.

Class 4 NICs are calculated on a sliding scale. The relevant rates can be found in the reference material in the exam.

(£50,270 – £12,570) × 9% = £3,393.00

(£57,514 – £50,270) × 2% = £144.88

Total: £3,537.88.

Task 4

(a) **True or false**

Statement	True	False
Lotus Ltd will be not be able to make a rollover relief claim for the gain on the factory as the reinvestment in the office is not a qualifying reinvestment.		✓
Assuming Lotus Ltd reinvests £400,000 in qualifying assets and claims rollover relief, £220,000 of the indexed gain on the factory will be rolled over.	✓	

The reinvestment in the office will qualify for rollover relief, as the office is a qualifying asset (land and buildings used in the trade) and the reinvestment takes place within the 12 months before the disposal of the factory.

In order to roll over all of the gain, Lotus Ltd must reinvest all of the proceeds of £550,000. If £400,000 is reinvested, only part of the gain can be rolled over. The rollover relief will be restricted by the amount of proceeds not reinvested (£550,000 – £400,000 = £150,000), so the amount rolled over will be £220,000 (£370,000 – £150,000).

(b) **Chargeable gain**

	£
Proceeds	280,000
Selling expenses	(3,420)
Cost	(120,000)
Enhancement expenditure	(70,000)
Unindexed gain	86,580
Indexation allowance (cost) (£120,000 × 0.218)	(26,160)
Indexation allowance (enhancement) (£70,000 × 0.080)	(5,600)
Indexed gain/loss	54,820

Repairs are not an allowable cost so the indexation factor from June 2012 should be ignored.

Task 5

(a) **Share pool**

Description	Number of shares	Cost £	Indexed cost £
August 2010 Purchase	40,000	88,000	88,000
Feb 2013 Bonus issue 1 for 1	40,000	0	0
Indexed rise to Sep 2015			
£88,000 × 0.156			13,728
Sep 2015 Rights issue 1 for 4	20,000	42,200	42,200
	100,000	130,200	143,928
Indexed rise to Dec 2017			
£143,928 × 0.071			10,219
			154,147
Feb 2024 Disposal	(75,000)	(97,650)	(115,610)
Balance c/f	25,000	32,550	38,537
75,000/100,000 × £130,200			
75,000/100,000 × £154,147			

(b) **Chargeable gain – share disposal**

Gain calculation		£	
Proceeds		350,000	
Less: Cost (a)		(97,650)	
Less: Indexation (a)			
(£115,610 – £97,650)		(17,960)	
Chargeable gain		234,390	

In the assessment you do not need to enter lines marking totals and subtotals.

Task 6

(a) **Long period of account**

	First period (12 months) £	Second period (4 months) £
Trading profit (12/16 × £1,728,000/ 4/16 × £1,728,000)	1,296,000	432,000
Property income (12/16 × £192,000/ 4/16 × £192,000)	144,000	48,000
Chargeable gains	21,200	
QCDs (date)		(6,500)
Taxable profits	1,461,200	473,500

The accounting period must be split into two for tax purposes. The first covers the first 12 months (1 March 2023 to 29 February 2024) and the second covers the balance (1 March 2024 to 30 June 2024)

(b) **Urban Ltd corporation tax payable**

The answer is £6,350.

The corporation tax upper and lower limits must be shared between associated companies:

Lower limit (£50,000 ÷ 4) = £12,500

Upper limit (£250,000 ÷ 4) = £62,500

As taxable total profits are between the lower limit of £12,500 and the upper limit of £62,500, marginal relief applies:

	£
Corporation tax at the main rate (£27,500 × 25%)	6,875
Less: Marginal relief 3/200 × (£62,500 – £27,500)	(525)
Corporation tax payable	6,350

(c) **Saints Ltd corporation tax payable**

The answer is £82,500.

The main rate (25%) of corporation tax applies as taxable total profits are above the upper limit of £250,000. Corporation tax payable is therefore £330,000 × 25%.

Task 7

(a) **Cherry self-assessment payments**

Date	Amount £
31 July 2023	0
31 January 2024 (£1,100 + £550)	1,650
31 July 2024	550
31 January 2025 (£800 + £950)	1,750

Cherry must make payments as follows:

31 July 2023

This would usually be the second payment on account for 2022/23. However, as Cherry's total income tax and class 4 for the previous year (2021/22) was less than £1,000, no payments on account (POAs) would be required for 2022/23.

31 January 2024

Balancing payment for 2022/23

This will be all £1,100 of the tax for 2022/23 as no POAs were due (see above).

First payment on account for 2023/24

Calculated as 50% of 2022/23 income tax and class 4 NICs.

£1,100 × 50% = £550

31 July 2024

Second payment on account for 2023/24

50% × £1,100 = £550

31 January 2025

Balancing payment for 2023/24

Calculated as difference between 2023/24 payments on account and actual amount owed for the year.

£1,900 − (£550 × 2) = £800

First payment on account for 2024/25

Calculated as 50% of 2023/24 income tax and class 4 NICs.

£1,900 × 50% = £950

(b) **True or false**

Statement	True	False
Cherry must keep her records supporting her 2023/24 tax return until 5 April 2024.		✓
If Cherry discovers an error in her 2023/24 tax return she has until 20 October 2025 to correct it.		✓
If HMRC discover an obvious error in Cherry's tax return they have until 20 October 2025 to correct it.	✓	
If HMRC wish to enter into a compliance check on Cherry's 2023/24 tax return they will usually issue notice of this by 20 January 2026.	✓	

Cherry must keep the supporting records for her tax return for five years after the due filing date, i.e. until 31 January 2030.

Cherry can correct any errors in her return within 12 months of the due filing date, i.e. by 31 January 2026. HMRC can correct errors within nine months of the actual filing date.

(c) **Maximus**

The answer is 31 October 2024

(d) **Gina**

The answer is £540.

The final/balancing payment for 2023/24 was due on 31 January 2025 so this is more than 30 days late, but not more than six months. The penalty is calculated at 5%.

5% × £10,800 = £540

(e) **Bonkers Ltd**

The correct answer is Bonkers Ltd must file its tax return by 30 November 2024.

The tax return must be filed 12 months after the corporation tax accounting period.

(f) **Khalid**

Khalid must notify by 5 October 2023.

(g) **True or false**

Statement	True	False
Donald submitted his tax return on 31 January 2024 but found an error on 28 February. Donald decided to tell HMRC. This is an unprompted disclosure of an error.	✓	
Grasmere Ltd made an error in its tax return which was corrected after being identified by HMRC. This is an unprompted disclosure of an error.		✓

Task 8

(a) **Implications for Zahera**

If Zahera extracts funds as salary this will be taxable as non-savings income meaning she will have to pay income tax on this at rates of 20% up to the basic rate band limit, then 40%.

A salary is also subject to employee's national insurance. This will be calculated at 12% and 2%.

If she extracts funds as a dividend she will pay tax at 8.75% then 33.75%.

National insurance contributions are not payable on dividends.

(b) **Implications for Lakeside Ltd**

Lakeside Ltd will have to pay employer's national insurance contributions on any further amounts extracted by Zahera as a salary. These will be payable at 13.8%.

The cost of paying any salary plus associated national insurance is an allowable deduction from Lakeside Ltd's trading profits. Corporation tax will be saved on this at 25%.

No national insurance is payable on dividends, but no tax savings are available for paying dividends.

(c) **Tax planning, tax avoidance and tax evasion**

Tax planning means maximising tax relief whilst acting within the spirit of the law and parliament's intentions.

Tax avoidance means maximising tax relief in a way that acts within the law but not as it was intended when passed.

Tax evasion is illegal. This means reducing tax liabilities in a way that is in breach of tax law. This action can lead to possible fines and/or imprisonment.

Task 9

(a) **Loss options**

Holly has made a loss of £24,000 in the 2023/24 tax year. Her options for loss relief are:

Carry forward

Holly could carry the loss forward and offset against future trading profits of the same trade only. Based on the information provided this would mean using £10,000 in the 2024/25 tax year. The remaining £14,000 could be carried forward indefinitely and set against the first available trading profits of the same trade.

The property income of £8,000 would use some of the personal allowance, with the remainder being wasted in 2024/25 if the loss was offset. Tax would be saved on income in excess of the personal allowance at the basic rate of 20%.

Current year

Holly could offset the loss against her total income in the tax year of the loss (2023/24). This would mean offsetting £8,000 of the loss against the property income for the year. This relief would waste the personal allowance and would not save any tax so is not recommended.

Carry back

The loss could be carried back to the 2022/23 tax year where a claim could be made against total income of £30,000 (trading income of £22,000 plus property income of £8,000). This claim would allow the full loss of £24,000 to be utilised, leaving income of £6,000 which would be covered by the personal allowance.

This claim would waste some of the personal allowance, and save tax on the remainder at the basic rate of 20%. This amount would be repaid to Holly.

Recommendation

Carry back relief seems to be the best option based on the information provided. It is better for cash flow as it will lead to a repayment of tax already paid, and it uses all of the loss.

(b) **True or false**

Statement	True	False
Keswick Ltd is able to offset its current period trading losses against its total profits before QCDs	✓	
Lina ceases trading on 31 March 2024. She has four years from 5 April 2024 to make a terminal loss claim	✓	
Savvas has made a trading loss in one of his first four tax years of trade. That loss can be carried back two years against total income.		✓

A company can claim relief for its trading losses against its own total profits of the same accounting period.

When an individual ceases trade, losses made in the final 12 months of trade can be carried back three tax years using terminal loss relief. A claim for terminal loss relief must be made within four years of the end of the tax year in which trade ceased.

When an individual starts trade, losses in the first four tax years of trade can be carried back three tax years on a FIFO basis using opening year loss relief.

Task 10

(a) Capital gain/loss

Asset	Capital gain/(loss)
Factory	Gain
Goodwill	Gain
Inventory	Nil

A gift of an asset is a chargeable disposal, with the proceeds deemed to be market value, so leads to a gain on disposal. However, the disposal of inventory will result in a trading profit/loss, not a capital gain/loss.

(b) Gift relief

Gain to Chad	£
Sale proceeds	998,000
Less: Cost	(320,000)
Less: Enhancement expenditure	(102,000)
	576,000
Less: Gift relief	(576,000)
Gain	0

Cost to daughter	£
Cost	998,000
Less: Gift relief	(576,000)
Base cost	422,000

On the gift of an asset we use deemed proceeds of market value.

The cost of repairs is not classed as enhancement expenditure, and cannot be deducted.

Claiming gift relief defers the gain for Chad against the cost for his daughter.

His daughter has a deemed cost of market value at transfer, although this is reduced by gift relief.

(c) **Business disposals**

The answer is D.

Abigail's disposal qualifies as it is within 3 years of the cessation of her business and she operated the business for more than 24 months prior to the date of cessation.

A is incorrect because the £1 million is a cumulative lifetime limit covering all disposals, not each disposal.

B is incorrect because business asset disposal relief would only be available if Manuel worked for the company.

C is incorrect because qualifying assets must be owned for at least 24 months before disposal.

INDEX